New Zealand and Japan
1945–1952

DATE DUE

New Zealand and Japan 1945–1952: The Occupation and the Peace Treaty

Ann Trotter

THE ATHLONE PRESS
London & Atlantic Highlands

First published 1990 by the Athlone Press Ltd
1 Park Drive, London NW11 7SG and
171 First Avenue, Atlantic Highlands, NJ 07716

British Library Cataloguing in Publication Data
Trotter, Ann, *1932–*
    New Zealand and Japan 1945–1952 : the occupation and peace treaty.
    1. New Zealand. Foreign relations with Japan, history 2.
    Japan. Foreign relations with New Zealand, history
    I. Title
327.93052

ISBN 0–485–11398–8

Library of Congress Cataloging-in-Publication Data
Trotter, Ann.
    New Zealand and Japan, 1945–1952 : the occupation and the peace
    treaty / Ann Trotter.
        p.   cm.
    Includes bibliographical references (p.   ) and index.
    ISBN 0–485–11398–8
    1. New Zealand—Foreign relations—Japan. 2. Japan—Foreign
relations—New Zealand. 3. Japan—History—Allied occupation,
1945–1952. 4. New Zealand—Foreign relations—1945–ation 5. World
War, 1939–1945—Peace. I. Title.
DU421.5.J3T76   1990
327.93052—dc20

Typeset by J&L Composition Ltd, Filey, North Yorkshire
Printed in Great Britain by Billings, Worcester

Contents

ABBREVIATIONS

ACJ   Allied Council for Japan
ANZUS   Australia, New Zealand, United States Tripartite Security Pact
BCAIR   British Commonwealth Air Group
BCOF   British Commonwealth Occupation Force
BRINDIV   British Indian Division
CFM   Council of Foreign Ministers
CRO   Commonwealth Relations Office
CSDIC   Combined Services Detailed Interrogation Centre
DO   Dominions Office
FEAC   Far East Advisory Commission
FEC   Far Eastern Commission
FO   Foreign Office
GATT   General Agreement on Tariffs and Trade
IMTFE   International Military Tribunal for the Far East
Jayforce   2nd New Zealand Expeditionary Force (Japan)
JCOSA   Joint Chiefs of Staff Australia
Kayforce   New Zealand Emergency Force (in Korea)
NATO   North Atlantic Treaty Organization
PACUSA   Pacific Air Command US Army
PRC   People's Republic of China
RNZAF   Royal New Zealand Air Force
2nd NZEF   Second New Zealand Expeditionary Force
SCAP   Supreme Commander Allied Powers
UKLIM   United Kingdom Liaison Mission (to Japan)

LIST OF MAPS

Acknowledgements

I am indebted to many people who willingly gave me their assistance and support in this project. I was able to carry out research in New Zealand, the United States, the United Kingdom and Australia during study leave granted by the University of Otago. I thank the University authorities for this and in particular the Assistant Vice-Chancellor, Humanities, Professor David McKenzie, for financial support which has helped make this publication possible.

The New Zealand-Japan Foundation has also been generous in its assistance. I thank the Foundation not only for its support but for the encouragement this has given me.

I would like in particular to thank Merwyn Norrish, formerly Secretary of Foreign Affairs, for permission to use files held at the Ministry of Foreign Affairs. Individual officers at the Ministry of Foreign Affairs were always helpful and co-operative and I thank the library and archive staff there for their patience.

I interviewed a number of former officers of the Ministry of Foreign Affairs who, without exception, readily gave helpful information and advice. I would like especially to thank Frank Corner, formerly Secretary of Foreign Affairs, for his help and for permission to use the McIntosh-Berendsen correspondence; Rod Miller, a former New Zealand ambassador to Japan who not only shared generously something of this knowledge and direct experience of Japan since 1945 when he was with the Occupation Forces, but read the manuscript and commented constructively; Malcolm Templeton, formerly Deputy Secretary of Foreign Affairs, who read the manuscript and has been helpful and supportive; and Sir Guy Powles who began his distinguished post-war career as New Zealand's representative at the Far Eastern

Commission. Other former members of the Ministry whom I thank are Colin Aikman, Charles Craw, Rex Cunninghame, Harold Evans, Sir George Laking, Tom Larkin, John Scott, Jim Weir. Their help was invaluable.

I thank also Ian Berendsen for permission to use his father, Sir Carl Berendsen's memoirs; Alison Quentin-Baxter for information about her husband Quentin Quentin-Baxter's work in Tokyo and permission to use his papers; the Honourable Sir Peter Quilliam for permission to use his father, Brigadier Ronald Quilliam's diaries; and Harold Evans for information about Justice Northcroft and material relating to the International Military Tribunal for the Far East.

I am also indebted to Professor Ian Nish, Emeritus Professor Angus Ross, Emeritus Professor Sir Keith Sinclair and the late Emeritus Professor F. L. W. Wood for help and information. Messrs. W. Anderson, M. Findlater and C. H. Irwin assisted with information about J Force.

I am grateful for assistance received from the staff of the Hocken Library, Dunedin; the National Archives, the General Assembly Library and the Turnbull Library, Wellington; the Canterbury University Library, Christchurch. I received help from the staff of the Commonwealth Archives, Canberra, the Public Record Office, London; the Columbia University Library, New York; the Mudd Library, Princeton; the MacArthur Memorial Archives, Norfolk, Virginia.

To Professor Erik Olssen and my colleagues in the history department at the University of Otago for their friendship and tolerance, and my sister Judith for her generosity and provision, over the years, of accommodation while I carried out research in Wellington, I extend my thanks.

Ann Trotter
Dunedin

Introduction

In the years since the Second World War, New Zealanders have contemplated Japan at different times with varying degrees of ignorance, interest, indifference and intensity. In these years Japan has gone from menace to major trading partner in the consciousness of New Zealanders.

The years 1945 to 1952 with which this study is concerned were years when, for the first time, New Zealand governments had seriously to consider a policy towards Japan. This intensity of concern over New Zealand-Japan relations and a New Zealand policy towards Japan was not matched after 1952 for another decade, by which time the menace of possible British entry into the European Community and the consequent need for New Zealand to find new markets caused New Zealand governments to reconsider Japan.

In 1945, however, New Zealand's primary concern was to secure itself against Japanese aggression. The Japanese advance after 1941 had reminded New Zealand and Australia that the Pacific Ocean connected them irrevocably to this expansionist Asian empire in the north and made evident the fact that the Royal Navy could never again be New Zealand's defender against 'Asian hoards' and other perils. This led New Zealand to look to the United States for security guarantees and it made United States policy in Occupied Japan of considerable interest to New Zealand.

The story of New Zealand's relations with Japan since 1945 runs parallel with the story of New Zealand's psychological and economic detachment from the United Kingdom. But in the period 1945 to 1952 this detachment was at most partial, foreshadowed rather than accepted. Psychological attachments had been strengthened by victory and wartime sacrifice in spite of the fact of demonstrated

British weakness in the Pacific. Economic ties remained strong. Throughout the period the Bulk Purchase agreements signed in 1939 under which the British took all New Zealand's surplus meat and dairy products remained in place and preferential tariffs were applied to British manufactured goods in New Zealand. These realities helped underpin New Zealand's reputation internationally as an economically dependent, generally undemanding and 'dutiful' daughter within the British Commonwealth family. Of course the dutiful daughter image was never entirely accurate as many historians have pointed out. New Zealand's loyalty to Britain was neither dumb nor blind and certainly from the mid-1930s New Zealand ministers were prepared to take an independent stance at Commonwealth meetings or in the League of Nations.[1] By 1945 there was a good deal of healthy scepticism in New Zealand official circles about 'mother's' demands and ambitions and some amusement at the reactions of some of mother's officials, but the fact remained that power which was both economic and political and ties which were sentimental resulted in the long run in a New Zealand stance which usually appeared at least to be 'dutiful'.

In Great Power manoeuvres, however, scant consideration, even in matters directly affecting them, is likely to be given to the small and the dutiful. For New Zealand this truth was illustrated in the Cairo Declaration of December 1943 in which Roosevelt, Chiang Kai-shek and Churchill set out their objectives in the war against Japan[2] and in the Potsdam Declaration of July 1945 setting out the terms on which Japan would be called to surrender.[3] On neither of these was New Zealand or Australia consulted or forewarned. In 1945 when peace came, New Zealand and Australia wished to be heard.

If it was not easy for a dutiful daughter to be heard in the family it was even less simple to make that voice heard by the United States. Here New Zealand had few cards to play. One seemed to be the 'Pacific' card. Although New Zealand's 'Pacific consciousness' was not at that time high, a Pacific connection between New Zealand, Australia, Japan and the United States was an obvious one. It was not, however, straightforward. The United States involvement with and concern for Japan after 1945 was, of course, in part a reflection of Great Power politics and the Cold War, but it was also a reflection of American priorities in their Pacific world. The American definition of the Pacific is an essentially north

Pacific one in which both Japan and China have traditionally played an important role. This is a view of the Pacific quite foreign to New Zealanders, sited in the south Pacific and conceiving of that Ocean in terms of small and scattered Polynesian and Melanesian islands and, in 1945, perceiving it as the route by which, without the British navy, an enemy might be expected to reach New Zealand's shores. New Zealanders and Americans thus had different images of the Pacific just as they had different images of Japan. In the period 1945 to 1952 Japan was central to American thinking first as the ex-enemy and then as a bulwark against the spread of communism. New Zealanders remained hostile and suspicious of Japanese intentions; but for the Americans, Japan quickly ceased to be seen as a potential threat. Quite apart from factors determined by its responsibilities as a Great Power, the American attitude to what a policy for the Pacific might be, and what might constitute security requirements in the Pacific, therefore started from basically different premises from those of New Zealand. New Zealand policy-makers were thus challenged in two respects. They had to develop their policy, essentially a security policy, towards Japan and they had to persuade the United States, without which a New Zealand security policy in relation to Japan could hardly be credible, to agree to be a player in the policy.

In the years 1945–1952 with which this study is concerned New Zealand's external policy was developing a new depth and complexity which involved dealings with both the United States and Japan. At the same time the British connection was still felt to be paramount and New Zealand's responses often seemed predictably co-operative with United Kingdom policy. Traditionally New Zealand had seen itself as a good Commonwealth team player prepared to shoulder burdens and take responsibility. In matters relating to the Occupation, New Zealand sought to be a player of this calibre and it was on this Commonwealth level that the actual Occupation of Japan itself was seen to be of real concern to New Zealand. The organizations relating to the Occupation in which New Zealand was involved and which are discussed in this study were the Far East Commission, the British Commonwealth Occupation Force and the International Military Tribunal for the Far East. The Far East Commission, in which New Zealand as a small nation had hopes of finding a 'voice' which might influence

Occupation policy, proved to be nothing but a 'talking shop'. There was no glory to be won in membership of the British Commonwealth Occupation Force nor honour, it transpired, in membership of the International Military Tribunal for the Far East. Involvement in the Occupation in these three areas was a considerable burden for a nation of less than two million people but as an independent member of the Commonwealth New Zealand saw this activity as necessary for the team effort. The historian of the British part in the Occupation suggests that British participation in the Occupation was both more substantial and more effective than has generally been recognized.[4] The New Zealanders who were disillusioned with those aspects of the Occupation in which they were involved might be comforted by and take some credit for such an estimate since they saw themselves as contributors to the general British and Commonwealth effort.

But of course it was no disadvantage to New Zealand diplomacy to be able to demonstrate that some Occupation tasks fell on New Zealand shoulders. While playing in the Commonwealth team in Japan, New Zealand sought to make American officials, who, unlike British officials, were unaccustomed to bothering themselves with the security concerns of lesser communities in the south Pacific, aware of New Zealand's merit and of what New Zealand saw as its needs. This was a challenge to New Zealand's fledgeling diplomatic service. It was necessary for New Zealand to emphasize that she was not only a Commonwealth member with responsibilities within the strategy of Commonwealth defence, but a Pacific nation. It was argued that, as a Pacific nation New Zealand was, in a sense, Japan's neighbour and therefore intimately concerned with and affected by the Japanese peace treaty and the fuure development and policies of that country. This was, as has been suggested, a view of Pacific neighbourhood which Americans found it hard to accept but was a matter of high policy for New Zealand. The nature of the Japanese peace treaty and the degree to which its provisions might restrict a possible resurgence of Japanese militarism were matters of central concern to New Zealand. New Zealand's persistence in its demand for security guarantees against future Japanese aggression represented a major diplomatic effort. The fact that the United States, albeit somewhat reluctantly, accepted responsibility towards New Zealand and

Australian security in the south Pacific in 1951 was the result, in part at least, of the persistent efforts of these two countries and to that extent, was something of a victory for them. In the long run, however, American participation in New Zealand's security policy had most to do with Cold War politics and almost nothing to do with any American concept of some kind of relationship and community with the south Pacific.

In looking at the Occupation and the Japanese peace treaty, through New Zealand eyes one is looking at events through the eyes perhaps, of the least significant player. The New Zealanders were, however, very independently-minded observers. Those involved in the Occupation Forces in Japan felt themselves to be better and more experienced soldiers than most there and saw no reason to be impressed by Americans of whose superiority they were not in awe and of whose abilities they were critical. The New Zealanders involved in the International Military Tribunal for the Far East were experienced legal professionals secure in their recognized qualifications and skills, and having a high sense of integrity. They made sharp criticisms from this position of strength. In Washington and New York, Sir Carl Berendsen, a diplomat of considerable knowledge and experience who feared no man, never hesitated to express an opinion whether or not it was unpopular or unfashionable. The most the New Zealand government could hope to gain from participation in the Occupation was American and British goodwill. The New Zealanders were untrammelled by a sense of mission or status, or by any awareness of possible future commercial gain. All this being so, the Occupation period through New Zealand eyes has a perspective rather different from that of most other participants.

A focus on the Pacific and on Japan is now accepted as central to New Zealand foreign policy. The years 1945–1952 were in a sense preparatory years when along with traditional diplomatic preoccupations with Britain and the Commonwealth, with the United Nations and the principle of collective security, New Zealand's security concerns were focused on Japan and the Pacific to a degree not before experienced in peacetime. The result of these years was a treaty with the United States which did not include the United Kingdom, the first such treaty that New Zealand had signed; and the establishment of diplomatic relations with Japan, the first Asian country with which New Zealand had had diplomatic relations and the first country which was neither a member of the Commonwealth nor a wartime ally, in which New Zealand had an official representative. The purpose of establishing diplomatic relations with Japan was to secure the convenience of a post in an area of acute diplomatic sensitivity at the time. New Zealand wanted to be able to 'watch' Japan. While this is a not uncommon reason for the establishment of a diplomatic post, for New Zealand it was a new departure and represented a more sophisticated attitude to the purpose of, and need for representation abroad.

At the time these things did not seem to mark the beginning of a new era, and New Zealanders were more preoccupied with domestic considerations in 1952 than with arrangements which portended change for New Zealand or the potential for changes in the international arena. It was, however, to be important to New Zealand in the next decade that these arrangements were in place. Then, as the situation in south east Asia became increasingly unstable, as Britain withdrew from east of Suez and as British negotiations to join the European Community, together, altered New Zealand's strategic concerns and undermined her markets, the changes which had been signalled in the period 1945–1952 could no longer be denied. The importance of both Japan and the United States to New Zealand and the centrality of the Pacific, rather than Britain, to New Zealand's world, all of which may, with hindsight, have been discerned by 1952, had to be accepted.

1
New Zealand and Japan: The Impact of World War II

The outbreak of war in the Pacific in 1941 drew attention in a new way to New Zealand's geographical position and to New Zealanders' perception of it as it related to them. If, as a recent writer has suggested, white New Zealanders had by then a sense of New Zealand as a nation and were already very clear that they were New Zealanders and not English, Irish or Scots,[1] it seems that white New Zealanders had very little sense of New Zealand as a specifically Pacific nation. Most, it was suggested in 1940, were in danger of forgetting that New Zealand was a Pacific country at all.[2]

It is true, especially in the last three decades of the nineteenth century and in the early twentieth century, that successive New Zealand governments had aspired to an imperial role in the south Pacific. Even before New Zealand became a British colony, supporters of the New Zealand Company had put forward the idea of New Zealand as the 'Britain of the south'.[3] For New Zealand politicians of the late nineteenth century, this role had appeal. In its imperialist phase New Zealand acquired the scattered Cook Islands and Niue, more than 1,600 miles distant from New Zealand, and the people of these islands became New Zealand citizens.[4] This was New Zealand's empire, an element of Britain's bigger and stronger empire of which New Zealanders were proud members.

It was, however, one thing for white New Zealanders to see New Zealand as one nineteenth-century politician claimed – using the language with which white New Zealanders referred to Britain – as 'a mother among the Pacific islands',[5] and another to recognize New Zealand as a south Pacific nation which, notwithstanding its historical connections with Britain, had priorities in the Pacific and kin relationships with other Pacific islands.

By the 1920s and 1930s imperialism was no longer fashionable. New Zealand governments had found that the responsibilities of a colonial power could be troublesome and expensive especially as New Zealand administrators were faced with the national aspirations of Samoans in the League of Nations Mandate, Western Samoa, which New Zealand had been pleased to be awarded in 1919.[6] Such interest as there was in the Pacific and Pacific Islands from the mid 1920s, therefore, was based rather more on problems of strategy than empire. The ocean tended to be regarded by New Zealand defence planners from a global perspective, as a factor in imperial defence policy. New Zealand would stand or fall with Britain, the Empire and Commonwealth, but New Zealand's remoteness and isolation could make it vulnerable.[7] In the late 1930s as the potential for air power grew, the islands assumed some importance as possible staging posts on reconnaissance routes. In the pre-war period, however, the main concern for New Zealand defence experts was to see the completion of the Singapore base from which a British fleet could patrol the Pacific ocean and keep New Zealand safe, thus enabling New Zealanders to do their bit for the defence of the Empire and Commonwealth. In this scenario, which was essentially a British one, the Pacific, and New Zealand's possible role in it as a Pacific nation, did not have priority. New Zealanders would serve in centres more vital for the preservation of the whole than their own land. The ocean was the route which took men to wars which might be fought on the other side of the world.

New Zealanders were, then, accustomed to thinking in terms of the 'tyranny of distance' which separated them at a sentimental level from 'kin'; which at the same time both made them vulnerable and distanced them from the significant centres of conflict; and which, on a practical level, separated them from the established markets for their exports in the United Kingdom. A 'very real feeling of remoteness' has been identified as part of the New Zealand psyche.[8] It has been suggested that their country's bush and the mountains enhanced New Zealanders' feeling of remoteness within their own land. Certainly the surrounding ocean with its empty horizons enhanced New Zealanders' sense of being remote from the world beyond that land. Of this ocean, of the peoples who lived on its rim and inhabited its small islands to their north, the average New Zealander knew very little. In October

1941, A. J. Campbell of the Christchurch Teachers' Training College said, 'The Pacific seems to be the part of the world of which New Zealanders know least and in which they are least interested. Perhaps it is because we think of ourselves in terms of Great Britain and not of ourselves as a Pacific power. ... It is necessary to think deeply of the Pacific'.[9] Few New Zealanders did. The truth was, as one leader writer commented in 1942 when the Japanese were advancing on Singapore, 'The strategical importance of various points in the Pacific, save Singapore, has never until now greatly interested the majority of us. We knew more about the Strait of Dover than the Strait of Malacca'.[10]

The identification by most New Zealanders of their country as a Pacific nation and the growth of a 'Pacific consciousness' is an important aspect of a more confident late twentieth-century New Zealand nationalism, the roots of which, perhaps, can be seen to go back to December 1941 and events thereafter in the Pacific. New Zealanders' psychological adjustment to the reality that their country is a Pacific country, that they are Pacific people living in a diverse Pacific world has, however, been a slow one.

'PACIFIC MINDEDNESS'

The reaction of New Zealanders to the traumatic events from December 1941 to February 1942 – the bombing of Pearl Harbor, the sinking of the *Prince of Wales* and *The Repulse* and the fall of Singapore – seems to have been one of numbed disbelief. Awareness of events in Japan was minimal. Nation-wide, press coverage of events in east Asia had been sketchy, only the *Press* in Christchurch having a regular Far East correspondent.[11] Of course in 1940 national attention was focused on events in Europe. The widely held belief at that time was that Japan was exhausted as a result of the war in China and, although mistrust of Japan increased as this war expanded into Indo-China in the latter half of 1940, it was generally believed that Japan would not risk antagonizing Britain or the United States. Those who warned politicians and the public in 1940 that Japan might have greater ambitions were generally ignored.[12]

Even after the fall of Singapore, which one wit in the Prime Minister's Department described as 'a new high in lows',[13] it seemed in spite of the exhortations of the press and the politicians, to be difficult for the New Zealand public to come to grips with the situation. While the *Press* claimed 'The fall of Singapore and the advance of Japan's military power southwards as far as New Guinea, the Solomons and the Gilberts has made New Zealanders conscious for the first time of their Pacific environment',[14] and the New Zealand correspondent to the *Round Table* reported 'increasing official awareness' of New Zealand's 'status as a Pacific country',[15] after the first fright, and once the assurance of American protection had been obtained, public attention switched back to the Middle East where New Zealanders were involved in battle.

In retrospect, this relative detachment from the more immediate dangers of the Pacific Front seems surprising but, quite apart from New Zealanders' ignorance of the Pacific by comparison with their knowledge of the theatres in Europe in which the war was being fought, there were reasons for this. Few New Zealanders were serving in the Pacific. Cumbersome procedures for clearance of news reports and heavy censorship resulted in poor press coverage of New Zealanders' activities there.[16] Severe censorship made for 'timid dullness' in local news reporting.[17] The main source of news, the BBC, inevitably focused primarily on events from the perspective of Europe. Even the Americans on the Atlantic seaboard stood 'mentally with their backs to the Pacific'.[18] A number of factors therefore combined to focus attention away from the Pacific. Besides, it became clear to New Zealanders before long that the Anglo-American plan was to defeat Germany first.

For most New Zealanders then, the heroes seemed to be in the Middle East. From November 1940 to 1942 when they were relieved by Americans, a New Zealand force had been stationed in Fiji. As their official historian wrote of the return of the New Zealand forces that year, 'These men bore no battle scars; they had no heroic tales to tell except those of endurance and boredom and toil in a climate as trying as any in the Pacific.'[19] Even after November 1942 when the Third New Zealand Division was sent to the Pacific and RNZAF squadrons were flying in the New Hebrides and the Solomons, the war against the Japanese in the Pacific lacked the 'glamour', and the heavy casualties, of the European theatre. Both the army and the airforce in the Pacific were ultimately under American command. The army had for the most part rather thankless guard duties and news of its actions at Vella Lavella, Treasury Island and the Green Islands in the Solomons group reached New Zealand belatedly. In terms of the strategy of the Pacific war these were clearly minor operations.[20] The RNZAF flew long sorties over miles of frequently empty ocean or against distant targets escorting the striking forces of American bombers. The constant enemies of all the men were the heat, rain, mud, malaria, dengue fever, yaws and hook worm, snakes and leeches which dogged them in the 'depressingly primitive' places in which they found themselves.[21] These did not make good news stories. It was hard for New Zealanders at home to focus on the Pacific when it seemed that neither the nation's news sources nor the Allied strategic planners were doing so. By the end of 1943 when the Japanese advance had been turned back at Guadalcanal, Japan was no longer regarded as a threat and New Zealanders felt, as Sir Harry Batterbee, the United Kingdom High Commissioner in New Zealand, reported, that 'their side was going to win'. The threat to the country had been brief; New Zealanders now had 'a feeling of security and absence from personal danger.'[22]

The result was, as the *Round Table* noted in January 1944, 'New Zealand has not become as Pacific conscious as once seemed possible', although it was felt that a 'discernible new interest in the affairs of the Pacific and America' was evident in the press.[23] In August 1944 in an editorial headed, 'We belong to the Pacific', the *Listener* commented that, if New Zealanders were not beginning to realize that Providence had placed them in the Pacific, not the Atlantic Ocean, it was their own fault. The editorial went on, 'Whether we realize it or not, like it or not, we have to find our place in a world occupied for centuries by tens of millions of Orientals'.[24] This was not a prospect New Zealanders cared for. It was one about which, it seems, most New Zealanders preferred to think very little, if they thought about it at all. In September 1945 the *Listener* again sought to encourage its readers to think about New Zealand's Pacific status claiming that signing the surrender document in Tokyo Bay had made New Zealand 'more consciously a Pacific nation'.[25] If it had, most New Zealanders had yet to absorb the fact.

Given New Zealanders' relative lack of interest in the Pacific in particular, and foreign policy in general, even at the end of the war, it was possible for the personality and predilections of a single individual to make a considerable impression on the entire policy-making process. Sir Harry Batterbee observed this when in September 1945 he reported on British prospects in the New Zealand scene and the degree to which wartime experience had affected the outlook of New Zealanders. He wrote to the Dominions Office:

> Despite the fright which New Zealand received from the directness of the Japanese threat in 1941–1942, New Zealand remains fundamentally more interested in European affairs than Pacific. . . . Pacific mindedness is, however, growing and will grow further. It is stronger amongst young than old 'progressives' than 'conservatives' and in the North Island than in the South Island.[26]

The weakness of Pacific mindedness in New Zealand resulted, Sir Harry claimed, in a policy determined more by the personal views of the Prime Minister, Peter Fraser, than by public opinion which he deemed to be generally non-existent. He believed that Prime Ministerial and public opinion alike could easily be influenced by outside pressure from the United Kingdom or Australia. New Zealand's specific interests in the Far East were, the High Commissioner reported, slight, and he believed its primary interest would be in the preservation of is own security against all comers. Given her lack of 'Pacific mindedness', he assured Whitehall, New Zealand would give general support to the power, influence and policies of the United Kingdom; would try to keep on good terms with the United States; and to co-operate with Australia in matters of common interest. All in all, he believed New Zealand would tend to give the United Kingdom the benefit of the doubt in disagreements over policies to be pursued. This estimate confirmed established opinion in the Dominions Office. The hard fact that the United Kingdom took 90 per cent of New Zealand's exports pre-war, was expected to keep New Zealand in the United Kingdom orbit in the long run.[27].

All the same, the Japanese advance after December 1941 had reminded New Zealand and Australia that the Pacific Ocean connected them irrevocably to Japan in the north. The Pacific War had made it evident that the Royal Navy could never again be New Zealand's 'shield and buckler' against a 'yellow peril' so that an aspect of New Zealand's dawning 'Pacific consciousness' and awareness of Japan was a new awareness of the importance to New Zealand of the United States, clearly now the major power in the Pacific.

NEW ZEALAND ATTITUDES TOWARDS JAPAN

Just as New Zealanders were low in general 'Pacific consciousness' before the war so too their consciousness of Japan was, at best, limited. Indeed, there is not much evidence that New Zealanders had given Japan serious thought before 1941 and a good deal of evidence that there was general ignorance about the country and its culture. 'New Zealand opinion about Japan', wrote one historian with careful restraint in 1940, 'has been a little uncertain, largely, no doubt, because of ignorance'.[28]

Of the Japanese most New Zealanders had no experience. There was no Japanese community in New Zealand where the 1936 census – the last census before the war – recorded 72 full-blooded Japanese and 30 Japanese of mixed race in a population of 1.5 million.[29] There was relatively little trade between the two countries partly because of the nature of New Zealand's exports, of which wool was the only item which Japan took in any quantity, partly because of inadequate shipping services between the two countries and partly because successive New Zealand governments concentrated on retaining New Zealand's share of the British market and did not seriously encourage initiatives elsewhere. In 1938 the Labour government, in office since 1935, announced increased duties on certain imported goods and in December 1938 introduced exchange control. Henceforth foreign exchange was available only for equipment, raw materials for industry and essential consumer goods not able to be produced in New Zealand. Moreover, where possible, imports were to be from Britain. The effect of these regulations was to bring about a decline in imports from Japan over the next two years. At the same time exports to Japan declined as a result of restrictions introduced by Japan after the outbreak of the Sino-Japanese war in July 1937.[30] The result was that, by 1940, New Zealand's exports to Japan represented only 0.11 per cent of total exports, and imports from Japan represented 1.5 per cent of total imports.[31] In the farming and business sectors of New Zealand therefore, there was no commercial reason to think positively, or indeed at all, about Japan.

New Zealanders had nevertheless very clear ideas about 'Asians' or, as they were more frequently described, 'Asiatics', in general. The Japanese along with the Chinese, who made up the largest pre-war 'Asiatic' community in New Zealand, were at the top of the list of the most undesired immigrants. Bitter anti-Asiatic feeling had in fact been characteristic of a lengthy period of New Zealand history.[32]

For most white New Zealanders race relations in their country are most probably seen as an issue of the 1980s. Hitherto white New Zealanders had generally prided themselves on New Zealand's good race relations. In the eyes of these New Zealanders, tolerance, racial harmony and freedom from racial prejudice characterized their society and their relations with Maori New Zealanders. But tolerance and harmony were not expected to extend to 'Asiatics', in which group were lumped Indians, Chinese, Japanese, and Malay peoples from the Pacific and south east Asia. New Zealanders' assumptions about these people were racist to a high degree and their attitudes little different from those of Australians with whom they tended to compare themselves favourably. Fear of the 'yellow peril' combined with feelings of racial superiority joined to put all Asians at the bottom of a hierarchy, at the peak of which were those New Zealanders of British origin. Successive immigration acts from the 1880s had reflected these attitudes and, as a Labour Department spokesman asserted frankly as late as 1954, immigration policy was based on the wishes of the New Zealand people as a whole, and it was their desire that 'people whose stock originated in Britain shall always have the overwhelming predominance in the total people of New Zealand'.[33]

It might have been expected that when the Labour government came into office the worst features of New Zealand's racially discriminating immigration policies would be alleviated. The Labour Party, after all, espoused internationalist causes in other areas. There was, however, as much racism in the Party and the trade unions as there was in other sectors of New Zealand society at the time. As it was explained to a Party conference back in 1920. 'Internationalism did not mean a reckless intermingling of white and coloured races'[34] and Michael Savage, who was Prime Minister when war broke out, was on record as saying he did not think New Zealanders wanted a 'piebald New Zealand'.[35] Clearly he was not alone in this belief.

From the point of view of the Labour Party there were also high moral grounds with which to reinforce any negative views of Japan. Since 1935 Labour had been strong in its support for the League of Nations and the principle of collective security. After the outbreak of the Sino-Japanese war the New Zealand delegation to the League and at the Brussels conference condemned Japan as a violator of this principle.[36] Although the government ultimately fell into line with a British policy towards Japan which they saw as 'appeasement', the events in China tended to reinforce the negative stereotype many New Zealanders held of the Japanese.

New Zealanders in 1941 then remained largely unaware of all but Anglo-Saxon culture and in the case of Japan their ignorance was combined with feelings of hostility towards Asian people in general. Japan furthermore was a country whose actions had violated the principle of collective security and undermined the credibility of the League of Nations, both of which the government and many New Zealanders held dear. The outbreak of war in the Pacific inevitably caused Japan's supposedly undesirable racial and national characteristics to be highlighted, and confirmed New Zealanders' prejudices against the Japanese.[37]

As an historian of the war years in the Far East has pointed out, individuals are quite capable of holding at one time, both anti-racist and racist views. Furthermore, these views may not operate to the same degree at all times and in all places.[38] If the outbreak of war in the Pacific confirmed New Zealanders' prejudices against the Japanese, it also required them to develop more positive images of the Chinese – in China at least, if not in New Zealand – since China had now become one of the Allies. In April 1942 when invasion was still seen as a possibility, the New Zealand *Listener*, a journal with some standing among intellectuals, published under the heading 'How to Tell Friends from Enemies', some 'rules of thumb' to enable readers to distinguish Japanese from Chinese. As might be expected the Japanese; short, stocky, lean, stiffly erect and 'hard heeled', with its close-set bespectacled eyes, positive, dogmatic, arrogant manner, and loud laugh ringing out at inappropriate times, suffered by comparison with the Chinese stereotype now seen as tall, fat, placid, kindly, open, relaxed and 'easy-gaited'. The more 'kindly' facial expression of the Chinese was said to be a way that those who knew them best could tell Chinese from Japanese.[39] If the *Listener*'s readers thought this simplistic stuff they chose not to comment. In an article entitled 'What to do with the Japanese' published in 1943, a writer in the *Listener* claimed that, while the Chinese thought 'like other people', the Japanese did not. This writer saw the problem in terms of whether the Japanese people could be 'reintegrated into mankind'.[40] Of course the fostering of crude images of the enemy was not confined to New Zealand or to the Allies, but in the case of New Zealand and Japan, the images for the most part enhanced an already distorted mental picture. New Zealanders were told, and readily believed, there were 'no nice Japanese' and the publication of Japanese atrocities in Hong Kong and Nanking confirmed this assertion.[41] Under the headline, 'Now we know the Jap.[sic] is a Beast, Hair! Knives! Toenails!' the *Auckland Star* urged readers in March 1942 to get ready to die fighting.[42] The idea that Japan must be pursued to the death, or until the 'necessary and desirable' process of laying her cities waste and reducing Tokyo to a 'handful of dust' had been completed, was part of the popular propaganda.[43] It was, a writer in the *Listener* suggested in April 1945, easier to teach Hitler and Himmler a lesson than to teach one to the Japanese. The Japanese militarists and all they stood for must be destroyed, although extermination of the whole race, it was conceded, was 'neither commonsense nor Christian'.[44] New Zealanders at home may, in spite of the propaganda, have been difficult to rouse to a sense of 'Pacific consciousness' in the face of the Japanese threat, but there is no doubt that they hated and feared these unknown people and thought of them, as one writer has put it, 'in terms appropriate to a newly discovered zoological species'.[45]

THE FIGHT FOR A 'VOICE'

In 1943 Sir Carl Berendsen, New Zealand's most experienced foreign service officer, then New Zealand High Commissioner in

Canberra, observed, 'I think we shall have to fight pretty hard to maintain a voice in the world. Churchill and Roosevelt ... are determined to run this war by themselves and I think it quite probable that Britain and America will attempt to run the world after the war', [46] a view entirely shared by Herbert Vere Evatt, Australia's dynamic Minister for External Affairs. Dr Evatt, the chief architect of Australia's Japan policy from 1941 to 1949, was deeply suspicious of British and American post-war ambitions and determined that Australia's voice should be heard.

It was their awareness of the danger that, in spite of their wartime efforts in the Middle East and the Pacific, and in spite of their geographical location, Australia and New Zealand might be consulted neither by Britain nor the United States about the Japanese peace treaty or post-war policy in the Pacific, which led, in 1944, to the Canberra conference between Australia and New Zealand.[47] Knowledge of this meeting, which was Evatt's brain-child, was deliberately withheld from the British and Americans by the Australians.[48]

The New Zealanders, who had merely been contemplating an exchange of views, were surprised and disconcerted to find the Australians contemplating a formal treaty. Peter Fraser, however, unlike many another politician, admired Evatt[49] and, of course, shared his 'Pacific consciousness'. Carl Berendsen, who as New Zealand High Commissioner in Canberra was a member of the New Zealand delegation, shared Evatt's awareness of the need for small countries to make their voice heard. The doubter in the team was Alister McIntosh, the recently appointed Secretary for External Affairs. He was always chary of the Australian connection and was later to declare himself 'sincerely and deeply ashamed' of the part he had played in the formation of the Australian-New Zealand Agreement.[50] In 1944, even had he sought to do so, he was of course in no position to stand out against Peter Fraser who at that time dominated foreign policy decision-making in New Zealand quite as firmly as Evatt did in Australia. On 21 January 1944 therefore, the Australian-New Zealand Agreement was signed, setting out the signatories' interest in all matters concerning the south west and south Pacific. The Agreement was accompanied by a proposal for a conference of all the governments with territorial interests in the south Pacific to consider problems of security, post-war development and the welfare of the indigenous

inhabitants.[51] Neither Britain nor the United States was amused
by this demonstration of independence and solidarity. The British
described the agreement as a 'deplorable monument of egregious
amateurism in international affairs'[52] and regarded it as 'unfortunate' that Australia and New Zealand should have organized
and carried out a conference without consultation with the United
Kingdom which had such 'immense interests in the Pacific'.[53] The
Dominions Office deplored the proposal for a south Pacific
conference and made this clear. On the British response Alister
McIntosh commented, 'I doubt if the Dominions Office have had
greater enjoyment in drafting a message in years. As a model of
frigidity I doubt if it has had its equal in all our years of
correspondence'.[54] Nevertheless, Peter Fraser, the Prime
Minister, McIntosh noted, 'took it quite calmly'.

The Prime Ministers of New Zealand and Australia had also to
submit to a dressing down by Secretary of State Cordell Hull; for
the Americans were equally outraged.[55] Evatt's comment was that
one couldn't make an omelette without breaking eggs, and the fact
that there were reactions from both the United Kingdom and the
United States indicated the importance of the Canberra decision.[56]
In the long run, however, the Agreement made only a ripple. The
reactions to its signing were nevertheless a portent of what was to
come.

Plans for post-war security were already being made in the
United States at Dumbarton Oaks by representatives of the Great
Powers. The Dumbarton Oaks proposals for the post-war world
organization were satisfactory to neither New Zealand nor
Australia. The excessive authority conferred on the Great Powers
through their veto challenged the right of small nations to an
effective voice in the world forum. Fraser and Evatt fought a
tireless and fruitless battle against the veto at the San Francisco
conference in May 1945 when the United Nations was established.[57] Berendsen, who was present, commented:

> We found ourselves being treated with that kind of friendly
> and patronising tolerance which adults extend to the frac-
> tious child. We were told, not of course in so many words,
> for that might be interpreted as impolite, that we were
> unrealistic, that we were not facing the facts of international
> life... we were urged, in the nicest possible and most indirect
> ways to be good children and not to rock the boat.[58]

THE QUESTION OF REGIONAL PACTS

Fraser and Evatt shared a determination to have a 'voice' and they shared a 'Pacific consciousness' which was more highly developed than that of many of their countrymen. By signing the Australian-New Zealand Agreement or Canberra pact they had signalled their special interest in the south and south-west Pacific but this was not seen by Fraser as a precedent for the establishment of wider regional security pacts in the future. Fraser made clear his lack of sympathy for the iea of regional security pacts and agreed when Berendsen, in his inimitable style, declared in 1943 'We must not be cribbed, cabined, coffined or confined to our own area'.[59] Fraser argued there were few problems that were 'purely regional'[60] and in any case felt that a pact in which New Zealand found itself allied with 'Asian' nations – which definition included the Philippines – would not have that 'intimate character' to which New Zealand was accustomed in its international relationships.[61] Notwithstanding the Canberra pact, therefore, New Zealand resisted the idea of a chain of regional pacts which raised its head from time to time after 1944. The concept of a Pacific or Asian region as a political unit, was, declared Fraser in 1944, 'unreal'[62] and the idea of regional security 'a mirage'.[63] A Southeast Asian regional pact to which Australia and New Zealand might belong, floated by the United Kingdom in 1949, was dismissed by McIntosh as 'designed more for artistic symmetry than for any practical purpose'.[64] Ironically, the idea of regional security arrangements has become more acceptable to New Zealand as the national outlook has become more independent and 'Pacific minded'.

NEW ZEALAND AUSTRALIA AND THE POTSDAM DECLARATION

As it was, in 1945, having declared their special interest in the Pacific and been admonished for this action; having battled publicly and in vain for their view of the post-war security arrangements, New Zealand and Australia were still ignored when the terms for the Japanese surrender were defined. These were worked out by the Great Powers at the Potsdam Conference in

July 1945 and New Zealand and Australia were informed of them in August, a week before Japan's formal acceptance of the terms.[65] The need for constant vigilance in the 'fight for a voice' had once again been demonstrated. Both New Zealand and Australia protested vigorously at the lack of consultation.[66] They were also alarmed by the suggestion at Potsdam that a Council of Foreign Ministers representing the Great Powers should be set up to deal with peace negotiations and territorial settlements. Supporting Evatt's stand on this, Fraser told the Dominions Office:

It is our view that the proposed peace terms should be examined by all those powers who have a direct interest in each settlement including not only the great powers but other belligerent states including the British Dominions which have contributed substantially to the defeat of any of the countries concerned.[67]

The final insult, resented particularly by Australia, was that they had to fight for independent status at the Japanese surrender. The Dominions Office advised that Admiral Sir Bruce Fraser had been designated to represent the United Kingdom government at the formal surrender ceremonies and invited the Australian and New Zealand governments to send a representative to be attached to Admiral Fraser at the ceremonies.

Partly, no doubt as a result of the known Australian attitude, the United Kingdom also asked Washington that agreement to the terms of surrender should be obtained from the Dominion governments before they were published. The terms of surrender were, however, an American affair and the views of the Dominions, no more than those of the United Kingdom, really counted. All were presented with a *fait accompli*.

New Zealand complied with the invitation to send a representative to the surrender ceremonies at once and designated Air Vice-Marshal Leonard Isitt, Chief of Air Staff, to join Admiral Fraser[68] but, having been ignored thus far, Evatt was determined that at least the Australian Government should be separately represented. When their request for separate representation was initially refused, further protests were made to the State Department and direct representations were made to General MacArthur who had been designated Supreme Commander for the Allied Powers

(SCAP). As a result it was agreed that the representatives of Australia, New Zealand, Canada, the Netherlands and France should separately sign the Instrument of Surrender.[69] New Zealand and others were thus the beneficiaries of Australia's determination to use every opportunity to establish its position as an independent Pacific nation. The signing took place in Tokyo Bay on 2 September 1945.

The Australians were aware that they had probably not endeared themselves either to the United States or to the United Kingdom in bringing about this result. Nor were they convinced that the result demonstrated in any way that the United States was now prepared to regard Australia or New Zealand as a party principal in all proceedings associated with the Japanese peace settlement. Vigilance would still be required.

THE COMMONWEALTH RELATIONSHIP

The apparent indifference of the United States to their interests was not simply a matter of New Zealand and Australia being small powers. There was a problem created by the Commonwealth relationship which was difficult for the United States, or indeed any other non-Commonwealth country, to understand. In 1944 Peter Fraser had described the relationship as a paradoxical one, the paradox being that 'the freer we become, the closer we draw together; the more our constitutional bonds are relaxed, the more closely we are held in bonds of friendship . . . the more truly we are one in spirit, one in peace as well as war'.[70]

Not surprisingly, outsiders required some education in the operation of this mystical union. If indeed this group was 'one in spirit', outside powers might have been forgiven for believing that the maxim 'one for all and all for one' applied. Of course it did not. There were difficulties inherent in this paradox for all parties concerned. For Whitehall, the relationship with Washington was all important in the post-war world. In these circumstances New Zealand or Australian importunity, where it appeared to challenge American plans for, and dominance of, the Pacific, could be a liability. A 'Commonwealth stance' could not be adopted by the United Kingdom at the cost of antagonizing Washington. Furthermore, notwithstanding his declaration of faith in the oneness of spirit in the Commonwealth, Fraser was well aware of the tension between the role of loyal Dominion and independent small state.[71] In an emergency, he knew from experience, the United Kingdom almost always failed to consult the Dominions and on most vital questions did not alter its policy to meet Commonwealth views in general, or those of Australia and New Zealand in particular.[72] Like Evatt, Fraser had no illusions about the capacity or willingness of the United Kingdom to meet Commonwealth wishes; even if his language was never as forceful or as colourful. The United Kingdom, declared Evatt, was always 'liable to double-cross' Australia and New Zealand; sometimes thought in 'four power bloc terms', and certainly 'couldn't be relied on to think consistently in United Nations terms'. The United Kingdom was, he said, 'not to be trusted in Pacific and Far Eastern matters' and in any case 'didn't know much about the Pacific'.[73] This was scarcely a reassuring demonstration of that 'oneness of spirit' commended by Fraser. According to reports, however, Fraser was 'very fond' of Evatt and regarded him as 'a much maligned and misunderstood man'. He was nevertheless a thorn in the flesh of the Foreign Office, and it was not easy for New Zealand officials to see Evatt in the 'angelic light' in which their Prime Minister regarded him.[74]

Evatt was not, of course, above calling for Commonwealth solidarity if he saw it as likely to promote Australia's interests and indeed Evatt was well aware that, rather than acting in isolation, Australia was likely, on many occasions, to have a better chance of promoting its interests by sustaining combined British Commonwealth authority and trying to influence the direction of Commonwealth policy in the Pacific from within.[75] Naturally Evatt sought New Zealand's support in his plans for the post-war Pacific. Responding to Evatt's promotion of one such scheme, Fraser asked whether it was right for Australia and New Zealand to attempt to have United Kingdom policy on particular subjects modified to meet Commonwealth wishes. 'We cannot', he wrote, 'extricate ourselves even if we wanted to, from the consequences of many United Kingdom decisions. Nevertheless there comes a point where we have to decide how far we can have it both ways; how far can we reconcile our status as independent nations with joint Commonwealth action?'[76]

The question for New Zealand, which valued, and, it was felt, as a small country, needed the extra leverage the Commonwealth team provided, was how far behaviour as a good team member could be reconciled with the desire for a 'voice'. It was a dilemma which was never really solved but simply ceased to be significant as the Commonwealth grew in membership and diversity and both Commonwealth solidarity and British power declined.

MAKING POLICY IN NEW ZEALAND

In 1945 Sir Harry Batterbee had drawn attention to the importance of the Prime Minister's personal views in the determination of foreign policy. In 1949 another United Kingdom High Commissioner made the same point:

> Mr Fraser alone determines the policy of the New Zealand government on every question of foreign affairs. No other member of cabinet is knowledgeable about or interested in such matters. Mr Fraser rarely consults his colleagues upon these subjects and quite frequently does not even inform them when he has taken important decisions . . . . Thus New Zealand's policy on international political issues is as personal as that of any dictatorship.[77]

In foreign affairs Fraser was an idealist, taking a high moral line and defining problems in black and white terms. 'Horse trading' in international affairs was to him, it was said, 'the height of political immorality'.[78] Arguments of expediency, were apt, one diplomat wrote, 'to appear in the guise of the powers of darkness, tempting Mr Fraser's conscience', and he resented those occasions when he felt he had been diverted from the 'paths of righteousness'.[79] For this reason the British tried as far as possible to draft messages to Fraser with the emphasis on moral rightness rather than expediency.[80] Fraser's idealism was, of course, reflected in New Zealand's stance at Commonwealth meetings and at the United Nations.

Fraser's ideas on the principles which must inform the conduct of foreign affairs by New Zealand jibed well with those of Carl Berendsen who for many years had guided prime ministers who, for the most part, had been little interested in New Zealand's external relations. Berendsen in fact, in later life 'recollected in tranquillity' that Fraser's judgement in matters relating to foreign and Commonwealth affairs was 'impeccable'.[81]

The administration of New Zealand's external relations in an organized way had begun in 1926 with the appointment of Berendsen as Imperial Affairs Officer within the Prime Minister's department. For the next ten years he alone with a clerk, T. J. Sherrard, and a typist, read and analysed incoming papers and prepared the speeches New Zealand prime ministers made at Imperial Conferences and representatives from New Zealand made at the League of Nations.[82] In 1928 responsibility for the administration of New Zealand's Mandate of Western Samoa was added to Berendsen's duties when he became, in addition to Imperial Affairs Officer, Secretary for External Affairs, at that time an office concerned exclusively with the Samoan Mandate. In 1932 Berendsen became permanent head of the Prime Minister's Department and in 1935 Alister McIntosh was appointed his deputy. Immensely hard-working, knowledgeable, able and opinionated Berendsen carried out these tasks and organized New Zealand's external relations from a small back room. When the war broke out Berendsen added Secretary of the War Cabinet to his duties.

Berendsen who believed, as he himself wrote, 'Right is right and wrong is wrong and it can never be wise to do wrong or tolerate wrong',[83] found himself at one with the high moral tone of Labour's foreign policy and applauded the government's support for Britain's war effort. He was, however, a man who disliked what he called 'shilly-shallying', made rapid and firm decisions, worked quickly and insisted on punctuality.[84] Fraser, who became Prime Minister in 1940 cared about none of these things. His day was completely disorganized, he would make no appointments and was, diplomats complained, 'at the beck and call of all and sundry'.[85] Having succeeded in obtaining an interview on an important matter, a frustrated British diplomat wrote:

one must expect to be interrupted a few minutes later in order that some Maori delegation may present its views to him on some matter of parochial significance. This may take two or three hours. Upon readmission, one may perhaps get a quarter of an hour of Mr Fraser's time, punctuated by almost unceasing telephone calls about the entertainment of some government guest, or the arrangements for a reception to some sporting body, or the affairs of some church in a vital constituency.[86]

Of course, in part, this state of affairs reflected the importance given by the Prime Minister to domestic over external matters but even in domestic matters it was difficult to extract a decision from him and he had no compunction about keeping his officials waiting about for hours. All this drove Berendsen, by his own admission, 'nearly to distraction'.[87] Once Japan came into the war and especially after the fall of Singapore in 1942, two things had become clear; the first was that New Zealand needed more extensive and sophisticated arrangements for its external relations since it now must forge a new relationship with the United States and to an extent Australia; the second was that Carl Berendsen and Peter Fraser could no longer work together. The clash of temperament between these two able men was too great given the strains of wartime. Berendsen therefore went to Canberra as New Zealand's first High Commissioner to Australia in 1943. McIntosh, Berendsen's protégé, became Secretary of a newly constituted Department of External Affairs which included the Prime Minister's Department. In 1945 McIntosh became Permanent Head of the Prime Minister's Department and the two departments were to remain under one head until 1975.

Berendsen had been very much a one man band. It was McIntosh who set about establishing a professional Department of External Affairs. He was an able, tactful and patient civil servant who could cope with the vagaries of the Prime Minister and attracted the loyalty and support of those he personally recruited to his department in the early years. When the war ended in 1945 the number in the Department in New Zealand had grown but was still very small.[88] Recruiting thereafter continued only slowly as priority was given to returned servicemen and in any case training of new staff presented problems given the small existing base of the Department.[89]

The new Department worked under a number of difficulties. Fraser dominated the political scene and determined foreign policy. It was difficult for the Department even to make recommendations on policy. In addition it was the target of attacks in Parliament from politicians of both parties who saw little reason for New Zealand to have an independent foreign policy at all. Nevertheless, in the face of these obstacles the United Kingdom High Commissioner observed, 'the Department of External Affairs preserves an outlook full of youth, zest, energy and independence'.[90] This then was the infant organization which tackled, for the first time in New Zealand's history, the task of formulating a coherent New Zealand policy towards Japan.

NEW ZEALAND POLICY AND THE OCCUPATION

A British historian has written that New Zealand's diplomacy in relation to the Occupation of Japan was marked by 'an air of unreality' and failure to comprehend the realities of power. New Zealand, he has claimed, apparently inhabited 'an idealistic world detached from harsh diplomatic realities'.[91]

Such a judgement, it might be argued, fails to take into account the realities as they exist for small powers. Inevitably their world view is different from that of the big players. Their problem in diplomacy is a timeless one: how the small may influence the great. There are a few ways in which this can be done. Idealism is one of several blunt weapons available. Gaining a reputation for impartiality; speaking one's mind; taking the moral high ground – unrealistic as these may seem to be, and irritating as they undoubtedly are for the players whose stakes are much higher – are ways in which a small power may make its presence felt.

In the matter of the Occupation of Japan, New Zealand's interest focused on the future security of the Pacific region, which at that time seemed likely to be threatened only by Japan. For New Zealand, the diplomacy of the Occupation of Japan itself, had no other more specific focus. Matters like possible future Japanese trade competition; or the resumption of trade with Japan; or leadership of British Commonwealth interests in the Pacific, which concentrated the minds of the British and the Australians respectively on 'realities' of power and self-interest – were of minimal interest to New Zealand in 1945. From its relatively detached position it is not surprising that New Zealand felt it could afford to concern itself with wider issues like international justice and co-operation and to take the high-minded ground with which, in any case, the New Zealand Labour government was most comfortable in international affairs. In 1945 New Zealand still had hopes that international forums where small-power interests might be represented and heard would yet be of account.

In the history of the development of New Zealand foreign policy, the years of the Occupation of Japan, 1945–1952, represent a transition period. While the war in the Pacific had demonstrated that the simple proposition of relying on the British for New Zealand's security was no longer enough, there was still a strong feeling among the public and in politicians' minds that New Zealand's security and interests were closely linked with those of Britain and the Commonwealth. Although desirous of maintaining the relations established in wartime with the United States, on 'the friendliest terms and the firmest basis', and aware of the need to develop that relationship, New Zealand's involvement in matters relating to the Occupation of Japan in 1945 arose as much from its desire to demonstrate itself a good Commonwealth team player as from a desire to win the goodwill and recognition of the United States, now the dominant power in the region. New Zealand emphasized its Pacific identity to both Britain and the United States as a matter of expediency, in order to establish its credentials as a small nation whose concern about possible Japanese aggression in the future was a legitimate one. This was a matter of tactics and not necessarily an indication that the New Zealand public or its politicians were a great deal more 'Pacific minded' than in the past. After the war, attention in New Zealand was again concentrated on Britain and Europe. There is no evidence of an increased desire to know more about Japan or the diverse Pacific world to New Zealand's north.

During the Occupation period, however, the Japanese peace treaty had to be formulated. This was a matter of high policy, distinct from the mechanics of the Occupation itself. The formulation of New Zealand's requirements of the peace treaty and the protracted negotiations relating to it which were carried out within the Commonwealth structure, and with the United States, were an important test for the officers of the Department of External Affairs. On the one hand New Zealand's needs were different from those of the United Kingdom so the fact of there being no Commonwealth solidarity on the issue had to be faced. On the other hand New Zealand officials had the task of making New Zealand's security concerns regarding Japan known and understood in the United States. The south Pacific was not normally seen as an area with which the United States need concern itself and American officials were unaccustomed to taking into account the requirements of small and distant states. The making of the Japanese peace treaty therefore represented for New Zealand and its Department of External Affairs, a challenge different in kind from other aspects of the Occupation period.

Before the Occupation was over, the Commonwealth had changed in composition, and with this its solidarity on defence matters had weakened; British interest in Japan, which was centred on British commercial concerns and prospects, was quite different from that of New Zealand; it had become evident that New Zealand's security priorities as a Pacific nation would only be met by more specific cultivation of the United States. By the time the Occupation ended and the peace treaty was finally signed New Zealand was committed to a new, if as yet publicly unrecognized era, in which the United States would be the arbiter of her security concerns. This era would also see New Zealand's focus on the Pacific and Japan change as the truth gradually penetrated that Britain would not only never again be the 'shield and buckler', but would also never again be New Zealand's all absorbing trading partner. By 1952 it had been recognized in official circles at least, that New Zealand needed the United States, a powerful nation in which she had only a limited constituency. In the next decade it would become clear that New Zealand needed Japan, a country in which she had no constituency at all. But already in 1952 the clear signs were that things would never be the same again.

In some ways then, much of the story of New Zealand's participation in the Occupation, which historically belongs to the end of an era in New Zealand's diplomacy, has an old-fashioned diplomatic quality, flavoured with that high-minded apparent disinterestedness which in retrospect might appear naive. It is peopled with characters like Peter Fraser speaking of principle and Carl Berendsen thundering uninhibitedly about the rights of small nations, men confident of New Zealand's place in the universe and demanding, without apology, a voice. In other ways the period can be seen as a period in which all the portents of change are already present.

2
The Occupation: Political Involvement: New Zealand and the Far Eastern Commission

The Occupation of Japan had for New Zealand three aspects; political, military and legal. The political aspect, represented by New Zealand's participation in the Far Eastern Commission (FEC), that body consisting of eleven nations and ostensibly having the task of advizing General MacArthur (SCAP), was the only one which the New Zealand government regarded with any real enthusiasm. It seemed that this might be a forum in which the views of a small Pacific nation carried weight. It was the kind of forum New Zealand knew and understood. The military aspect was represented by New Zealand's contribution to the British Commonwealth Occupation Force (BCOF). The New Zealand government participated in this operation with the greatest reluctance and out of a desire to demonstrate solidarity with Britain and the Commonwealth. Jayforce as the New Zealand brigade was known, was always unpopular in New Zealand. Finally, New Zealand was involved in a legal aspect of the Occupation by reason of the participation of a New Zealand judge and prosecutor in the International Military Tribunal for the Far East (IMTFE). The New Zealand government saw New Zealand's representation in the IMTFE in terms of a duty and responsibility to be borne by those nations which were members of the FEC and had signed the Instrument of Surrender. Some hopes were expressed that the fact that New Zealanders were involved in the Tribunal's proceedings, would stimulate New Zealanders' interest in the outside world and lead them to ponder questions of political responsibility and international law. The Tribunal was thus seen, optimistically, to have wider implications for New Zealanders than that of seeing justice done to those who were deemed to have led Japan into war. In New Zealand, as elsewhere in the West, however, the drawn-out and complex proceedings of the IMTFE were largely ignored and its findings, when they appeared finally in 1948 were received with little interest.

In 1945, however, the New Zealand government accepted responsibilities associated with the Occupation of Japan with hopes of a positive spin-off, both domestically and also in terms of New Zealand's relations within the Commonwealth and with the United States.

ESTABLISHMENT OF THE FEC

The establishment of the FEC owed everything to United States initiative. The American plan for an international commission was already well advanced when the war ended. An alternative 'detailed and ambitious' British proposal for a control commission based in Tokyo which was submitted to the United States and other interested parties in August 1945 was soon pushed aside.[1] The American proposal was for a Far Eastern Advisory Commission (FEAC) to be composed of the United States, the United Kingdom and the USSR plus Canada, Australia, New Zealand, France, the Netherlands and the Philippines. It was to be based in Washington.

New Zealand was, from the beginning, pleased to accept the idea of the FEAC. Furthermore, since it was decided the Commission should sit in Washington, New Zealand had on the spot a man with experience of just such forums who could represent the country effectively and with style. Sir Carl Berendsen, who had years of experience at Commonwealth conferences, the League of Nations and, more recently, as New Zealand's representative at the United Nations, was a skilled operator on the conference scene. He was also well known in the relatively much smaller diplomatic circles of Washington at that time. For Berendsen, as for the New Zealand government, the FEC was about participating in international decision-making on the future shape of the Japanese government, about the elimination of the militarist elements in Japanese society and the construction of a democratic state, about control in what he expected to be a long occupation. He therefore approached his FEAC task with initial enthusiasm and certainly endorsed the sentiments of Alister McIntosh who wrote of New Zealand's role in this forum:

> We are fortunate that our distinctive national interests are not so powerful as to endanger the wider interests we have in international justice and security; and when we come to political issues our views may carry more weight if we have established a reputation for impartiality.[2]

Berendsen of course knew little about Japan and shared the prejudices of most New Zealanders against Asians. He was impressed, however, when he went to Japan with members of the FEAC in January 1946, with many aspects of Japanese culture, though he was, and remained, deeply suspicious of the militaristic potential of Japan which he believed, like the leopard, would not change its spots, and of the Japanese people whom he found strange and unattractive.[3] But the Commission was as much about international relationships in the post-war Pacific world as about Japan, and Berendsen was all too soon to be disillusioned about the part which New Zealand could play in it and about how much influence this international organization could wield in shaping Japan's future.

Since Berendsen was in place and was to add representation of New Zealand at the FEC to his other duties, this aspect of New Zealand's participation in the Occupation of Japan had the merit of being uncostly, an important consideration at the end of the war. The small New Zealand office in Washington was, however, unreasonably stretched by the addition of this work. In December 1945 therefore, 'Dick' (later Sir Guy) Powles, an experienced lawyer who had served in the Third New Zealand Division in the Pacific during the war, was recruited by McIntosh and Fraser, first as a member of the New Zealand FEAC delegation to Japan in January 1946 then as First Secretary, (later Counsellor), at the New Zealand Legation in Washington, to do much of the FEC work.[4]

The FEAC held its first meeting in October 1945 but the Soviet Union was not represented. The Soviets favoured four power control of Japan and it was not until the Council of Foreign Ministers meeting in Moscow in December 1945 that American proposals for a Commission were finally agreed. The price for this agreement was a four-power Allied Council for Japan to sit in Tokyo and 'advise' SCAP. In January 1946 the FEAC evolved into the Far Eastern Commission (FEC) with the Soviet membership of the group confirmed.[5] The New Zealand government saw it as, or perhaps simply hoped it would become, 'the supreme organ' for deciding the policies governing Japan which General MacArthur would put into effect.[6]

The terms of reference of the FEC as finally laid down were much criticized, evidently with justification, by Berendsen, a lawyer and an expert and experienced draftsman. As a result of what Berendsen regarded as shoddy draftsmanship, the Commission was to be plagued by recurring and tedious arguments about the meaning of certain expressions and provisions in the terms.[7] It had more than enough problems without this.

The functions of the FEC were threefold: 'to formulate policies, principles and standards in conformity with which fulfillment by Japan of its obligations under the Instrument of Surrender might be accomplished'; to review directives issued to SCAP; to consider 'such other matters as may be assigned to it by agreement between participating governments'. These apparently substantial powers were limited by the agreement that the United States might issue interim directives on most subjects, by the fact of American power and by the fact that the United States recognized SCAP's authority as total in almost all circumstances.[8]

Whatever the limitations of the Commission might prove to be, the New Zealand government knew in 1946 it had to be content. Moreover given the limitations of New Zealand's diplomatic representation at the time, the FEC was a welcome vehicle for the provision of firsthand information about Occupation policy and a platform where concerns might be expressed about the implementation of the Potsdam Declaration and New Zealand's future security in relation to Japan.[9] New Zealand therefore prepared to take the FEC seriously. In welcoming its establishment, the Minister of External Affairs had noted: 'At least New Zealand can be consulted and voice its views on the treatment of Japan and it meets our need for direct information from our own representative about the situation in that country.'[10] – an assessment of the value of the FEC for New Zealand which said much about the problems of representation and information gathering which plague small countries. New Zealand had no official government representative in Japan at the time, and in Wellington, information about Japan was sparse.

The FEC was of course to be based in Washington, though Berendsen thought this was a mistake. He reported, however:

> General opinion appears to be that it is better to have the Commission in close touch with the United States Government even with the disadvantages of less immediate contact with conditions in Japan, than to have it involved in difficulties with MacArthur at close quarters. Experience has shown that MacArthur can only be handled through the American Joint Chiefs of Staff and the President, and that the Commission is therefore strategically best placed here.[11]

These comments might have served as a warning. New Zealand's concern was that small nations be accorded their 'appropriate and proportionate voice' in the decision-making process at the Commission.[12] In the light of this, the news that one of the conditions agreed at Moscow when Soviet entry in the Commission was secured, was the right of veto by the Big Four; the United States, the United Kingdom, China and the USSR, was particularly disappointing. Berendsen's 'hydra-headed veto monster', much hated and feared by small countries had appeared again.[13] Its effect was, that controversial matters were not put to the vote, rather, the veto operated covertly, issues were discussed endlessly and seldom resolved in the FEC.[14] Another disappointment for New Zealand was the exclusiveness of the administrative organs of the FEC. New Zealand had hoped the FEC, its secretariat and the executive department of SCAP, might be 'truly international in character' as a good example to the Japanese and as a check on the Big Four and on the 'personal pecularities' of SCAP.[15] This was not to be. Apart from one Australian who was Economic Secretary, the Secretariat of the FEC was all American[16] and of course SCAP brooked no interference with his appointments.

In the long run the New Zealand government knew it must accept what was offered. This, however, was not seen, particularly by Berendsen, as a reason for not expressing New Zealand's views at any time.[17] Moreover, New Zealand saw itself as having some rather specific expertise to offer. In those days New Zealand was accustomed to seeing itself as the social laboratory of the world and, on such matters as labour organization and social security where, as Berendsen put it, 'the United States did not shine', he thought, optimistically, the benefit of New Zealand's experience should be welcomed.[18] But the American Occupation was already established by January 1946 when the FEC came into existence and had begun to boast of its achievements in revolutionizing Japanese society. There was little prospect of advice from New Zealand or any other country being sought seriously on these or any other topics. In the event the FEC found itself most often reacting to a series of *faits accomplis*.

At the first meeting of the FEC Berendsen was elected chairman of the Steering Committee, one of seven committees into which the work of the FEC was divided. This committee was responsible for organizing the Commission business, co-ordinating the functions of the working committees and considering their recommendations and proposals. Berendsen had a reputation as a first class chairman and tried to inject some dynamism through the Steering Committee into the work of the FEC as a whole.[19] He did not succeed.

THE WORK OF THE COMMISSION

The major issues of discussion in the first year soon illustrated the limitations of this so-called 'experiment in international co-operation'. It quickly became clear that balancing the commission's right to 'formulate policies' for Japan against the special position of the United States would be a difficult and delicate matter. Only when proposals had the blessing of the United States was there the slightest chance of their being adopted. This meant that anything that implied criticism of, or offered alternatives to existing policies, was inevitably stalled. It is true that a surprising number of policy decisions were reached in the first year including the Basic Post-Surrender Policy for Japan agreed in June 1947 but, by and large, these were non-controversial.[20] It was a situation designed to try sorely Sir Carl Berendsen's admittedly limited stores of patience.

When the FEC convened, a new Japanese constitution and the question of the date for Japanese elections were immediately major issues. Constitutional revision was already underway in

Japan and the evidence suggests that MacArthur was anxious to push this through before there was any chance of FEC interference. On the elections, Berendsen believed, two issues were involved. In his opinion the FEC rather than SCAP should have jurisdiction over when the elections were to be held, and he believed that early elections would unduly favour the old ultranationalist elements.[21] But it was soon evident that the Americans favoured no interference with SCAP on this, and the issue was dropped.[22] The FEC, which the non-American members had assumed would frame the constitution, had held only one meeting, when in March 1946, MacArthur approved a draft constitution, basically American in origin, and the date of the election was announced.[23] The FEC believed it had the right to consider the constitution to determine whether it met the requirements of the Potsdam Declaration. It also believed the Japanese people should be given time to study it. This led to 'wearisome' debates, a struggle between the members of the FEC to produce an agreed policy and a battle with General MacArthur.[24]

Berendsen reported the United States government and its officials 'working strenuously to achieve a situation in which the due legislative processes in Japan' would not be interfered with by the FEC.[25] In these circumstances the FEC made little impression and in the end accepted the constitution. In the final debate Berendsen, reflecting the general feeling, observed that no representative could express complete satisfaction with the draft constitution but that further discussion of it would be useless.[26] The members of the FEC, large and small, were being ignored. It is not surprising therefore that the FEC also failed in its attempts both to get a review of the Japanese constitution after two years and to get the legislation implementing the constitution sent to it before it was passed by the Japanese Diet.[27].

Another absorbing issue of the first two years was the question of the amount and distribution of reparations. On this the FEC failed to reach agreement or produce a result, and in the long run, a change in United States policy resulted in the whole issue becoming redundant. The New Zealand government from the beginning felt New Zealand's claims should be minimal and made persistent efforts to be 'reasonable and fair', qualities frequently not demonstrated by a number of other delegations. For two years, New Zealand delegates participated, to no real purpose, in endless discussions about materials which might be claimed, and percentages of the whole reparations pool which might be due each of the allies.

On food policy, on which again the FEC failed to influence SCAP or the United States government, New Zealand was more actively engaged. New Zealand's sympathies were, of course, with the plight of Britain and Europe. New Zealand was also a world food supplier. Given this background New Zealand inevitably had strong views about food distribution in a world 'menaced' by famine. United States and SCAP food policy, which was felt to favour Japan before some of its victims, brought forth some of Berendsen's more florid contributions to the debate. He would, he said, be 'betraying his manhood' and betraying his 'every conception of all that is decent and proper and just in the relationship of man to man' if he failed to uge that Japanese responsibility for the world food shortage was not borne in mind when allocations were made.[28] The United States government doubted that the FEC had jurisdiction in the matter of the allocation of food supplies to Japan and was concerned lest an FEC policy paper should be construed as a criticism of MacArthur or the United States government.[29] Nevertheless the FEC persisted and after many 'difficult and prolonged discussions' agreed to a policy paper so amended by the United States that Powles described it as 'not even half a loaf', the original paper before the FEC having been reduced, he said, to 'one slice'. Nonetheless this was better, as he conceded, than no bread at all.[30] Powles made a formal statement when the food policy decision was finally passed in order to place on record the New Zealand government's continuing concern that Japan's victims should not suffer greater food shortages than the Japanese and that the Japanese should be aware that their shortage of food was largely their own fault.[31] The rather admonitory tone of New Zealand's message was a typical response to what were seen to be increasingly 'soft' policies towards Japan and, typically, the message fell on deaf ears.

The one issue over which New Zealand felt its own substantial interests were at stake was the question of Japanese whaling expeditions to the Antarctic. On this matter the United States exercised its authority each year, against the strong opposition of the other delegates on the Commission, to permit the Japanese to whale in the Antarctic. In August 1946 SCAP authorized a

Japanese whaling expedition to the Antarctic for the 1946–1947 whaling season. The New Zealand government protested on the grounds both of Japanese known indifference to international agreements for conservation of the whales and on grounds of security problems arising from the penetration of Japanese shipping into Antarctic waters. This was seen as an area of great importance to New Zealand because of its proximity to New Zealand's shores and to those of the Ross Dependency, the sector of the Antarctic continent to which New Zealand lays claim.[32] Neither New Zealand nor any other interested member of the FEC had been consulted about the expedition. New Zealand, Australia and the United Kingdom wanted the FEC to consider policy on Japanese whaling but the Unied States, in reply to a joint protest from them, made it clear that SCAP was acting entirely within his authority.[33] This was reality. Objections to this expedition could not be pressed. New Zealand was assured that interested governments would be consulted in future. SCAP, however, made it clear that he resented any limitation on Japanese whaling.[34]

A year later another expedition was authorized. Further bitter protests were made by New Zealand, Australia and the United Kingdom. New Zealand once again emphasized the security aspect, this time suggesting that a Japanese whaling fleet might be adapted for warlike purposes and thus represented a potential security threat.[35] In the FEC itself where a proposed policy paper on Japanese whaling was also being discussed there were also protests. The United States government, however, made it clear that it would not approve the paper and would support SCAP.[36] By this time, in the opinion of the New Zealanders in the FEC, the United States government was being stiffened in its determination to support the whaling expedition by a concern to demonstrate to an economy-minded Congress that such expeditions would have benefits in dollar terms. It became clear that if the matter was pursued in the FEC there would be an American veto. Faced with this threat the United Kingdom took the lead suggesting that, in spite of feeling badly about this expedition, the protestors should all look at the issue in the context of general relations with the United States. This was the voice of experience and pragmatism. The FEC policy paper and all protests were dropped.[37] When further expeditions were proposed for the 1948–1949 and

1950–1951 seasons, New Zealand registered its disapproval and its desire to be consulted without any expectation of influencing SCAP or the United States government.[38]

On neither the issues relating to Japan in which it had a practical interest nor on those in which it was concerned on matters of principal could New Zealand influence the United States government or SCAP. Neither of course could the FEC, as a whole, influence them. By 1948 American officials had made it clear to the New Zealand representatives that they were prepared to go it alone in Japan and did not contemplate the FEC taking any part in the formulation of policy, except possibly on very broad lines. Their attitude, described by Powles as 'quite aggressive although of course reasonably courteous' was in effect, 'He who pays the piper should call the tune'.[39]

THE NEW ZEALANDERS AT THE COMMISSION

Both Berendsen and Powles were lawyers by training, they were and able and articulate, they were good committee men and unafraid of taking an unpopular line if they believed it to be right. They were usually operating without specific instructions from New Zealand although the generally rather high-minded line they took was approved there.[40] The result was that in the FEC New Zealand probably had a higher profile than might have been expected from its size and its degree of interest in the matters with which the FEC was dealing. New Zealand's 'voice' was certainly heard in the FEC, perhaps to a greater degree than either New Zealand or the organization warranted. The Secretary for External Affairs had hoped that a 'reputation for impartiality' might add weight to New Zealand's views. This may have been a not unreasonable stance for New Zealand to take in January 1946, but an impartial stance was increasingly anachronistic and difficult to sustain as the Cold War closed in after 1948.

In the Steering committee of which he was chairman, Berendsen had tried to spur the FEC into action. He soon reported that the Commission was being used as a shield to give the impression of international control but was in fact being 'elbowed out'.[41] Frustration, exasperation, annoyance and feelings of futility most frequently described the response of the New Zealand delegates to proceedings at the FEC. As early as June 1946 Berendsen was writing to McIntosh that the Commission was 'nothing but a joke' and its members 'MacArthur's stingless gadflies'.[42] By mid-1947 Berendsen described himself as 'contemptuous' of the Commission and wrote, 'It is by all odds the least satisfactory and the least efficient body with which I have been connected.'[43] For this situation Berendsen blamed the American delegation which he described in these early days of the Cold War as both 'un-American', and as 'the MacArthur Protection League'. He also blamed the 'shadow of the veto', and the fundamental problem of the relationship between SCAP and the FEC.[44] The fact was, that while the FEC debated, SCAP, as Powles observed dryly, 'with the attribute of Old Man River just goes rolling along – and there is nothing that anybody can do about it'. Powles added, 'This does not mean that one can't protest, which I shall do.'[45]

The New Zealanders in fact became famous for their protests and, in Berendsen's case, for the 'vigour' and 'frankness' with which these protests were presented. With his experience as a delegate, his ability as a chairman, his aptitude as a public speaker with a flair for the telling phrase, his belief in the rights of small countries, and his strong sense of right and wrong, there was no way in which Berendsen could accept quietly the flagrant disregard of the FEC both by the United States government and SCAP. This led him to clash spectacularly more than once with General McCoy, the much criticized American chairman of the FEC. Berendsen claimed that McCoy regarded any difference of opinion with him 'with the heated resentment of a Cavalry Officer being opposed by a Junior Lieutenant'.[46] Berendsen was, no doubt, sensitive to this since he was himself not inexperienced in pulling rank and believed that an ambassador 'should never allow himself to be ignored or directly or indirectly insulted or imposed upon'.[47] In any case he could hold his own in any verbal battle.

On one torrid occasion McCoy accused Berendsen of consistently throwing 'monkey wrenches' into the machinery of the FEC, of opposing everything proposed by General MacArthur and generally adopting an obstructive and irresponsible attitude. He subsequently apologised.[48] After another bitter encounter Berendsen made a lively defence of the right of the representative of a small nation to be heard:

The word 'admonished' has been used this morning. ... I personally am not disposed to submit to admonishment and insults. And if I were, I am not appearing here as a private and undistinguished individual. I am appearing here as representing a government which is a member of this Commission, and in that capacity I will not submit to admonishment.[49]

In a world dominated by the Super Powers few representatives of small nations have since felt able to declare their independence so openly. On the other hand, even in 1947, encounters like these while no doubt adding colour and excitement to otherwise rather stultifying proceedings, except in so far as they heightened awareness of New Zealand's existence, can hardly be said to have furthered New Zealand's interests. Nor of course did they add substance to the work of the FEC.

NEW ZEALAND AND THE ALLIED COUNCIL FOR JAPAN

The final plans for the control of Japan agreed in Moscow in December 1945 included in addition to the FEC, an Allied Council (ACJ) to sit in Tokyo. This arrangement represented a compromise. The Council had its origins in a Soviet suggestion for a four-power control body to supervise the Japanese surrender. The British had independently already suggested that Australia, in recognition of the part it had played in the war against Japan, should be a member of a five power control body for Japan. In the event the Council which was set up consisted of members representing United States, USSR and China plus a British Commonwealth member who represented Britain, Australia, New Zealand and India.[50] Under some pressure from Dr Evatt, Minister for External Affairs in Australia, who was determined that his country would play an independent part in the surrender and occupation of Japan, the British agreed that, 'in view of Australia's special interest in this area', the British Commonwealth member should be nominated by the Australian government.[51] The Council was to 'advise the Supreme Commander in regard to the implementation of the terms of surrender, the occupation of Japan, and of directives supplementary thereto'.[52]

When the proposal was first mooted the New Zealand reaction was that there was little need for this Council. A four power body was regarded with some suspicion as likely to reduce the standing of the FEC where New Zealand hoped to play a significant part. If the FEC was effective it was difficult to see what role the Council was expected to play and when the terms of reference of the Council were announced there was criticism of their drafting and scepticism about what they actually meant. The arrangement by which one representative acted for, and in the name of, the British Commonwealth, was not considered desirable by New Zealand but, since the British approved, had to be accepted. The proviso was that the representative should be directly responsible to New Zealand as well as the other countries concerned.[53] New Zealand proposed to attach a New Zealand adviser to the British Commonwealth member's office, though in the long run staff shortages in Wellington were to make this impossible.

The first British Commonwealth representative on the ACJ was Macmahon Ball, Head of the Department of Political Science at the University of Melbourne, who had been a consultant to the Australian delegation at the San Francisco conference in 1945 and had recently returned from a special mission to Java on behalf of the Australian government. New Zealand immediately concurred in this appointment which was accepted with the greatest reluctance and under protest by the British and by General MacArthur who made it clear that he thought the British must have little interest in the Council if they were prepared to so weaken it by having an Australian as the Commonwealth member.[54] Ball's known social democratic views made him even more of an anathema to MacArthur.

In addition to any idealogical differences MacArthur may have had with Macmahon Ball he was from the beginning hypersensitive to the Council's existence in Tokyo and as Ball reported after the first meeting, made it clear that all initiative should rest with SCAP. The tension between Soviet and United States members was also immediately obvious.[55] In the circumstances it was impossible for the Council to 'advise' SCAP or achieve anything much although Macmahon Ball made a real but unacknowledged contribution to the Occupation land reform policy.[56] By and large, however, the work of the Council quickly became an exercise in futility and the resignation of Ball in August 1947 – when Evatt who was visiting Japan and seemingly influenced by MacArthur's criticisms of Ball withdrew his support[57] – in no way changed matters. His replacement, Patrick Shaw, an Australian diplomat and a man more acceptable to the British and to MacArthur, could be no more effective.

New Zealand could only observe these events belatedly and at a distance. The Department of External Affairs was too small to provide an adviser to Ball. Ball's reports reached Wellington via Canberra and were forwarded from there to the New Zealand representatives on the FEC, so there was no co-ordination between the New Zealand delegation at the FEC and Ball. When necessary, New Zealand government views were transmitted to the Commonwealth ACJ member through the same indirect route via Canberra, although by and large the government felt unable to comment on Council matters since it hadn't its own man on the ground in Tokyo.[58] But the New Zealand government believed that both Ball and his successor, Patrick Shaw, had followed a 'highly commendable' line in the Council. They had both been 'generously appreciative' of SCAP's achievements while expressing 'honest differences of opinion' on particular issues.[59] In terms of New Zealand's interests these were legitimate diplomatic positions. The British, however, ascribed Ball's attempt at impartiality in diplomacy to his 'innocence'.[60] Soon after his arrival in Tokyo, Ball requested instructions on various matters and wrote:

> I assume I should do whatever possible to reconcile American and Russian points of view, in particular that I should openly support those declarations of democratic principles which the Russian member seems anxious to make while showing caution in committing myself to supporting specific requests to SCAP.[61]

The Australians proposed to concur in this assumption and in Wellington it was felt the proposed Australian reply to Ball could be supported.[62] But the British objected most strongly. They were, of course, concerned with the implications of any of difference with the Americans over Japan, for Anglo-American relations elsewhere.[63] They had no wish to be committed in advance to a general policy of mediation in Japan. When the British views were known in Wellington it was felt there that outright support for the Australians would seem like a snub to the United Kingdom government and a cable was drafted which took account of the United Kingdom view and provided a sop to the Australians by suggesting that what had been intended was that governments would be consulted as occasions arose and each situation would be judged on its merits.[64] Less directly involved in the implications of the Cold War, New Zealand was inclined to find 'honest differences of opinion' less menacing than the British did, and in any case, Wellington was less dismayed by Ball's political opinions and their effect on MacArthur than was Whitehall.

In 1948, the impotence of the FEC having been amply demonstrated, the New Zealand government urged that the Allied Council should be brought to life and make every effort to 'exercise in fact was well as in form' the functions for which it was established. SCAP, it was suggested should be given the 'helpful' independent advice and criticism which would stimulate his administration. Any expectation that resuscitation of the Council was a possibility was, however, unreal and, given that New Zealand had not been able to appoint an adviser to either Macmahon Ball or to Shaw it was not possible to press the matter. Shaw reported 'anything short of a general laudation of the SCAP reports would be regarded as playing into the Soviet hands'. The deterioration in the international situation and MacArthur's sensitivity to criticism of the Occupation (made all the more acute by his Presidential ambitions), made it impossible to make anything of the Allied Council.[65]

The Council limped on until 1952, at its best little more than a debating society, more often its meetings a farce.[66] In September 1949 Colonel William Hodgson replaced Shaw as British Commonwealth representative at the Allied Council.[67] Of him MacIntosh wrote, 'He is more Australian than most and should never be handled with kid gloves'. He was, MacIntosh thought, 'an able chap', 'despite his crudities'.[68] The New Zealand Department of External Affairs seems not to have cared for this appointment any more than the Foreign Office had liked the association with Macmahon Ball. But it no longer mattered. The ACJ had ceased to be of real concern to the New Zealand government.

The political results of New Zealand's policy in relation to the Occupation of Japan were clearly disappointing. Its voice may have been heard but certainly wasn't listened to. As a vehicle for international co-operation the FEC had proved a broken reed and the ACJ a joke. If New Zealand's expectations had been unreal in 1945, the reality of American dominance and the implications for small powers of the post-war rivalry of the United States and the Soviet Union had been made plain in the impotence of these two bodies.

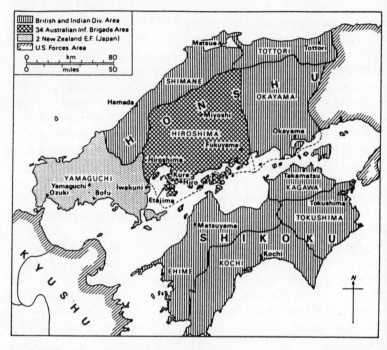

Southern Japan: Regions Occupied by British Commonwealth Forces 1946

Source: *R. Singh, Official History of the Indian armed forces in the Second World War, 1939–45: post-war occupation forces. Japan and south-east Asia* (Kanpur, 1958).

3
The Occupation: Military Involvement
New Zealand and the BCOF

New Zealand's military involvement in the Occupation of Japan, if it has been remembered at all, has not been remembered as of much account. It has in fact been suggested that the British Commonwealth Occupation Force (BCOF) in Japan, of which a New Zealand brigade was a part, is a 'forgotten army'.[1] Garrison duty is of course distinctly unglamorous especially when it must compete in the national memory with deeds of heroism in the trenches, in the desert or on the beaches, but the lack of interest taken in this army by New Zealanders and others at the time and since is the more ironic in that, the New Zealand government at least, participated in this venture in the face of some political difficulty, and with the laudable intention of demonstrating yet again its willingness to be a good team player.

THE BACKGROUND

New Zealand's participation in the BCOF had its origins in negotiations, which had been taking place during the last year of the war in Europe, with the United Kingdom government over the size and the area of operation of the forces which New Zealand accepted it should contribute to the war against Japan. The New Zealand government accepted that, as a Pacific nation and a signatory of the Australia-New Zealand Agreement and in the interests of maintaining New Zealand's relations with the United States on 'the friendliest and firmest basis', New Zealand should make its full contribution to the war against Japan.[2] There were, however, all sorts of logistical problems associated with organizing such a force given that the main body of New Zealand forces was in the Middle East and there were manpower shortages at home. None of these problems had been resolved in July 1945 when the British government proposed a 'striking demonstration of Commonwealth solidarity' in the form of a joint force of British, Australian, New Zealand, British-Indian and possibly Canadian divisions to share with the Americans the burden of the assault on Japan.[3] At the Potsdam Conference which took place later that month the British government assured the Americans of Commonwealth support in the plans for the invasion of Japan although at that stage New Zealand had not actually committed itself to ground forces in the proposed 'demonstration of Commonwealth solidarity'.[4]

In New Zealand the question of committing troops to the invasion of Japan had become a political issue and, after such a 'long and arduous war', the Prime Minister felt national unity was imperative before embarking on fresh military undertakings.[5] General Bernard Freyberg, Commander of the New Zealand Expeditionary Force (2nd NZEF), reported that operation Coronet, one of the invasion plans for 1946, envisaged a British and the New Zealand division moving from Europe to the United Kingdom and on to the United States where they would draw American equipment. After a short period of training they could expect to move to the Pacific.[6] No decisions had been made on this plan when Japan surrendered.

When the Japanese surrender was imminent the United Kingdom government approached the Commonwealth governments again, drawing attention to the 'many tasks' which would now have to be done in Japan. 'We trust', Prime Minister Attlee wrote, 'that we may rely on your assistance, and indeed we regard your assistance as indispensable'.[7] Agreement in principle was asked for a Commonwealth force to take part in the Occupation of Japan, the force to be formed from one brigade group each of Australian, British, British-Indian, Canadian and New Zealand troops with a tactical airforce contingent. The United States had accepted in principle the participation of British ground forces but the details and necessary consents had yet to be hammered out.[8] In these early days of August 1945 it was expected that the Occupation might be a difficult and lengthy affair.

In the context of shrinking opportunities for flying in post-war New Zealand, the provision of an airforce squadron made up of volunteers did not present a problem and the New Zealand government immediately agreed to this.[9] The provision of a brigade group was more difficult. The futher participation of New Zealand troops in post-war activities overseas was already a political issue and the Labour government was anxious in the interests of national unity, and the unity of the Labour Party, that a New Zealand brigade group should, if possible, be made up of volunteers. Freyberg was asked whether 5,000 volunteers from all ranks could be found for a period of up to twelve months in Japan from the single men in the Middle East in the 11th to 15th reinforcements. These reinforcements had left New Zealand at intervals between January 1944 and April 1945. They contained over 1,000 men who had seen service in the 3rd New Zealand Division withdrawn from the Pacific in mid-1944.[10] Freyberg was adamant that 5,000 volunteers could not be found from these reinforcements in which there were only 7,500 single men. He considered compulsion the only answer. When asked whether volunteers might be found from all categories of men in the 11th to 15th reinforcements Freyberg cited the general war-weariness as the reason for his belief that, even from a wider group, there would be insufficient volunteers. It had been as he said, 'a long war'.[11] Faced with this conclusion the Cabinet decided that New Zealand should provide a brigade group which would have to be drawn from the single men of the 13th to 15th reinforcements plus suitable volunteers from all categories of men outside these reinforcements. As an incentive the proposed length of service in Japan was reduced to six months.[12]

When this decision was brought before the Labour caucus, however, there was 'considerable opposition' which forced the Prime Minister to go back to Freyberg and ask him to reconsider his assessment of the numbers of volunteers who could be expected to come forward.[13] Freyberg, who was in London, returned to Italy and consulted with his senior officers. None of them thought numbers anywhere near 5,000 could be obtained. Freyberg pointed out that New Zealand's case was different from that of other possible participants in the Occupation force. the Australians, volunteers, were already in the Pacific where they had been fighting. The two British brigades were already in India and had been fighting the Japanese. The American troops were volunteers who were to be given 90 days home leave before going to Japan.

The New Zealanders would be the only force to move directly from the European theatre to the Pacific. VJ Day he said, reflecting the facts of New Zealand's war efort, meant far less to the New Zealanders than would the day when they left Italy for home. He noted, 'The general desire of everyone to get home and re-established in their new life is most pronounced'. Apart from the suggestion that the New Zealand force should be reduced to 4,000 men, he could not help the New Zealand government in its dilemma.[14]

With the greatest reluctance the Prime Minister faced the apparent necessity for compulsion. This was still bound to be resisted by a significant number in the caucus and by the Opposition. The task of persuasion was all the more difficult in that the United States had so far merely accepted the idea of a BCOF 'in principle' and there was no concrete plan, to the details of which the government could point. Furthermore Japan itself was remarkably quiet so that the military function of the Occupation was evidently less significant than had been anticipated. It was all very well for the United Kingdom to express the hope that New Zealand could be 'counted on' whatever the composition of the BCOF but the Prime Minister was faced with a real political problem. The leader of the Opposition was adamant in his opposition to compulsion and made much of the disadvantageous situation of New Zealand troops to which Freyberg had drawn attention. The position was made no easier when the BBC Rome correspondent reported that it was understood that 5,000 volunteers from the 2nd NZEF would be required for garrison duty in Japan and roused further Opposition, press and public concern about the boys 'away overseas'.[15]

In the meantime there were troubles elsewhere in organizing the Commonwealth force. The Australian government had announced shortly after Japan's surrender that it wished to take part in the Occupation of Japan with Australian army, navy and airforce units operating under an Australian commander subordinate only to SCAP. The British resisted this on the grounds that a joint force would be a valuable demonstration of unity and would carry more weight with the Americans than two smaller independent forces. As a carrot to the Australians Prime Minister Attlee proposed that the Commander-in-Chief of the Commonwealth force should be an Australian.[16] To this the Australians eventually agreed in late

September 1945.[17] Headquarters in Canberra were to be staffed by Australians and administrative decisions and inter-governmental matters, it was agreed, should be the responsibility of the Joint Chiefs of Staff in Australia (JCOSA) in which each of the participating forces would be represented.[18]

The New Zealand government had now faced the fact that the New Zealand contingent for the Occupation force would initially have to be made up of men from the late reinforcements in Italy. It was expected that the men would leave Italy in November or December 1945 and after six months in Japan be relieved by volunteers from New Zealand.[19] This was announced amid protests from the Opposition which continued to assert that the force could and should be a voluntary one. It was a good issue for the politicians, one designed to rouse public emotions. The men in Italy should be brought home at the earliest possible date, the Leader of the Opposition, Sidney Holland declared, and the complex problem of their rehabilitation tackled.[20] The Prime Minister, in response, repeated the opinions of Freyberg and the Service Chiefs in New Zealand on the impracticability and possible embarrassment of attempting to organize a volunteer force. He concluded, 'We could not risk, far less court, failure at this critical hour in the destiny of our Commonwealth'.[21]

Critical as the hour might have been declared by the Prime Minister, the fact was that nearly two months had passed since the surrender of Japan. Only the basic questions had been settled. The actual details of how the BOCF might be deployed had still not been worked out with the United States. President Truman's Directive of 6 September 1945 had laid down as the first objective of the Occupation the complete disarmament and demilitarization of Japan. On 30 September 1945 it was estimated that full demobilization would be completed by 15 October. Arrangements had also been made for the speedy repatriation and demobilization of Japanese forces outside Japan. Not only did the Japanese military authorities co-operate but the Japanese population as a whole proved unexpectedly submissive. It was quite clear by the end of September that far fewer troops than anticipated would be required in the Occupation forces and proposed reductions in the American contingent had already been announced by General MacArthur.[22]

The organization of the Occupation had so far been an entirely

American affair and given that it was going so smoothly under the leadership of an autocrat like MacArthur, it is not surprising that the arrangements for the participation of the BCOF in the Japanese Occupation were not a high priority with the United States. The Australian government opened negotiations with the State Department on the basis of a BCOF land force consisting of one British and one British-Indian brigade, one Australian and one New Zealand brigade and an air contingent composed of British and Australian squadrons and a New Zealand squadron. The force was to be led by Lieutenant-General John Northcott, Chief of General Staff, Australian Mobile [military] Forces. Approval for participation of the BCOF and details of its role and location in Japan were sought. Command and administrative arrangements in relation to United States occupational layout should, it was suggested, be completed directly between SCAP and Commander-in-Chief of BCOF.[23] In spite of repeated requests for an early reply to these proposals time dragged on. There was no reply from the United States.

Having struggled in his Party and in Parliament to win an agreement to the direction of troops to Japan, the New Zealand Prime Minister was considerably embarrassed by the delay. When the United States reply finally came at the end of November, the time when the government had hoped the New Zealand troops would be on their way to Japan, it was still not definitive. The Americans continued to accept only 'in principle' the participation of British Commonwealth forces and appeared now to be suggesting that Commonwealth forces would be integrated operationally into the United States forces.

The New Zealand government liked these developments no more than the delays which had preceded them. It was not prepared to see the New Zealand brigade integrated operationally with the Americans and thus risk losing its identity. Any such arrangement, which was without merit from either the point of view of national or Commonwealth pride, was bound to cause an outcry from the New Zealand public given that the question of the New Zealand contingent of the BCOF was already a political issue.[24] Discussions on the detail of arrangements was obviously required. These proceeded in Washington, led, on the Australian side by Dr Evatt, Minister for External Affairs, with Lieutenant-General Lavarack, head of the Australian Military Mission in

Washington. At the same time Lieutenant-General Northcott left for Tokyo for discussions with General MacArthur. Even in Australia enthusiasm for the BCOF was waning.[25] Having studied the detail of the general principles for the participation of the BCOF proposed by the Americans, the Australians concluded that the only way the BCOF might work in Japan was if some compromise was reached by which the force remained under the administrative control of Commonwealth officers while being technically under American command.[26]

Lack of enthusiasm for the general principles enunciated by the United States was compensated for by the detailed arrangements worked out in the talks between MacArthur and Northcott in Tokyo. Their agreement, known as the MacArthur-Northcott Agreement assigned the BCOF the Hiroshima prefecture in southern Honshu and the role in that area of military control and demilitarization and destruction of equipment, arms and other defences. The force was to be subject to the direction of MacArthur on policy matters, responsible to the US Eighth Army for operational and local control but with control of administrative matters resting with Force Headquarters. Northcott 'strongly recommended' the acceptance of these terms and this recommendation was endorsed by JCOSA and ultimately accepted by all participants in the BCOF.[27] The New Zealand government, however, recorded that enthusiasm for the Force, never strong in New Zealand had 'flagged very considerably'. The not unreasonable feeling was that the Force was not needed and that it was questionable whether, in the circumstances, it was likely to yield any increase in British Commonwealth prestige, the most obvious justification for New Zealand's participation.[28] Consequently, in spite of leaks in the Australian press and pressure from Australia, the New Zealand government, anxious not to be seen to be committed until a firm agreement with the United States had been reached, held out against any detailed official announcement about the BCOF until the MacArthur-Northcroft memorandum had been cleared by the United States government. In the meantime arrangements had to be made for the movement of troops and stores in Italy. Since inevitably this led to further publicity in New Zealand the continued delay on the part of the United States government greatly embarrassed the New Zealand government which was criticized in the press for its failure to keep the public informed about the negotiations.[29] The official announcements were finally made on 1 February 1946 and were accompanied by an apparently enthusiastic message of welcome from General MacArthur.[30] The New Zealand brigade sailed from Italy on 21 February 1946.

THE RATIONALE

Although he must in fact have felt far from confident, New Zealand's Prime Minister told the country on 1 October 1945:

> I feel sure that the people of New Zealand will agree that this opportunity [to take part in the BCOF] of proving our unity and solidarity with the mother country, and of sharing in the responsibilities of the British Commonwealth in the Pacific, should be accepted . . . . It will be generally agreed that New Zealand should undertake this duty not only because it is in our interests as a Pacific country to do so but also because, in common with the other members of the British Commonwealth of Nations, we have been invited to do so. . . . Indeed Mr Attlee said. . . . 'We trust we may rely on your assistance and indeed we regard your assistance as indispensable'.[31]

The impact of these loyal words was somewhat reduced by the confident and much publicized assertion of the Leader of the Opposition that if the question of a voluntary or compulsory force had been submitted to a free vote of Members of Parliament there would have been a substantial majority in favour of a voluntary force.[32] Nevertheless it is interesting to note that, in making his rather emotionally loaded appeal to the country, Prime Minister Fraser chose to stress Commonwealth ties and solidarity above Pacific responsibilities and the fact that Japan was New Zealand's 'only enemy in the Pacific'. Clearly it was his perception that on a controversial issue, which the direction of men from Italy to the Occupying Force in Japan had become, the Commonwealth tie had, from the political point of view, the best public appeal. When the Department of External Affairs or the Prime Minister, considered questions relating to New Zealand's participation in the Occupation, the fact that New Zealand was a Pacific nation with a special interest in the peace of the region and hence in Japan, seems to have been a fundamental consideration. But apparently for the public, this argument was felt to have a less compelling ring. In spite of the war in the Pacific, New Zealanders' interest in post-war Japan for itself and as a Pacific country was marginal. This, and the negative publicity the BCOF received in New Zealand throughout its existence, was bound to make recruiting for the New Zealand brigade difficult.

Commonwealth solidarity, co-operation and duty were seen by the politicians as the elements most likely to make the BCOF palatable to New Zealanders. When on 1 February, Acting Prime Minister Nash released the official announcement on the arrangements for the BCOF, he stressed the significance of co-operative effort in the attainment of a victory which would not be won until Japan's peaceful development was assured. This he suggested, with more rhetoric than accuracy, would only happen when General MacArthur was provided with the means to put into effect the policies formulated by the Far Eastern Commission. The intervention of armed forces was, he said, the only way of doing this, and, as New Zealand took responsibility for deciding policy concerning Japan, it was part of New Zealand's job to help put these policies into effect.[33] General MacArthur might have found these assertions surprising, coming as they did at a time when the purely military phase of the Occupation was over and his reform programmes already launched. Nash's claim, 'New Zealand is vitally concerned with the maintenance of peace in the Pacific' was more modest and made more sense.

New Zealand's 'vital interest in the peace of the Pacific' was touched on in a speech by the Minister of Defence in which responsibility, co-operation and Commonwealth partnership were again themes. Calling for volunteers to serve in the BCOF he said:

> we have been joined during the war with our partners in the Commonwealth in many enterprises . . . so too in this task . . . of establishing conditions which will preserve peace in the Pacific, we are joined again with our Commonwealth partners. . . . We are discharging our share of the political responsibility in this area; we must also accept our responsibility in those measures which are necessary to secure the defeat of Japan and the establishment of peace.[34]

It all sounded good and made the Occupation of Japan and the BCOF's part in it sound like the joint enterprise with the Americans which it could not be, given American numerical superiority and their already well-established position in Japan.

THE NEW ZEALANDERS' EXPERIENCE

The area of Japan assigned to the BCOF under the agreement worked out by MacArthur and Northcott was that of Hiroshima-Kure in southern Japan on the Inland Sea. This area was subsequently expanded to include neighbouring prefectures. When the final arrangements were made, New Zealand occupied Yamaguchi, an area of 2,000 square miles, the Australians Hiroshima, the British Shikoku and the British Indian Division (BRINDIV) Okayama, Shimane and Tottori, geographicaly the largest area.

In his meeting with the New Zealand Cabinet in January 1946, Lieutenant-General Northcott had described the area 'selected' for the BCOF as an 'excellent' one. With one good port, Kure, it was 'ideal for the purpose'. There were, he said, good barracks with fittings of a high standard and good facilities for recreations such as boating, yachting and football.[35] Taking their cue from Northcott, Nash and the Minister of Defence, in their recruiting speeches, rejoiced in the 'good area' where, in a healthy climate, every provision would be made for the 'recreation and comfort' of the New Zealand forces.[36] In fact the area in which the BCOF was stationed represented Hobson's choice. While no specific zone had been asked for, it had been hoped that BCOF could participate in the occupation of the Tokyo prefecture, but there was no chance that MacArthur would allow anything other than ceremonial guard duties to be undertaken there. Of the remaining areas of significance, Nagoya, the industrially developed area south of Tokyo was earmarked for the Chinese (who in the event did not come), the Kobe-Osaka area, which contained the first major port of the American forces, was declared unavailable to the BCOF by SCAP, and this left Northcott the Hiroshima-Kure area, predominantly rural and remote from Tokyo, as the only one on offer. He had had no opportunity to reconnoitre thoroughly any of the areas, although he made a brief visit to the Hiroshima-Kure area and to Osaka in the few days he had in Japan.[37] Subsequently a reconnaissance team provided some details of the terrain, the 'less than adequate' roads and the less than favourable aspects of the climate – summer humidity, typhoons and occasional snowfalls. Accommodation was described as 'sufficient'.[38] On the basis of this sketchy information the occupation by BCOF was planned.

Northcott visited some sections of the BCOF before the move to Japan, and he visited Wellington in January 1946 to stiffen the lukewarm government. He was unable to visit the New Zealand brigade forming in Italy which, he reported later, remained, as a consequence, 'somewhat insular in outlook as they were out of touch with progress in the organization of the BCOF until arriving in Japan.'[39] An early contact with the New Zealand commander might have assisted liaison at Headquarters but could not have changed the realities in the Yamaguchi prefecture to which the New Zealanders were assigned. One New Zealand Member of Parliament was subsequently to describe this area as equivalent in New Zealand terms, to being stationed in Westland, New Zealand's most remote province, with the chief town Hokitika, a community not noted for the sophistication and variety of its diversions.[40] Veterans of the Italian campaigns who went to Japan agreed that it was the equivalent of being posted to Siberia, or perhaps the south coast of western Southland, an area as unknown to most New Zealanders as Siberia.[41] The result of the advance and shakily-based publicity was that the expectations of the first New Zealand contingents were unrealistic and the discontents consequently greater.

The New Zealanders finally embarked for Japan on 21 February 1946. They had been enjoying the delights of Italy since the New Zealand Division had been withdrawn from Trieste in the summer of 1945. The men directed to 2nd NZEF(Japan) or Jayforce as it became known, had been in good accommodation in Florence and Sienna since October. There they had enjoyed leave on a generous scale with some units giving general after-duty passes. Most of the men drafted from the 13th to 15th reinforcements had served not more than twelve months overseas. Most officers, who came from 11th reinforcements or later, had served not more than two years. Some of the brigade had seen little or no fighting, but all had left New Zealand with the training and expectation that they would be used as frontline troops. They were commanded by Brigadier

Keith Stewart, a highly regarded officer who had had a distinguished record before being captured in Italy in 1944.[42] He took command in November 1945 and had the task of forging into a coherent group, men who came from different units whose loyalties had been formed in wartime conditions and were now being asked to perform a task which none of them regarded with any enthusiasm. They embarked at Naples.

The *Strathmore* on which the Force travelled from Italy called at Port Said, Colombo, Singapore and Hong Kong before arriving at Kure on 19 March. Any hopes that prolonged service would be compensated for by a chance to see more of the exotic east than Japan were dashed when a serious measles epidemic developed on the second day of the journey. No leave was granted at any of the pots.[43] After their month cooped up on board, the New Zealanders viewed the 'staggering' mass of twisted steel and rusting debris that was the bombed out Japanese naval base of Kure, their port of disembarkation, with some dismay. They travelled from Kure to the Yamaguchi prefecture, a number of them via the devastated city of Hiroshima. The landscape was discouraging as were the billets in Chofu, Yamaguchi and Mizuba. Japanese military barracks were generally of a poor standard especially as far as water supplies and drainage were concerned and the barracks of the Kobe steel works and Mitsubishi aircraft factory at Chofu where the headquarters were established and the 22nd Battalion were accommodated, had been bombed. In every case a good deal of repair work was immediately necessary. The barracks and the facilities were, to say the least, 'disappointing', especially after the public relations build-up and by contrast with the amenities available in Italy.[44]

Apart from accommodation problems, the initial contingent was faced with difficulties because the brigade arrived in advance of is stores and, to the irritation of the Commander-in-Chief, Lieutenant-General Northcott, had immediately to be supplied with a variety of essential items from the newly established headquarters set up by the Australians.[45] By and large the New Zealand soldiers had arrived with the minimum of personal equipment. In their months in post-war Italy where everything was tradeable, the New Zealanders had cheerfully bartered away food, cigarettes, their gear and much of the army's stores.[46] They expected a plentiful supply of clothing at least when they arrived in

Japan and the lack of it was a source of some hardship and considerable grumbling. The New Zealanders also arrived without medical stores and with 150 hospital cases which had to be farmed out, temporarily, in the Australian and British-Indian hospitals. There was a general shortage of medical equipment and in the humid summer which was soon upon them, irritating skin conditions of various kinds became common among the troops.[47] When equipment did arive much of it was battle-scarred. The trucks of the New Zealanders were obsolete and needed constant life-giving attention. Spare parts were scarce and cannibalizing of vehicles was necessary to maintain those sufficiently serviceable to travel the dreadful roads. It was said moreover that, by army standards, the New Zealanders' weapons should have been condemned before they left Italy. In the event, this was less important than the clothing shortage which continued for months, since the weapons were not required in operations in Japan anyway.[48]

It was all a come-down after Italy, but perhaps most difficult of all for these men, who had been trained as fighting soldiers, was to find themselves in what was for them such a very strange land with little to do and nowhere to go. In Italy they had had opportunities at bars, restaurants, hotels and in the countryside to supplement their army diet. This was forbidden in Japan. Fresh fruit and vegetables could not be purchased, partly because of the acute food shortages in Japan and partly because Japanese methods of fertilization made this undesirable. Supplies had to be brought from Australia which presented logistical problems. Refrigeration plants had to be built. The much touted recreation facilities did not exist apart from the swimming pool at the Kobe steel works which was popular in spite of the skin rashes it appeared to promote. Initially, sports and training at Chofu had to be carried out on the open road. It is true that rest camps were soon established on the beaches but they were patently a 'far cry from Albergo Daniele in Venice or the Bagnoli in Florence'.[49] An ambitious programme of building new barracks and reconditioning old ones had to be embarked upon. This involved complicated requisitioning procedures and permissions from Headquarters and the American authorities. The buildings and facilities were not ready before the first arrivals left.

The New Zealanders were amazed by the submissiveness of the Japanese and disliked the fact that it was not simply their uniforms or the flag marches undertaken to impress the population that made them a terrifying spectacle to many Japanese. The Japanese found the New Zealanders 'strict looking and stern' and their Occupation regime 'far more military' than that of the Americans whom they succeeded. Tales of the cruelty of New Zealand troops had also been spread.[50] Of course New Zealanders had a low opinion of the Japanese as ex-enemies noted for their cruelty, and as Asians, the racial group against which there was most prejudice in New Zealand. Of Japanese culture they were largely ignorant. But it was sobering to some of these veterans to be regarded as 'hulking uncultured barbarians'.[51] In Italy they had been welcome among families and friendships had been formed. Here the society was so foreign as to discourage all but the most formal relationships. In any case, except on matters of official business Japanese homes were off limits for members of the BCOF. The fraternization rules were always a problem. General Northcott issued a directive requiring each member of the BCOF to 'remember he is a representative of the British Commonwealth of Nations and all that it stands for in the world' and to be 'formal and correct' in relations with the Japanese. The framing of more detailed orders was considered impracticable.[52] When Brigadier Leslie Potter replaced Stewart as Commander of the New Zealand force in July 1946 he was clearly concerned about the varying interpretations of Northcott's directive and its vagueness, possibly because by that time it was amply clear that the Occupation force had no military function and the troops who were under his command were now younger volunteers who had most frequently joined Jayforce in a spirit of adventure rather than concern for the good name of New Zealand or the Commonwealth. Potter, a Regular Army officer and stickler for the rules, had seen service in the Pacific but not in the Middle East, and was not highly regarded by some of the more battle-hardened officers under his command.[53] He issued a detailed clarification of the principles underlying the non-fraternization policy. This relaxed the rules forbidding visits to Japanese houses and theatres and recognized that propaganda work among the Japanese was desirable but had much to say to discourage association with the rural population by whom the New Zealanders were surrounded – 'little more than serfs' in Potter's opinion.[54] Such association as he had had with the Japanese had clearly not made him more tolerant of cultural differences.

When Potter's memorandum on fraternization arrived in Wellington it was the subject of considerable criticism. His analysis of the class structure of Japan was found 'extremely offensive and wrong-headed'. The one member of the Department of External Affairs who at that time had direct knowledge and experience of Japan wrote:

> There are many better ways of discouraging soldiers from spending all their time in low dives than slandering the largest and most important class among the Japanese. Working in excreta covered paddy fields is no sign of lack of morals or education ... it is merely a sign of careful agriculture.[55]

This officer thought that 'propaganda' rather than 'good marching' should be regarded as the most important work of the Occupation Force but this was not an easy message to get across to Brigadier Potter. The Department suggested to him an alternative directive stressing the need to 'act decently' and both to teach and learn from the Japanese.[56] Potter was unimpressed. He justified the rigid line he took on the ground of the 'positively staggering' incidence of venereal and other infectious diseases in the rural population. He was also trying to restrict New Zealanders' involvement in the flourishing black market operations which he saw as 'the first step in a process of moral disintegration' which could lead to major crime.[57] The non-fraternization rules were the more trying because the Americans, who had the best billets, the best recreation areas, the best food and the best pay were not subject to such restrictions.

The original contingent from Italy was replaced from July 1946 by volunteers from New Zealand whose tour of duty was to be twelve months. It is not unreasonable to suppose that the change-over was welcomed by Potter. He reported that, with the departure of the last of the troops from Florence, the atmosphere among the troops changed overnight. This would not be surprising. The men of the first contingent had been, on the whole, reluctant soldiers in Japan counting the days to their release. The new men were, by contrast, volunteers, younger, green, trained for and expecting garrison duty. Potter reported extravagantly that he considered the new volunteers to be 'among the most promising body of young men who have left the shores of New Zealand'. The highest standard of amenities and living quarters were, he said, to be provided for them. They were also to be helped to 'widen their outlook, improve their education, and form their characters'.[58] One of the chief concerns of the Commander had to be to provide sufficient diversions for a force which was less than fully occupied.

By contrast with the army contingent, the New Zealand airforce squadron which went to Japan received little publicity and, throughout its time there, remained uncontroversial. This was partly because the men were all volunteers.[59] Furthermore the squadron came from New Zealand so the men hadn't the sense of having been deprived of an opportunity to go home. Although their physical conditions seem to have been little better than those of the New Zealand army units,[60] pilots are usually happy when they can fly which is what they are trained to do. They are also interested in aircraft. The patrol work and flying exercises required of the squadron brought it into contact with members of the other squadrons in British Commonwealth Air Group (BCAIR) and with American pilots whose aircraft were different and some of them new to the New Zealanders. Visits were made to other squadrons. Thus there was the possibility of more mobility and more variety in the lives of the men in this part of the Force. The atmosphere at Iwakuni near Hiroshima where the New Zealand No. 14 Corsair Squadron was based, seems to have been, in the manner of the airforce, more relaxed than in the army stations.

The RNZAF also made a good impression from the beginning with BCOF HQ by arriving well equipped. General Northcott who was less than pleased with the demands the New Zealand army brigade had made on the administration as soon as it arrived reported, perhaps to underline the contrast, that 'The New Zealanders arrived complete with their 24 Corsairs, stores, transport and canteen supplies for the New Zealand component. An excellent example of inter-service co-operation'.[61]

The squadron arrived at Kure on 24 March 1946 and was one of ten in BCAIR. It was under the command of Squadron Leader J. J. Willimoff. He was responsible to the Air Officer Commanding BCAIR, Air Vice-Marshal Bouchier RAF, but could communicate direct with the Commander of New Zealand land forces and RNZAF Wellington on domestic matters. The whole air component, BCAIR, was assigned to the general operational control of the Commanding General Pacific Air Command US Army (PAC

USA).[62] The men of the first RNZAF group were relieved after a year.

THE TASKS

By the time the BCOF arrived it was clear that the military tasks of the Occupation Forces would be limited to the collection and disposal of armaments and the dismantling of military installations. This became a matter of routine which was carried out by and large without any hindrance. Intelligence units worked with the Japanese police and informers to discover arms caches which were often considerable in size. A great deal of time was spent in the confiscation of ancient family samurai swords, the weapon with which the Japanese were most consistently reluctant to part.[63] In the New Zealand area 107 'targets' or arms caches of various kinds were disposed of in the first year and large quantities of arms and explosives were dumped. Materials such as engines and motors were reconditioned and put into service by the army and material which could assist in the rehabilitation of the Japanese was handed over to the Japanese Home Ministry.[64] The search for hidden arms and war supplies gave intelligence units the opportunity to move about, to see Japanese homes and to learn something of the way the Japanese lived. This was an opportunity denied the majority of soldiers.

As arms caches were discovered and disposed of, the main work of the intelligence units became anti black market operations in support of the Japanese police. There were acute food shortages in the town and shortages of clothing and other necessities in the villages. A traffic between the two developed. But government policy required that a percentage of a farmer's output of rice should be made available to the government or its agencies. Since rice was a more stable currency than the yen, farmers tried to evade the rice requisition as far as possible. Searches and checks for hoarded rice were undertaken by BCOF forces in conjunction with the Japanese police in support of government policy. It was not an easy or particularly pleasant task and it was evident to those involved that the Japanese police were frequently in collusion with black marketeers.[65]

In fact most of the work carried on by the Occupation force

more properly came under the heading of policing rather than
military activity. The New Zealanders supervised the repatriation
of Koreans, recruited before and during the war by the Japanese
as forced labour, who opted to return to Korea. At the same time
they had to deal with illegal Korean immigration. Encouraged
away by the economic chaos in Korea and attracted by better food
conditions and the possibilities of black market operations in
Japan, Koreans from the southern part of Korea tried to land in
Japan from fishing boats under cover of darkness. The nearest
coastline was that of Yamaguchi, the New Zealand area of
responsibility. Patrolling the coast, detaining and repatriating
illegal Korean immigrants was one of the tasks of the force. Aerial
searches for boats carrying illegal immigrants were also carried out
by the New Zealand squadron of the BCAIR based on the south
coast at Iwakuni.

Another policing task was the supervision of repatriated
Japanese soldiers who were processed through a Japanese agency
in Hiroshima. These soldiers were mostly resigned and caused no
trouble in the poor rural area to which they now were returning
but, in the early days, their supervision was an Occupation Force
task which was taken seriously. Troops, accompanied by Japanese
police, regularly patrolled and checked for any signs of unrest or
illegal activity, but there was relatively little crime. It was of course
a reflection of the co-operation and docility of the Japanese
population that such a relatively small force – which soon was
diminished even further both in its New Zealand component and
overall – could control such a large area. In Yamaguchi prefecture,
the original New Zealand brigade of 4,000 men was outnumbered
343 to 1.[66]

The arrangements for establishment of BCOF included the right
to perform guard duties in Tokyo. In this the New Zealanders took
their turn to the great pride of any New Zealanders who happened
to be in Tokyo.[67] The opportunity to go to Tokyo was sought-after
and efforts were made to give those who went there on guard duty
reasonable leave. But special permissions were required for others
to take leave in Tokyo because it was in the American area of
occupation and it was of course more than 600 miles from the New
Zealand base. Many of the New Zealanders therefore saw only
rural Japan and the devastated cities of Hiroshima and Kure which
were in the BCOF area. Their impression of Japan was therefore

somewhat distorted and, although travel may broaden the mind, for most of the New Zealanders involved, contact with the Japanese was so limited and the times in Japan so exceptional that membership of the Occupation force did little to improve perceptions of Japanese culture.

One of the roles of the BCOF was 'to illustrate and to impress upon the Japanese people as far as possible, the democratic way and purpose of life'.[68] The Department of External Affairs suggested to Potter that men should be 'tireless' in propagating among the Japanese whatever they knew about democracy. Encouraging the liberals and enlightening the under-privileged, good social democratic goals, were seen as desirable activities in which New Zealanders in Japan might be engaged.[69] All this was rather more easily said than done when contacts were so severely limited. One of the many unanticipated duties of the Force, was, however, the supervision of the parliamentary elections in April 1946. The elections were extremely complex since they were for both the upper and lower house. For the first time suffrage was universal. Within the BCOF area the responsibility for ensuring elections were conducted in a 'manner completely in keeping with the traditions of freedom and democracy' lay with the Commonwealth forces. Teams were organized to visit polling booths to ensure the secrecy of the ballot and prevent any intimidation of voters. If they did not prove to be ardent propagators of democracy, at least the New Zealand soldiers who observed the orderly behaviour at the polling booths were observers of democracy at work.

The founding members of Jayforce, however reluctant, had been challenged in various ways. They had established themselves in an area which was both devastated and culturally alien. The skilled among them had had to perform feats of engineering, building and refurbishment. The tasks that brought them in contact with the Japanese required patience and diplomacy rather than military skills in which they had been trained. Although their discontents received a good deal of publicity it was acknowledged by administrators that the brigade performed well under exceptionally difficult circumstances. For the volunteers who went to Japan in late 1946 and in 1947 the chief tasks were those related to policing the black market and checking that SCAP's directives, such as those relating to school text books were being implemented. It was a less interesting if easier time. At all times, however, the chief enemy for the New Zealanders in Japan was not the Japanese, but boredom.

THE PROBLEMS OF THE BCOF

The BCOF was billed as an experiment in Commonwealth co-operation and the integration of Commonwealth forces. The British in particular were keen on this idea.[70] But in fact the uncertainties which preceded the creation of the Force and its establishment in Japan meant that understanding of what was meant by integration was by no means clear to all parties. The machinery by which integration was supposed to be achieved was clumsy at best. The Joint Chiefs of Staff Australia (JCOSA), which consisted of the Australian Chiefs of Staff and representatives of the Chiefs of Staff of New Zealand, the United Kingdom and the Commander-in-Chief of the three Indian services, had the right to control and administer BCOF, subject to the control of the governments concerned, but the responsibility of implementing JCOSA policy was vested in the Australian Defence Ministry. The lines of authority were not clearly drawn and the machinery for communication with the respective governments was complicated. There was constant friction between the Australian Defence Department in Canberra and the overseas members of JCOSA, who felt that Australia was trying to dominate policy-making.[71]

Integration between the different elements of the BCOF was not any more satisfactory in Japan. 'Psychological variations' as well as differences in organization made the policy of integration for all elements common to the BCOF, including Headquarters, Movements Control, Canteens and so on, difficult to achieve. There was often friction, and appointments at BCOF's HQ were unpopular and difficult to fill.[72] Adding to BCOF HQ's problems was the fact that BCOF was under the command of the United States Eighth Army which in turn was under SCAP. Liaison with SCAP HQ was through a Tokyo headquarters known as British Commonwealth Sub-Area Tokyo and pressure was put on national commanders to provide staff officers for this establishment. Fortunately, perhaps, the New Zealand commanders were always reluctant to detach officers for BCOF establishments and consequently New Zealand took very little active part in this structure.[73]

The Prime Ministers' directive to the Commander of the New Zealand force in Japan issued in October 1945 gave him considerable powers and the right to communicate direct with the New Zealand government.[74] This was inconsistent with an integration policy. When Northcott spoke to the New Zealand Cabinet in January 1946 he said that, while the officer commanding the New Zealand force might communicate direct to his government, such communications must be made through his Headquarters to JCOSA and from there to the government. Brigadier Stewart, who remained ignorant of this, and any integration policy, until he visited Wellington in March 1946, was reassured by the Prime Minister that he was nevertheless to be guided by his directive and NZEF regulations and that he had the full support of the government to command and administer 2nd NZEF(Japan) on the same lines as had General Freyberg with 2 NZEF. Then it had operated as a self-contained national army under British command.[75] When Stewart arrived in Japan he found, to his indignation, that orders had been issued to his services which he regarded as tantamount to taking them from his command. Stewart, who was a great fighter for his brigade, had a wealth of experience and personal contacts which enabled him reassert his command but his outstanding impression of the BCOF was coloured by what he saw as 'the misuse, misinterpretation and undue emphasis placed on "integration"'.[76] Clarification was obviously required. Stewart argued that the 2nd NZEF(Japan) should be maintained as a self-contained national unit with 'co-operation' and 'combine' substituted for 'integration'. The integration policy had of course been agreed but the Chiefs of Staff in New Zealand did not think it was necessarily incompatible with the Prime Minister's directive and believed the Commander, after consultation with the Commander-in-Chief, had the right to communicate direct, on matters of policy with the government, and could correspond direct on matters of domestic administration and welfare. This, it was thought, should be sufficient protection for New Zealand's national interests.[77] The rather unsatisfactory situation remained. When Northcott wrote his final report as Commander-in-Chief in July 1946 he drew attention to the difficulties created by the separate directive of the New Zealand Commander which made him virtually independent in all matters except operational control.[78]

Potter, who was temperamentally less likely than Stewart to

question regulations nevertheless agreed with Stewart that 'maximum co-operation' rather than integration should be the 'key note' of relations between national formations and the BCOF. He implied that integration as originally conceived would only result in a 'confused mess' and suggested that only by a 'nice adjustment of the various spheres and duties of its indivisible components' could a mixed Commonwealth force become a real success.[79] Integration, however, continued to be official policy and in October 1946 a new directive, which set out the lines of authority more clearly was issued to Colonel Potter.[80] Relations between the New Zealand Force and BCOF evidently ran satisfactorily thereafter and it seems indeed that for one reason or another that New Zealand may have had an easier passage in its relations with BCOF than some of the other elements in the Force.[81]

At the last meeting of JCOSA when the record of the BCOF was being assessed, it was generally agreed that, while the experiment had been a valuable one, the Control of BCOF and any other Force would be much simpler if the excessive integration which was the essence of the BCOF experiment had not been attempted. The experience of the New Zealand Force was cited as the best evidence of this. Its commander had a clear-cut directive and, having very little active part in the base organizations, New Zealand's relations with the Force and with JCOSA had been much simplified.[82]

THE DECISION TO WITHDRAW

The New Zealand government had undertaken that the men who were directed to Japan from Italy in Jayforce would be relieved by volunteers after six months. The first draft of 1,600 of all ranks arrived in June 1946 and the change-over was completed in August. No sooner were these men settled in, than in November 1946 the United Kingdom government warned that its military commitments would have to be reduced world-wide. The United Kingdom brigade of 3,500 was to be withdrawn from Japan in February 1947.[83] This represented a partial withdrawal only, and would leave the United Kingdom element of BCOF at 6,500 men, but the decision was a severe blow to the whole concept of a Commonwealth force.

The publication of Britain's decision led immediately to rumours that the New Zealand force would also be withdrawn. These were denied by the Prime Minister who insisted publicly that New Zealand must continue to 'do her utmost to play a full part in international action to secure peace, and to fulfil commitments which had been entered into for the joint policing of Japan'. He referred to New Zealand's 'vital interest in securing peace in the Pacific' which, he argued should be able to be reconciled with the shortages of manpower being experienced at home which were leading to the calls for the return of Jayforce.[84] But there was no doubt that the case for Jayforce, never strong in the eyes of many Members of Parliament on both sides of the House and never strongly supported by the public, was greatly weakened by the departure of British troops. Furthermore, according to the United Kingdom High Commissioner in Wellington, notwithstanding his brave words, Fraser was pleased to hear of the British decision for partial withdrawal because he regarded BCOF 'as serving no sufficient purpose in Japan today, where the Australians rule the roost anyhow and ride roughshod over the members of the British Commonwealth force'.[85]

The publicity the Force received in New Zealand continued to be negative.[86] The army component of Jayforce had to be relieved in mid–1947. When the appeal was made for volunteers in February it was immediately clear that there would be too few to replace the 4,000 troops in Japan. At first sight it looked as if the New Zealand Force would be as small as 1,200 all ranks. Subsequently 2,000 volunteers were secured in New Zealand and 400 volunteered from among the force in Japan.[87] Informing the Minister of External Affairs in Australia of these developments, the New Zealand government suggested that the time had come for a complete review of the position of the BCOF. Serious doubt about the value of continued participation in the military occupation of Japan was expressed. Further, it was noted, none of the governments participating in the BCOF had any share in the military government of Japan and no opportunity therefore of influencing directly the development of democratic institutions and a way of life in Japan which would not be a menace to the future security of the Pacific. 'It is doubtful' the message concluded, 'whether the existence of the force is of any value to us in the advocacy generally of policies affecting Japan, while its maintenance in a position of substantial inferiority to the Americans tends to diminish our prestige in the eyes of the Japanese'.[88]

The tone of these comments was in line with an article from *The Times* recently republished in New Zealand which had argued that the BCOF had neither prestige nor influence in Japan and that the big question among British troops was, 'Why are we in Japan?'[89]

For New Zealand, withdrawal from BCOF at this stage carried the risk of losing a 'proper voice' and vote at a future peace conference, an outcome against which Sir Carl Berendsen warned from Washington. The view from Washington was, of course, rather different from that of Wellington. Berendsen thought that withdrawal would be unpopular with MacArthur and with a Congress anxious to make cuts in the defence budget.[90] Berendsen's view was supported by the Australians who also believed that the BCOF must be maintained at least till the peace treaty was signed. The review for which New Zealand had asked did not therefore take place.[91]

Nevertheless the case for the retention of Jayforce and BCOF continued to be undermined. In March 1947 the government of India announced that, in view of the impending constitutional changes and consequent reorganization within the Indian army, all Indian troops would be withdrawn by 15 September 1947.[92] At the Canberra conference on the Japanese treaty which Fraser attended in August 1947, New Zealand let it be known unofficially that the reduced New Zealand contingent, which would have to be relieved in June 1948, would probably not be replaced.[93] It was thus evident that the 'experiment in Commonwealth co-operation' was ready to fall apart when in September 1947 the United Kingdom advised that all its troops would be withdrawn immediately.[94] This had serious implications for the future design of BCOF and the Chiefs of Staff in New Zealand were most annoyed to be informed by the Australians that the withdrawal of the United Kingdom element was not a matter which need concern New Zealand.[95] It was a further example, of which there had been many, of Australia trying to dominate proceedings. But the Australians were now quite clearly in charge. At the end of 1947 JCOSA was dissolved and the control and administration of BCOF became the responsibility of the Australian government with a New Zealand representative having the right to attend meetings of the Defence Committee when matters relating to the BCOF were discussed.[96]

BCOF was now a shadow of its former self. A definite decision had to be made on the future of Jayforce since the troops had to be relieved in June and six months notice was required if the contingent was not to be replaced. The Australians were keen for the New Zealanders to remain even if in a further reduced capacity but the government had to decide whether Jayforce was worth the effort from either a political or a military point of view. General Horace Robertson, who had replaced Northcott as Commander-in-Chief BCOF in April 1946, met the New Zealand Cabinet in February 1948. He thought that if the New Zealanders withdrew completely the Americans would have to be asked to take over Yamaguchi prefecture and this would be unfortunate for British prestige which, he claimed, was higher than even that of the United States in Japan. He seemed to suggest a 'small battalion' of about 700 New Zealanders would be sufficient to prevent the side being let down in this way.[97] Brigadier Potter had, however, recently reported:

> The dominating influence of American Military Government combined with the strategical disposition of her military forces are the two main factors which have hardened Japanese opinion in favour of the USA. Conversely BCOF participation in the occupation is regarded as negligible and has no influence on Japanese public opinion except locally, where it is regarded as of value only in the prevention of large-scale black-marketing and the maintenance of law and order.[98]

Robertson's claims, therefore, cannot have impressed already sceptical politicians, nor did they impress the army or airforce. The Chiefs of Staff were clear that, from a military point of view, the continued stationing of forces in Japan could not be recommended. Robertson's proposal to maintain one New Zealand Infantry Battalion was firmly rejected on grounds of inefficiency, logistics and finance. The airforce also wished to withdraw the New Zealand squadron on the grounds that the Corsair aircraft with which they were equipped had to be replaced and suitable aircraft could not be made available without special financial provisions.[99]

In the last resort, however, the decision on withdrawal had to be a political one. Any convincing political reasons for participation had by now been swept away. Commonwealth solidarity had disintegrated, prestige had evidently not been enhanced and there was no evidence that the presence of the BCOF had established closer ties and greater friendship with the United States. The Cabinet accepted the recommendation that the army component of Jayforce be withdrawn in mid-year and not be relieved, and that the participation of the New Zealand airforce squadron should cease at the end of the year.[100] The United States was so informed, and the last of both the army and airforce personnel left in November 1948. In retrospect what is remarkable is that they had stayed so long.

THE EXPERIMENT ASSESSED

The BCOF was a 'unique experiment' in Commonwealth co-operation and one which, in the end, found few supporters. Part of the problem was that there had been a lack of real inter-governmental discussion of the aims and objects of the Force in advance and no clear lines of responsibility and machinery of control established. Australia's predominance in command positions came to be resented by the other participants and the procedures for policy-making were clumsy and slow. In the opinion of the official Indian historian the routing of decisions from JCOSA to its agents, the Australian Chiefs of Staff, and then on the GHQ BCOF was 'a circuitous channel' often liable to 'considerable delays and misunderstandings'.[101] Even Australian Prime Minister Chifley was to admit that he did not consider Joint Chiefs of Staff Australia to be a 'suitable model' on which to base future Imperial Defence developments.[102]

If BCOF failed in its object of promoting Commonwealth co-operation and the integration of Commonwealth defence forces, so too did it fail in its aim of raising Commonwealth prestige in the eyes of the Japanese. The dominating influence of the American Military Government was so complete and its presence in Tokyo and the heavily populated areas so evident that it would have been surprising had the Japanese regarded the BCOF as anything more than a peripheral aspect of an essentially American affair. The limitation of the BCOF to marginal areas, by what seems to have been deliberate American policy, meant that BCOF influence on Japanese public opinion could only be local and whatever respect the force commanded locally, carried no weight in the circles which counted in Tokyo.

By 1947 BCOF had no job to do, and indeed it was argued in London that it had never had a real job.[103] This contributed in part to its failure because the lack of urgency about any of the activities in which it was engaged exacerbated frictions at HQ and contributed to the discontents of troops and consequently bad publicity. In these circumstances it was not surprising that the Force fell apart and came to illustrate differences between Commonwealth members rather than their solidarity. The individual and collective decisions to create and send the BCOF to Japan had been, essentially, politically based and political considerations caused the Force to break up. The British recognized that diplomatic contacts in Tokyo represented a better investment both in terms of Anglo-American relations in Japan and elsewhere and in terms of the promotion of economic opportunities in Japan itself. The Indians withdrew to pursue in their independence a policy of non-alignment. Once the cracks began to appear it was impossible for the New Zealand government to justify Jayforce. The grounds for New Zealand's participation, i.e., solidarity with Britain and other Commonwealth members and co-operation with them in the promotion of Commonwealth prestige, no longer applied. Furthermore, while New Zealand's interest in the security of the Pacific remained strong, the advance of the Cold War reinforced American determination to preserve as much control over Japan as possible. This meant that New Zealand's security concerns, as far as the Pacific and Japan were concerned, were likely to be better fostered in Washington and by making contacts in Tokyo than by continued participation in the remnants of BCOF. It meant that sooner, rather than later, New Zealand would need diplomatic representation in Japan.[104]

The only positive winner out of BCOF was Australia. Its commitment had been complete and sincere from the start even if not always appreciated by its Commonwealth partners. One historian judged, that 'By its commitment it demonstrated a new maturity in its Pacific foreign policy. The presence of Australian troops supported Australian claims to be taken seriously as a regional power'.[105]

Obviously it was no bad thing for New Zealand if Australia forced the United States to look south before making policy decisions. New Zealand aspired to play a role in the Pacific, but by itself had little leverage with the United States, the dominant power in the region in the decades after 1945. Although Australian dominance of BCOF had frequently been resented and although New Zealand's relationship with Australia on other matters was not always an easy one, as the negotiations over the peace treaty were later to show, the association of New Zealand with Australia in political dealings with the United States tended to work in New Zealand's favour. The New Zealand government gained nothing in domestic, political terms as a result of participating in the BCOF and in terms of enhancing Commonwealth defence co-operation the BCOF was a failure. But in terms of the changing balance of power in the Pacific and the role the United States was likely to play in the future, given that New Zealand had aspirations to be seen looking outwards as a Pacific power, New Zealand's contribution in Japan need not be regarded as an entirely wasted effort.

4

The Occupation: Legal Involvement New Zealand and the Tokyo War Crimes Trials

While the Far Eastern Commission and the Allied Council for Japan struggled vainly to make some impact on SCAP policies for the Occupation of Japan and the BCOF played out its peripheral role in the Occupation, there was at work in Tokyo yet another international group concerned both with Japan's past and its future in which New Zealanders were taking part. The International Military Tribunal for the Far East (IMTFE), set up in 1946, was designed to mete out 'stern justice' to Japan's wartime leaders, to impress upon the Japanese people the evils of these men and, by doing this through judicial trials, to command maximum public support at the time, and, it was hoped, ultimately the respect of history.[1]

In October 1945 the United States informed those countries which had signed the Instrument of Surrender with Japan of its policy with regard to the punishment of war criminals in the Far East.[2] The basis of this policy was the Potsdam Declaration of 26 July 1945 which read in part:

> We do not intend that the Japanese shall be enslaved as a race or destroyed as a nation but stern justice shall be meted out to war criminals, including those who have visited cruelties upon our prisoners.[3]

The establishment of an International Military Tribunal to try war criminals was based on this declaration. The Supreme Commander for the Allied Powers, General MacArthur (SCAP), was given the authority to set up such a tribunal and in January 1946 declared the establishment of the tribunal for the Far East and announced its Charter.[4] The International Military Tribunal for the Far East thus derived its authority from SCAP who acted as agent for the powers who had signed the Instrument of Surrender. As one of the powers which had signed this document, New Zealand had a direct interest in what followed.

By the time the Charter was announced, the New Zealand government, as a signatory of the Instrument of Surrender, had indeed already received an 'urgent' request to nominate a judge and a prosecutor to the proposed court. It was expected in December 1945, that trials would begin 'at the earliest possible moment'.[5] The government took the request seriously, a selection committee consisting of the Chief Justice, the Attorney General, the Solicitor General, the President of the New Zealand Law Society and the Deputy Secretary of the Department of External Affairs was set up and nominations were considered.[6]

By that time the general attitude in New Zealand to the trial of war criminals seems to have undergone some change. At the end of the war the idea of summary justice had appeal and the view that war criminals should be shot on sight had some support in New Zealand.[7] Criminal trials were seen simply as a waste of time. But by the end of 1945 the Nuremberg trials were in progress, New Zealanders had become familiar with the idea of a war crimes trial and not displeased to see, in newspapers and journals, the faces of German leaders like Goering and Hess, whose names and deeds were familiar to them, in the dock. No doubt partly as a consequence of Nuremberg, the idea of Japanese war crimes trials, and New Zealand's participation in them, seems to have been accepted without question although very little was known in New Zealand about Japanese wartime leadership.

In any case the New Zealand government was, of course, anxious to be involved in matters relating to Japan in the post-war world. A role in the trials would underline New Zealand's significance as a Pacific nation. Announcing the nomination of Justice Northcroft, a judge of the Supreme Court,[8] as a member of the international military courts to be established in Tokyo and of Ronald Quilliam, barrister, of New Plymouth,[9] to serve on the prosecution staff at the headquarters of SCAP, the Acting Prime Minister, Walter Nash, referred to New Zealand's 'special interest' in the settlement in Japan and in the maintenance of peace and security in the Pacific. New Zealand's representation at the trial would, he believed, identify the country in a 'special way' with the punishment of war criminals. Thus lofty principles were seen to be involved. Nash said the government hoped that the action would establish once again and ensure recognition for all time of the rule of law in 'the relations between nations and the peoples of the world'.[10] The New Zealand government evidently felt conscious of obligations imposed by international law and wished to identify New Zealand with that demonstration of justice, and the punishment which, it was assumed, would be the outcome of the trials. This kind of sentiment was echoed elsewhere in New Zealand where the value of the trials 'from the point of view of empahsizing to the whole world that sense of the principles of justice with which the British Empire, in conjunction with its allies, had conducted the war'[11] was expressed. Righteousness and self-satisfaction rather than any desire for vengeance seems to have been seen as the justification for New Zealand's participation in the trials.

None of the New Zealand team could be expected to have any background in matters of Japanese history or politics. Nor were the New Zealand judge and prosecutor, both of whom were well qualified and experienced in legal proceedings in New Zealand, experts in international law. As Quilliam, the New Zealand prosecutor who practised in a provincial New Zealand town, New Plymouth, commented wryly before he left, 'I have not had many clients consult me on matters of international law.' He also conceded, 'There will be a lot of agreements and pacts with which I shall have to make myself familiar.'[12] He need not have worried. As it transpired, there was plenty of time for preparation. It was to be months before the trial began.

THE NUREMBERG MODEL

The International Military Tribunal for the Far East (IMTFE) which was now being set up cannot really be understood in a vacuum. New Zealanders accepted the IMTFE as a logical development after Nuremberg and the structure and Charter of the IMTFE owed everything to the Nuremberg model.

The Nuremberg tribunal, the first in history to try individuals for crimes against the peace of the world, owed its origins to American determination to employ judicial proceedings against war criminals. This determination caused heated debates between America and its allies. British preference was for executive action or at most a 'short quick trial' with neither defence nor prosecution able to call witnesses. Churchill himself wanted the Nazi leaders summarily shot. There was, in the Foreign Office, considerable doubt whether many Nazi transgressions could properly be described as crimes under international law.[13] In the end, however, the British deferred to American opinion and the realities of power. A conference was held in London in June 1945 at which British, Soviet and French representatives met with the American negotiators to discuss the American proposals for a war crimes trial. The Soviets and the French resented American pressure for their agreement and were in unfamiliar legal territory, particularly over the suggestion of prosecuting conspiracy, a charge unknown to them in law. There was a good deal of tension and resentment of American pressure for agreement: the Americans were forced to make some compromises and an 'Agreement' and 'Charter' were finally signed in August 1945. The trial at Nuremberg began in November and was thus well launched by the time the Tokyo trials began in May 1946.[14]

The Nuremberg Charter which served as the legal foundation for the trial contained three prosecutable offences; crimes against peace, war crimes and crimes against humanity. The first and last of these were categories of 'highly uncertain status' in international law. Crimes against peace were defined as the 'planning, preparation, initiation or waging of a war of aggression ... or participation in a common plan or conspiracy for the accomplishment of the foregoing'. The conspiracy charge, included at American insistence, much criticized and familiar only to Anglo-Saxon law, enabled a wide net to be cast and allowed certain procedural regulations and rules of evidence to be relaxed.[15] The term 'war of aggression' caused problems since it was argued, as it is still argued, that launching a war was not a crime in international law. Furthermore the term 'aggression' could not be satisfactorily defined. Nevertheless this count was finally agreed. It had been necessary to maintain that international conventions, such as the 1928 Pact of Paris, also known as the Kellogg-Briand Pact, had established 'aggressive war' as a crime recognized by all 'civilized nations', another term which defied definition. War crimes referred to violations of the traditional laws of war such as mistreatment of prisoners of war and was well understood. Crimes against humanity included murder, extermination and 'persecution on political or religious grounds' whether committed 'before or during the war'.[16] This count was also much criticized on the ground that there was no code of law or international agreement in existence which made it illegal to persecute religions or exterminate populations undesirable as such activities might be. The count of crimes against humanity, it was argued, amounted to an exercise in *ex post facto* prosecution, declaring an act to be a crime after it had been committed and punishing it as such. Furthermore the prosecution of policy-makers as distinct from perpetrators was an issue which had hitherto been carefully skirted by international lawyers. This count was, however, so worded as to make individuals prosecutable and to remove the denial of superior orders as a legitimate defence.[17] This wide and much debated interpretation of international law accepted at Nuremberg established a precedent for the Tokyo trials.

THE IMTFE

There was no desire to re-examine the difficult legal and political issues raised during the formulation of the Nuremberg Charter when the creation of a tribunal for the Far East was mooted. Hence the reliance in Tokyo on the Nuremberg precedent is immediately evident. The Charter which MacArthur issued in January 1946 from which the authority of the court derived, set out the crimes for which individuals were to be tried. These were the same counts as Nuremberg, similarly worded and justified by six broad principles of international law.[18]

The most obvious difference between Tokyo and Nuremberg was the greater number of states involved. There were four at Nuremberg. Ultimately there were eleven in Tokyo, the nine signatories of the Instrument of Surrender, plus India and the Philippines.[19] This made the bench unwieldy, made for difficulties of co-ordination and added to the probability of split decisions. These were all the more likely given the shaky legal ground on which the Charter was based and the ambiguities of the indictment when this was finally drawn up.

New Zealand chose not to submit a list of Japanese war

criminals, asking merely for the right to comment on any lists submitted. In contrast to Australia, New Zealand, in spite of its geographical position, had been relatively detached from the events of the war with Japan because the main thrust of its war effort had been in the Middle East. Accurate information about the wartime leadership, and on the subject of war criminals was hard for the government to come by.[20] With the exception of the Emperor, General Tojo's name was the only one with which the general public was likely to be at all familiar and there seems to have been no public outcry immediately after the war for the punishment of either of these two.[21] The American records suggest that, in October 1945 at least, some in the Department of External Affairs and perhaps the Prime Minister believed that if trials were to be held, the Emperor should be tried as a war criminal.[22] If this is correct, it seems this was never official policy.[23] Press claims, in January 1946, that the government favoured the trial of the Emperor were denied[24] and the Prime Minister, as Minister of External Affairs, informed Sir Carl Berendsen in Washington, 'As we see it Hirohito has served a useful purpose both with respect to the surrender and in aiding the task of the occupation forces. The nomination of him as a war criminal would we feel require the most careful consideration'.[25]

Berendsen endorsed this view although he personally felt that the emperor should qualify as a war criminal. When the Far Eastern Commission visited Tokyo in January 1946 SCAP stressed that any attempt to try the Emperor as a war criminal would lead to a violent reaction in Japan and put the whole Occupation at risk. Berendsen reported General MacArthur's argument that the Emperor was 'a cypher, a puppet rather than a leader'.[26] This view, which was accepted in Washington and met the wishes of the British who favoured the retention of the emperor,[27] went unchallenged in government circles in New Zealand and ultimately the press appears also to have accepted that the indictment of the Emperor would have been politically unwise.[28] As it was, New Zealand accepted the individuals proposed by other powers for trial.

THE NEW ZEALAND TEAM IN JAPAN

The New Zealand team had been carefully chosen. Both the judge and the prosecutor had distinguished records in both the First and Second World Wars. Both were experienced lawyers and highly respected in legal circles. Northcroft had been on the bench of the Supreme Court since 1935. Quilliam, who had a legal practice in New Plymouth, had been an examiner in criminal law for the University of New Zealand and Deputy Adjutant-General of the New Zealand Army before his release at the end of 1943 when he returned to his legal practice.[29] It is not surprising that men of this calibre and background approached their task in Japan with a high sense of duty or that they expected both 'honour and satisfaction' from their appointed roles rather than material rewards.[30] It was inevitable that they should see themselves not simply as part of the judical process set up to prosecute and judge Japan's wartime leaders, but as representatives of a country steeped in British law and justice, now establishing its identity as a Pacific nation with special interests in Japan. In the sense that they were 'showing the flag' for New Zealand, the New Zealand judge and prosecutor could not but be conscious of their political as well as their judicial function.

Justice Northcroft, his associate, Flight Lieutenant Harold Evans, a young officer of the Department of External Affairs who had a legal training and experience as a judge's associate before the war,[31] and Brigadier Quilliam, arrived in Tokyo on 5 February 1946. They were all shocked by the devastation of Tokyo 'the scene beggars description', Quilliam wrote. He was amazed by the numbed docility of the Japanese people. 'I often wonder what they think about us' he added, 'I have not seen any evidence of hostility but I cannot help thinking they must hate us'.[32] If the general scene in Japan was depressing, equally depressing for the New Zealand party was the fact that they found very little had been done by way of preparation for the trials. Only one other judge, the Australian, Sir William Webb, with whom the New Zealanders had travelled from Brisbane, was in Tokyo. The material for the prosecutors had not been collected. It had not yet been decided who was to be arraigned. It was clear that it might be months before the court could function.

In the intervening weeks the prosecutors were very busy collating material, studying and preparing the case. Inevitably the judges were rather isolated in these enforcedly idle months. Northcroft sent for books, enjoyed fishing and with Webb played a good deal of not always amicable golf.[33] As the other judges arrived, there were administrative matters to attend to. Northcroft was concerned by suggestions that SCAP might be contemplating giving instructions to the court, thus compromising its integrity, and accompanied Webb in a call on General MacArthur to clear up this matter. If the 'principles of British justice' were to be observed, SCAP had to be kept away from the Tribunal.[34]

In February 1946 General MacArthur named Sir William Webb President of the IMTFE. Initially this appointment seems to have pleased the New Zealanders well enough. Quilliam wrote of Webb, 'He has a keen sense of justice and is well imbued with its principles and traditions'. Quilliam suggested that the choice was probably due to MacArthur's wish to pay Australia, from which he had begun his successful campaign against the Japanese, a compliment. Besides MacArthur knew Webb well from those days. Quilliam also speculated that the choice relieved MacArthur of the dilemma as to whether it should be an English or an American judge who should preside. Since the Americans had charge of the prosecution it might have been thought undesirable to make the court too much of an 'American show'.[35] A recent American writer has, however, suggested that the choice of Webb was forced on MacArthur because the American nomination to the Tribunal was so weak that he could not be named President. He argues that the choice of Webb was forced on MacArthur who did not want a British President.[36] Be that as it may, Webb was President, and once the court was in session both Northcroft and Quilliam became very critical of him on the grounds of both his professional skills and his personality. Northcroft came to work closely with other Commonwealth judges, Lord Patrick the British judge and McDougall, the Canadian judge. They all disapproved of Webb.

Unlike the Commonwealth judges, the Commonwealth prosecutors seem quickly to have developed a rapport. For most of the first year they all had accommodation at the Canadian Legation and one of the advantages of this was that they had the opportunity to discuss matters relating to the prosecution 'quietly and fully'.[37] As a group, they took their complaints to Joseph Keenan, the American Chief Prosecutor and to Webb. Partly as a result of this, no doubt, they had the not unfamiliar problem of persuading the Americans that they must be treated as individuals and that the United Kingdom prosecutor did not in some way represent and speak for them all. They were all impatient of the delays, of the failure to consult and of the lack of direction from the Chief Prosecutor, Keenan, whose publicity seeking, lack of leadership, inefficient and frequently drunken behaviour they found increasingly abhorrent.[38] The New Zealand prosecutor, along with the rest of the prosecuting team, was dependent on the Americans for documentary evidence on which to base a satisfactory prosecution and was most critical of procedures. Quilliam was worried about the inadequacy of the 'interrogations' of prominent Japanese, about failure to give priority to examination of documents and of the failure of the American prosecuting team generally, to 'get down to brass tacks'. Keenan had neither the drive nor the expertise to prepare the indictment which, in the end was largely the work of Comyns-Carr, the British prosecutor. He had the dynamism, skill and experience to drive matters forward although, as Quilliam pointed out, this had the not altogether desirable effect of protecting Keenan. The prosecutors' meetings on the draft indictment were, Quilliam recorded, 'very difficult'. His impression was that the Chinese, Dutch and French prosecutors didn't understand some of the disputed points of law at all. He was moreover disgusted when a policy of appeasement was adopted towards the prosecutor from the Philippines, who threatened to resign unless his addition, couched 'in picturesque extravagant and loose language' was added to the original draft of the indictment.[39]

Northcroft had other worries. He found it 'embarrassing', given that English and Japanese had been designated the languages of the court, that the Russian judge spoke not a word of English, so that quite often on important matters one was not clear whether he and the other judges were discussing the same things. The French judge and prosecutor spoke very limited English and this too was to cause problems. Northcroft was tactful about his colleagues on the Tribunal but clearly found the qualifications of some of them rather dubious.[40] Northcroft was not alone in this feeling.[41] Once the trial was underway and the strain of the long hours and generally poor performance of the President and court was felt, Northcroft's impatience grew.

The list of twenty-eight defendants was finally determined on 17

April. Two of these, diplomat and former foreign minister
Shigemitsu Mamoru and General Unezu Yoshijiro, had been
added at Russian insistence. Both men had been notably anti
Communist before the war.[42] Quilliam was opposed to the addi
tion since these men had already been considered, and it had been
agreed by the prosecutors before the Russians arrived that they
were 'less culpable' than the twenty-six individuals they had finally
named. The majority of prosecutors, however, led by Keenan
thought it advisable to make this concession to the Russians. The
Soviet press had had much to say about the Emperor's war guilt so
there was a good deal of apprehension among the prosecutors tha
there might be a drawn out debate and divisions on this issue
Keenan had already made it clear that what he termed 'the higher
levels' would not approve of the Emperor's inclusion in the list. To
Quilliam's surprise the Russians made no attempt on this, or any
other occasion, to have the Emperor's name included.[43]

The twenty-eight defendants were charged in the period from 1
January 1928 to 2 September 1945 with planning, preparing
initiating and waging wars of aggression in violation of international law and treaties, committing wholesale murder and instigat-
ing numerous 'crimes against humanity' in a fifty-five count
indictment. Proceedings finally began on 3 May 1946.

THE LEGAL PROCESS

While the New Zealanders had no doubts about the justification
for, and legality of the trials, they were extremely critical of the
legal process. In the case of both the judge and the prosecutor
their criticisms were to lead them both, at different times, to ask
the government for permission to resign before the trial was over.

Both Northcroft and Quilliam were shocked by the 'unseemly'
behaviour and limited abilities of many of the American defence
counsel a number of whom, Quilliam thought, were out simply to
obtain as much notoriety as they could from the trial. Northcroft
considered the incompetence on the part of some of the American
counsel amounted 'almost to childishness',[44] Northcroft was critical of the 'Hollywood' atmosphere of the trials and thought the
Americans had made 'a very bad job' of conducting them. It was
not, he thought when the trial had been underway a bare two

months, a 'very good show'. Keenan he declared showed 'every
sign of being an exceedingly incompetent lawyer'.[45] 'So much of
our time in court', he wrote 'is little more than a sheer waste'.[46]
Part of the problem was that the prosecuting team was predominantly American and, it has since been suggested, generally not of
as high a calibre as the legal representatives sent from other
countries. In addition, as some of the defence lawyers were to
admit later, the defence was frequently deliberately obstructive,
dragging out the trial in the expectation that the allies would
eventually fall out among themselves, so that their clients' claims
would be enhanced.[47] The patience of the judges was frequently
sorely tried. For the New Zealanders, for whom there was little or
no personal, and certainly no financial mileage to be gained,[48] the
protracted and disorganized proceedings were exceedingly
frustrating.

But the standard of the prosecution and defence lawyers was
only part of the problem. Soon after the trial began both
Northcroft and Quilliam became critical of Webb as President of
the Tribunal. According to Quilliam, Webb, 'time and again',
demonstrated his 'unfitness' for his admittedly difficult task.[49] No
excuse could be found for his bullying of witnesses and counsel, or
for his demonstrations of bias. One of the problems was that Webb
alone had the microphone and could control or, more often, hold
up proceedings. Within a short time Northcroft reported that he
thought there was 'not one member of the bench' who was not
thoroughly disheartened' over the personality and inadequacy of
the President.[50] The difficulties were compounded by the fact that
this was no ordinary court where standard practices were normal
to all judges and dissatisfaction with the President could be dealt
with as a domestic matter. The judges had no common concept of
what the President's role should be, most had no experience of a
composite court, and consequently no notion of the *primus inter
pares* status of a President. According to Northcroft, Webb didn't
understand this concept either, and was not amenable to suggestions for ways in which the workings of the court might be
improved. Northcroft came to feel that Webb had 'an indifferent
knowledge of the rules of evidence', was 'unreliable', vain and
stupid too.[51] For Northcroft, a judge of more than a decade's
experience, Webb's deficiencies were all the more difficult to take
since, not without reason, he felt himself to be better qualified than

Webb to act as President of the Tribunal and was also inevitably associated with him as a member of the Bench.[52] After the trial had been underway for a year Northcroft found Webb's behaviour so unsatisfactory that he requested permission from the Prime Minister to resign. He indicated that the Canadian and British justices were equally dissatisfied, that they too wished to resign and that they had also communicated this to their governments.[53]

Faced with Northcroft's request, the Prime Minister sought an opinion from the recently retired Chief Justice of New Zealand, Sir Michael Myers. Myers was firmly of the opinion that the resignation of the judge so far into the trial might have serious consequences, by giving the defendants a legitimate sense of grievance.[54] If the announced ground for resignation was Northcroft's failure to agree with the President, both Northcroft and Webb seemed likely to be enveloped in criticism and derision and the Tribunal as a whole brought into contempt. Furthermore, a scandal of this kind would inevitably affect detrimentally New Zealand's relations with both Australia and the United States.[55] Northcroft, whose sense of duty to the law, 'the cause of international justice' and his country was strong, stayed on. It seems, however, that at the Commonwealth conference on the Japanese peace treaty which was held in Canberra later that year, 1947, Prime Minister Peter Fraser complained to the Australian Prime Minister about Webb's behaviour. In October 1947 Webb was summoned back to Australia, ostensibly because of 'important' proceedings forthcoming in the Queensland Supreme Court. He was away two months, his return being engineered apparently, by MacArthur who was considerably embarrassed by the absence of the President of the Tribunal at that late stage of the trial. In the two month interim an acting President had had to be appointed. Ironically Northcroft was the next most senior judge, but MacArthur thought him unsuitable in view of the 'insignificance of New Zealand as a world power'. The American judge, General Cramer, who had himself been challenged by the defence because he was a late substitute for the original American member of the Tribunal, John P. Higgins (who had resigned in July 1946), was appointed. MacArthur admitted later that, from the standpoint of experience and knowledge of jurisprudence, Cramer was not really suitable'.[56] It was a less than satisfactory situation from Northcroft's point of view.

Quilliam, like Northcroft, a man with a strong sense of duty and of strong opinions, was quite as frustrated by the inefficiency with which the trial was run and the way in which matters were allowed to drift. Within a month of the trial's opening he recorded, 'all sense of urgency has gone'.[57] Full of righteous indignation, he was in the forefront of various unsuccessful moves to have Keenan, whose deficiencies were legion, removed. Quilliam also regularly cited and protested against various irregularities which, in other circumstances, might have led to calls from the defence for a mistrial.[58] There was, however, little chance that the concerns of the New Zealand prosecutor, representing as he did the smallest country involved, would receive much attention, particularly when the British prosecutor, more aware no doubt of the realities of power, chose to work with Keenan. Quilliam was charged with the responsibility of presenting the prosecution's case in respect of Japanese 'General Preparations for War'. Under this heading, naval, military, fortifications, financial and production questions had to be taken into account. It was an extremely wide and difficult brief, in the preparation of which Quilliam complained that his American assistants were an embarrassment rather than a help.[59] Within his brief Quilliam was responsible for the prosecution of Admiral Nagano who died in January 1947 before his prosecution had taken place. Quilliam's dry comment was, 'I had done a great deal of work ... There was a strong case against Nagano and I am inclined to regard his demise as somewhat inconsiderate to me personally'. The competence of Quilliam's work was welcomed by the judges,[60] but Quilliam had not endeared himself to Keenan and had the feeling that he and the other British prosecutors were being side-tracked.[61] By the end of 1946 Quilliam was considering resigning. He left Tokyo in November 1947, by which time he felt he had done all he could usefully do in the trial and by way of assisting in the prosecution and representing New Zealand at the trial.

In the meantime Northcroft's life had been made somewhat easier with the arrival, in June 1947, of Quentin Quentin-Baxter, a young solicitor from Christchurch, to join the New Zealand team. He came as a result of Northcroft's request in July 1946 (after the trial had been running for just two months), for an assistant with legal training to compile summaries of the mountain of evidence which was accumulating. By that time, Northcroft reported, 197 exhibits had already been filed and the record was already 2,294 pages of typescript. The prosecution was, he said, in effect, 'hurling masses of material at the court, leaving the court to do the best it can with it'. Since the court sat from 9.30 a.m. to 4 p.m. and the transcript of the day's proceedings could not be produced before 8 p.m., there was no time for a judge to maintain a current summary of the case under its various headings. In order to avoid the court 'wandering in a wilderness of exhibits and/or evidence' when it came to consider questions of guilt and innocence, Northcroft asked for someone who 'has a clear, analytical and enterprizing mind, one who is industrious and, if at all possible, one who has assisted in a good office or with counsel in a substantial practice in preparation of cases for trial.'[62] The 'wilderness' of evidence became ever more impenetrable in the eleven months it took to find and deliver Quentin-Baxter to Tokyo, but miraculously he fulfilled all Northcroft's requirements. He was a graduate in law and philosophy from Canterbury College (as it then was), a Senior Scholar in Law, had practical experience including two years court work with a leading Christchurch firm, and was highly recommended by his employers for his intelligence and diligence. In making this appointment, an official in the Department of External Affairs noted, prophetically as it happened, 'we have some possibility, if the young man turns out well, of getting some benefit, even if only indirectly, for New Zealand'.[63]

Quentin-Baxter described later how he spent his first twelve months in Tokyo reading the accumulated evidence and making notes. This in itself was a Herculean labour. He, like most of those involved in this trial, had no background in Japanese history, and his task was so formidable that he made a conscious effort not to clutter his mind by reading anything about Japan except the evidence before him. His particular task was to sift this evidence in order to assess the justification for the charge of conspiracy to commit crimes against peace.[64] Northcroft was unstinting in his praise of the results of Quentin-Baxter's unremitting toil.[65]

THE LEGAL ISSUES

At Tokyo the contest was between defence lawyers who adopted a strict interpretation of international law and prosecution lawyers

who employed the Nuremberg claim that the sources of international law were much wider. The defence argued that the wider
interpretation amounted to retroactive legislation and questioned
whether existing international law could be applied to individuals
rather than states and whether, if offences were judged to have
been committed, the court had the right to enact punishments.
Defence arguments were accepted entirely by the Indian member
of the Tribunal, Justice Pal, who wrote an erudite and lengthy
dissenting judgment.[66] He held the view, moreover, that the
IMTFE charter had insufficient authority to try the accused.

The majority, however, accepted that the IMTFE had a basis in
international law and was bound by the directions of its charter
from which alone it derived its jurisdiction. The Nuremberg
tribunal was claimed as a precedent. The court had sat for two
years and was in effect conducting the trials of twenty-odd persons
upon a large number of alleged crimes in each case.[67] The
transcript ran to more than 50,000 pages. Judgement had to be
reached.

In May 1948 Northcroft wrote:

> Some of us are working very hard in preparation for the
> judgment of the tribunal. This is a long business ... The
> tremendous width of the topics canvassed before us and
> which in turn we must discuss in our judgement, together
> with the mass of evidence which it is necessary to examine,
> prevents the task being done, if properly, quickly.[68]

He reported that Quentin-Baxter was working 'tremendously
hard' giving assistance to him and to the other judges with whom
Northcroft was collaborating. He explained that the work of
writing the judgement was really being done by a very small group
of three or four people. They submitted portions of the work as
they were completed from time to time to a larger group who,
although not active themselves, were in general agreement with
the active group. When this conference had taken place and the
separate parts had been settled, these parts were then distributed
to the rest of the judges who, Northcroft felt, when the final day
came, would accept their work, 'Indeed', he commented, 'there
will be nothing else for it, because no other work is going forward

but ours, with the exception of one judge who, apparently will write a dissenting judgment on the whole matter.'[69] Northcroft's account seems, if not entirely to refute, at least to modify and qualify a recent claim that the majority judgement was reached without discussion by the whole bench.[70] It also explains why part of the judgement can be recognized by those who know his style well, as the work of Quentin-Baxter.[71] He helped write, assemble, check and organize the material for the small 'active' group of judges. Northcroft wrote at the time:

> He [Quentin-Baxter] is producing material for use by a few of us who are the drafting committee for the Judges in the preparation of the judgment. This work is so good that, unlike the contributions of others similarly employed, we are able to adopt his treatises on difficult and important aspects of Far Eastern historical developments in large measure with only slight alteration in either substance or expression. One of our number and the best brain among us and a really distinguished Judge has remarked at times that he would have been happy to have produced it himself.[72]

It is evident that Quentin-Baxter's later reference to having taken 'a substantial part in the preparation of the opinion of the court', is in fact a modest claim.[73]

It took seven months to write the majority judgement to which Northcroft and eight other justices were parties. Two of these, Webb, from Australia and Jaranilla from the Philippines filed separate but essentially concurring opinions dealing with specific problems. Webb argued that the Emperor should have been tried and, since he was not, none of the essentially less criminal defendants, the Emperor's subordinates, should receive the death sentence. Jaranilla argued for harsher penalties. Apart from the Indian judge who dissented entirely and accepted the arguments of the defence, the Netherlands and French judges wrote dissenting judgements dealing with particular issues. The former wanted five of the accused, including both the civilians Hirota and Shigemitsu, acquitted of all charges. Bernard from France also argued that the Emperor should have been indicted and cited this as one of the reasons for his opinion that all the accused should be acquitted on the grounds that the procedures of the IMTFE had been invalid.[74] The disunity among the judges which was soon widely known did little to enhance the court in the eyes of the Japanese or to convince them and many others that this court had been an instrument of justice. Seven of the accused were sentenced to death, sixteen to life imprisonment and two, diplomats Shigemitsu and Togo, to lesser terms if imprisonment.

THE OUTCOME

The New Zealanders involved, certainly believed the trial to be justified and its legality undoubted. They had sought to act according to the 'best principles of British justice'. But inevitably both Northcroft and Quilliam were painfully aware of very real legal, political and logistical problems associated with the trial. Defending the Tribunal against the allegation that it had made an improper use of is power, Northcroft maintained that one of the important results achieved by the Tribunal was that:

> it conducted an historical inquiry into the actions of Japan, and it traced the proximate causes. There is set upon its findings a seal of authority and, I trust, impartiality which cannot attend the work of any historian of recent events, for the Tribunal's decision was reached upon all the available evidence and after the fullest opportunity had been afforded for the presentation of opposing views.[75]

While Northcroft's sincerity is not in doubt, forty years later neither historians nor jurists would be inclined to accept his view of the Tribunal's results wholeheartedly.[76] In spite of his confidence in the Tribunal, however, Northcroft was quite aware that a dangerous precedent had been established. He therefore argued, not very realistically in the Cold War atmosphere which already prevailed by 1948, for the setting up of a permanent international criminal court as a matter of urgency.[77]

Quilliam was equally convinced that the trials were legal, were justified, and their outcome proper. As a prosecutor he had, however, particular concerns. He noted the serious difficulties in international law of the charge, 'crimes against peace' and specifically of the charge that waging 'aggressive war' was a crime in international law. He recommended that, should such trials be held in future, serious consideration should be given to the wisdom of laying this charge.[78]

For his part, Quentin-Baxter was optimistic about the Tribunal and its results. He believed that it had 'established a chain of reasoning and a standard of objective enquiry which refutes the allegation that the nations which established this Tribunal have made improper use of their power'. He concluded a speech to the New Zealand Law Conference in April 1949, 'The judgment of the Tokyo Tribunal does not purport to absolve the Japanese people from the responsibility for their country's conduct, but it does show where that responsibility chiefly lies. In so doing, it makes a constructive contribution to the task of rehabilitating the Japanese nation'.[79]

The Tokyo trials could hardly be said to have given New Zealanders a greater awareness of their international obligations and of the importance to them of all matters relating to Japan and the Pacific. This had been one of the justifications for participation but, from the beginning, the coverage of the trial in the New Zealand press had been very thin. Lamenting this fact McIntosh, the Secretary of External Affairs noted that, while the Nuremberg trials figured largely in the press, topics of 'more pressing interest' like the Palestine problem and American loans to the United Kingdom kept the Tokyo trials out of the papers.[80] Later the Department of External Affairs encouraged Evans to write accounts of the trials and circulated the material to the press. Little or no use appears to have been made of this. Shanahan, Deputy Secretary of External Affairs wrote:

> I am anxious if possible to develop a public opinion in support of our participation in the Tribunal and trial proceedings. Our people are singularly apathetic to matters of this kind and, in view of the importance of the Pacific, I feel we should do everything we can to develop and stimulate interest.[81]

By 1948 when the judgement was announced, however, few New Zealanders were much interested in the esoteric niceties of international law or the outcome of the trials in Tokyo. Nor were these readily seen as an aspect of New Zealand's 'Pacific' responsibilities and identity. By and large the New Zealand press seem to have reported the Tribunal's sentences with little comment. The debate about whether the Emperor should have been tried was noted as was the fact that the decision not to try him was a political one.[82] The lack of unanimity among the judges over the verdicts and the appropriate sentences, which cast an uncertain light on proceedings, was not debated.

In fact in the long run participation had simply associated New Zealand with a rather 'sorry affair'. By 1948 there was no disposition by the New Zealand government to take part in any further trials.[83] When in 1950 a Soviet proposal to try Emperor Hirohito surfaced in the Far Eastern Commission, McIntosh described the charges as 'vague, irresponsible and mischievous'. The view of the Department of External Affairs at that time was that the allegations against the Emperor, even if fully substantiated, would not justify a decision to put him on trial. In any case it would obviously have been highly undesirable on political grounds to have done so.[84]

From the point of view of the New Zealand government, the nomination of a New Zealand judge and prosecutor to participate in the war crimes trials had been an expression of New Zealand's willingness to participate with its allies in shouldering the responsibilities of the post-war world and in particular it had been a demonstration of New Zealand's interest in the future of the Pacific world. To this extent the government could feel New Zealand had done its bit and its participation in the trials where decisions of historical importance were made had been worthwhile. It had, nevertheless, been a 'dreary business' rather than a clear demonstration of the operation of those 'principles of justice' by which Walter Nash had set store. Furthermore it could scarcely have been said to assist in the education of New Zealanders to recognise the importance to them of the lands beyond their horizons in the rest of the Pacific world.

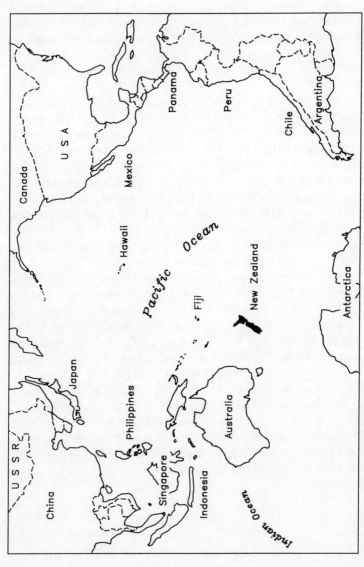

New Zealand and the Pacific Rim

5
The Peace Treaty Debate
1945–1949

The FEC, BCOF and IMTFE operated beyond New Zealand's shores and dealt specifically with matters relating to Occupied Japan. New Zealand participated in them as one of the smallest of the allies out of a mixture of high-minded motives: to demonstrate her willingness to accept responsibility; to be part of the team; to participate as a Pacific nation in the reformation of Japan. She also participated in order to establish, should this be necessary, her right to participate in the fomulation of a peace treaty with Japan, that is, her right to a 'voice'.

The Occupation had for New Zealand an international perspective and an aspect of self-interest. The organizations relating to it operated beyond New Zealand and in the overall picture, New Zealand's role was a very minor one. In the case of BCOF, New Zealand was even a rather reluctant participant. But the matter of the Japanese peace treaty was seen to be different. From the beginning it was seen as of central interest and central to New Zealand's security. The planning of New Zealand's priorities in any peace treaty had to be a matter of importance for Wellington.

The calculations and negotiations involved, of course, New Zealand's relationship with both the United Kingdom and the United States. Inevitably New Zealand's perspective was different from that of the United Kingdom and, while there was merit in Commonwealth solidarity in the bargaining process, there was always the possibility, given the post-war preoccupations of Britain and its need for the United States, that in Evatt's words, New Zealand and Australia would be 'double crossed' and find their concerns ignored. To add to the uncertainties, New Zealand had no real constituency in the United States which was bound to exert the major influence. Learning how to make New Zealand's mark with the United States was also to be an aspect of New Zealand's experience in the prolonged process of making a treaty with Japan.

The Potsdam Declaration confirmed fears New Zealand and Australia already held that wartime recognition of their interest in the Pacific and in the Far East settlement might not be translated into an invitation to participate in the process of peace-making. From the beginning New Zealand had wanted to participate in this process.

EARLY PLANNING

Study began in early 1945 in the Department of External Affairs to establish the principles on which New Zealand policy towards Japan would be based. It was no easy task to prepare background papers and assessments of the position with regard to Japan and the east Asian theatre. There were few in New Zealand with first hand knowledge of east Asia and such 'experts' as New Zealand then possessed were mostly 'old China hands' of missionary background. Little was known of the nature and origins of Japanese militarism, and the Department of External Affairs was largely dependent on rather scarce printed resources for most of its information. The young official who was responsible for preparing the early position papers has described how, starting without any background on the subject, he read everything on Japan that he could find and shared material with his opposite number in the Australian High Commission in Wellington.[1] They were on their own. Whitehall, the usual Commonwealth source of background material, was not yet planning its policy for the Japanese peace.[2].

The Japanese advance from 1941 to 1943 had brought a foreign war closer to New Zealand than at any time in its history. Though the danger then receded and New Zealanders relaxed, it is scarcely surprising that in 1945 Japan should be seen as the chief obstacle to Pacific peace and New Zealand security. If Japan was eliminated as a military power there was, it was argued, a good chance of that 'condition of peace in which the territorial integrity and political independence of every country in the Pacific was protected against aggression', being achieved. The removal of Japan's overseas possessions was seen as an important security measure and, since it was assumed that plans for expansion would continue to be fostered by an influential nucleus of the Japanese population, radical changes in Japan's political social and economic institutions were seen as necessary to foil these plans. The old 'rightest elements' were considered to be well organised and well entrenched. The Japanese government must therefore be suspended until the allies were satisfied that Japan's capacity and desire for aggressive expansion had been removed.[3] New Zealand wanted a tough peace. The long Occupation for which New Zealand called, was one way of protecting such 'moderate elements' as might exist in Japan against a resurgence of aggression. New Zealand called for 'a mental change' and re-education in Japan. Predictably, with its social democratic tradition, there was concern in New Zealand that, in the long run, agrarian reform, more extended ownership of the means of production and the breakup of monopolies of the great corporations should be instituted in Japan.[4] A long Occupation was, therefore envisaged in 1945 though a long and thorough Occupation would be, for New Zealand, a heavy commitment.

NEW ZEALAND AND AUSTRALIAN STYLE

The problem was whether or not New Zealand and Australia would be consulted about the peace treaty. Evatt had boasted in December 1945 that he had said to President Truman, 'We must be partners even if junior partners.' to which Truman replied 'No, full partners',[5] but 1946 brought no evidence that New Zealand and Australia were considered anything other than sleeping partners. In October, arrangements, in which neither New Zealand nor Australia were consulted, were made for the disposal of the Japanese fleet. This was seen as a serious and ominous slight by both countries and New Zealand hurried to associate itself with the Australian protest. New Zealand asked for recognition, with Australia, of its right to a 'direct voice' as a 'party principal' in any decisions on matters relating to the peace settlement.[6] The long-standing fear that Britain and the United States would 'sew up' the post-war world between them had in no way been allayed by events so far.

Australian protest over the disposal of the fleet, and the Australian response to a mollifying interchange which subsequently took place between Evatt and the US Ambassador in Canberra, were seen by the Dominions Office as an indication of Evatt's desire to lead the British team.[7] He had, of course, such ambitions, and had already indicated to New Zealand that he thought the position had been reached where Australia and New Zealand 'would take over from the United Kingdom the leadership of the British Commonwealth in the Pacific.'[8] There was, however, no sign that such a transfer of power was in the offing. Evatt's fear was that, unless Australia and New Zealand worked together, the Japanese settlement would take place piecemeal and bargaining points would disappear, an outcome which would be quite as damaging to Australia and New Zealand ambitions as the proposal for a 25-year Four Power treaty on the disarmament and demilitarization of Japan which had earlier been floated.[9] The indefinite state of affairs which applied by 1947 was unsatisfactory to all those, like New Zealand and Australia, wishing to participate 'fully and effectively' in the peace settlement.

Rather than the head-on confrontational style which characterized the Australian approach, New Zealand had somewhat naive hopes that support for an internationalist approach might give it a voice in the peacemaking. New Zealand saw in the eleven countries of the Far Eastern Commission (FEC) a valuable representative grouping where the basic work of shaping the peace treaty could be done.[10] New Zealand's experience of working in international organizations made this an attractive proposition. Moreover given Berendsen's fearless advocacy of the right of small nations to be heard, Wellington knew it had a delegate who would lose no opportunity to present New Zealand's case. Berendsen himself expressed doubts about entrusting the drafting of the treaty to the FEC but Wellington had hopes that the FEC would be the forum for preliminary discussions and the airing of views.[11] Enthusiasm for the FEC was, however, not shared in Australia where it was recognized as likely always to be overridden by MacArthur and the United States Government and hence 'useless'.[12]

The difficulty for Australia and New Zealand was to get themselves represented in forums that counted if the FEC did not. Evatt's fear was that the Soviet Union's insistence (since the Moscow conference of December 1945), that the Council of Foreign Ministers ought to determine how a peace conference might be summoned and a treaty signed with Japan, might finally be accepted. This would exclude Australia and New Zealand from the proceedings. He tried without success to enlist New Zealand support for a proposal that the United Kingdom representative at the Council of Foreign Ministers should give place to a joint British Commonwealth representative.[13]

Fraser's response to this idea was a model of good sense. He agreed with Evatt that New Zealand's and Australia's position in relation to the peace settlement was unacceptable and that they must consider some action to secure recognition of their 'dignity and rights as active belligerents who contributed to victory as much proportionally as the Big Powers and more in real value than some.' But if, as Evatt suggested, there was to be a 'British Unit' in which members of the Commonwealth formed a team which counted as one unit in the Council of Foreign Ministers, how was joint policy to be reached? What weight was to be attached to the views of each Commonwealth member? Evatt's scheme would no doubt strengthen the United Kingdom's voice in the Big Four; at the same time it would leave it open to other powers to maintain that, if the Commonwealth was a single unit, its members should not have independent representation at international meetings. New Zealand and Australia could not expect to have it both ways. Furthermore such a plan would also, Fraser thought, lead to the perpetuation of the existing dual arrangement of a relatively ineffective international body made up of all sizes of equal and sovereign, small and large states, dealing only with small problems, and a smaller Big Power grouping which settled the really large and important problems and weighted the views of its four members according to the strength they disposed of. Neither Fraser nor Evatt wanted this. Fraser felt that the United Kingdom had probably gone as far as it was prepared to go to limit its freedom of action to meet the views of the Dominions. In his judgement the best way to make an impression, and the way most likely to reduce Russian suspicion, was to make direct representation as independent nations to the Council of Foreign Ministers like other independent non-members of the Commonwealth.[14] At the heart of this exchange lay the crucial problems for New Zealand and Australia in those post-war years. How could they resolve the tension between their aspiration for independent nationhood and their desire for Commonwealth defence solidarity; how most effectively could they, as nations, make their voices heard?[15]

PREPARATIONS FOR THE CANBERRA CONFERENCE 1947

It seemed from General MacArthur's statements in March 1947 that a peace conference was imminent. New Zealand and Australia were concerned to play a part. Given the problems that had already occurred, the Foreign Office and Dominions Office were concerned to convince them that this wish was fully supported and that they would be consulted before any discussions with other countries were entered into. A Commonwealth conference was proposed, Whitehall's less than disinterested aim being to avoid the danger of the United States springing a Japanese peace treaty on an unprepared Britain.[16] Disagreement arose over the venue, London, Washington and Canberra being proposed, but Canberra eventually won, to New Zealand's relief. It was also a relief when an American proposal for a peace conference, to be held shortly after the Canberra meeting, fell through. The political situation in New Zealand was such that it was almost impossible for any minister to be spared. The Government's majority was precarious and it was expected that as soon as the House met in June the government would be defeated many times. It remained to be seen Alister McIntosh, Secretary of External Affairs thought, whether Prime Minister Peter Fraser had 'the guts' to carry on. In these circumstances it was not too surprising if not much thought was being given to foreign affairs by the New Zealand Government and McIntosh thought the conference might well 'go for a skate' as far as New Zealand was concerned.[17]

The Department of External Affairs was, however, trying to prepare itself. A request to Whitehall for any Foreign Office or Dominion Office preliminary studies on the Japanese peace settlement drew a blank. 'Comprehensive studies', New Zealand was informed in April, had not gone very far and such views as had been formed in the Foreign Office Japanese Department, were 'embryonic and bits and pieces'. The Foreign Office was reluctant to 'let them out'.[18] Consequently it was decided that the best thing New Zealand could do was to concentrate on one or two issues of major importance to New Zealand and not to attempt to cover the whole treaty in detail. Perhaps it was as well that New Zealand was left to determine its own priorities. Foreign Office officials had never been interested in 'massive social engineering' in Japan, but to New Zealand officials 'democratization and allied questions', and the machinery for achieving these objectives seemed to be most important questions.

As it contemplated the question of Japan's future, the New Zealand Government was concerned about the degree of responsibility it might have to assume in the maintenance of its fundamental requirement, the disarmament and demilitarization of Japan. On the one hand it was accepted that, if New Zealand was to make demands, it must expect to pull its weight in their implementation. On the other hand there were manpower shortages at home and the public was already unenthusiastic about supporting the New Zealand contribution to the Occupation. Given the political situation, the government was understandably restive about assuming further burdens.[19]

As preparation for the Canberra conference went ahead, different points of view on New Zealand's needs in relation to the peace treaty emerged among the government's advisers. From the point of view of the Joint Planning Committee, a sub-committee of the Chiefs of Staff, the strategic position of Japan was of vital importance and the continuance of the Occupation of Japan desirable. Japan itself was not seen as likely to be a military threat in the next twenty-five years. The military potential and warlike ambition of the USSR were, however, thought likely to threaten Pacific security within a decade. Soviet ambitions were seen to include China and Japan. It was, therefore, in New Zealand's interests that the Occupation of Japan by American and, if necessary, British Commonwealth forces, should continue until Japan emerged as a self-sufficient and democratic nation and that, after the withdrawal of the Occupation Forces, Japan should remain a sphere of American influence and a barrier to Soviet expansionism. The full participation of the United States in the matters of Pacific security should, the Chiefs of Staff maintained, be encouraged by every possible means. New Zealand could not defend itself by standing alone against a major invasion and in any conflict south of the equator it would be vital to its safety that the United States entered on the side of New Zealand and the British Commonwealth as soon as possible. Bound to the USA by 'mutual interest and by necessity', the policy of the British Commonwealth should be to support any reasonable strategic interest of the USA in the Far East.[20]

If the Joint Planning Committee focused on the big picture and did not see Japan itself as a threat, the attitude of the Department of External Affairs to New Zealand security was rather different. Here there was clearly considerable suspicion of Japan. New Zealand's primary aim, it was suggested, should be to impose 'rigorous' control on Japan. New Zealand had no particular investment to safeguard, no desire to extract large reparations and no wish to cripple the Japanese economy needlessly but the lesson drawn from New Zealand's experience was that no action that might be taken was likely in itself to make the Japanese feel goodwill for New Zealand. Trust in Japanese promises of good faith or peaceful intentions was likely to prove misplaced. New Zealand wanted to see military disarmament, industrial disarmament and mental disarmament. The latter would involve a continuation of purges of ultranationalists and ultranationalist societies, protection of human rights and the rights of trade unions. Under SCAP, it was complained, the conservatives were still in controlling positions and the political pendulum had never been permitted to swing left, so there seemed to be a danger that it might never finally come back to a 'healthy' central position.[21]

Of the countries at the peace conference, only Australia seemed likely to join New Zealand in insisting that security must be the overriding consideration. There had been, New Zealand observers felt, an 'amazing softening' in attitude towards Japan elsewhere in the previous eighteen months and now security arguments were being outweighed by other considerations, particularly economic ones. It was noted:

> The argument that high production by Japan is necessary to the well-being of the Far East is received with approval, especially in this period of scarcity; it is hard now to advance the contrary argument, that the raising of standards of living in the Far East might well await the industrialisation of India, China, the Netherlands East Indies the Philippines etc., if the price that must be paid for quick improvement is Japanese economic and political domination.[22]

Estimates of how much industry should be left to Japan were becoming larger every month. The collapse of any serious attempt to constrain Japan was a definite possibility.

Fear of Japanese economic revival was not shared by all the government's advisers. From Washington where, as Counsellor at the New Zealand Legation, he most frequently had the often thankless task of representing New Zealand in the FEC, 'Dick' Powles was a voice arguing that one of the main objects of the Japanese peace treaty must be to secure the rehabilitation of the Japanese economy. A permanently depressed Japan was bound, he said, to cause trouble sooner or later whereas a thriving Japan might not do so. 'We should be opposed to anything in the nature of an "economic cesspool" in Japan', he wrote, 'and should consider whether or not a greatly increased output of consumer goods from Japan will not advance our general objectives in the Far East'.[23]

In a lengthy despatch on the long term aspects of the peace settlement, he wrote:

> We who live in the Pacific must, in the interests of our future generations, do everything we possibly can to assist our yellow friends and to maintain and strengthen whatever goodwill now exists between us. These people seem to me to be peculiarly susceptible to the psychological approach, and if we adopt a constant and active policy of friendship I honestly believe that our children and grandchildren will have nothing to fear. If we don't the contrary may be the case.
>
> It is with a somewhat grim humour that one is irresistibly drawn to the conclusion that one of the main objects of the Japanese peace settlement is to secure the rehabilitation of the Japanese economy'.[24]

In Wellington it had been suggested that New Zealand and Australia might be so much in a minority in pressing the 'security' viewpoint as to need to exaggerate the security implications of every proposal in an attempt to secure what they considered to be minimum requirements.[25] Powles commented, 'I am frankly apprehensive of the possible consequences of Australia and New Zealand on so-called security grounds taking a line more repressive of Japan than may be the wish of India, China, Indonesia and the Philippines'. It seemed to Powles that even the Australian line might be softening and that New Zealand should be certain of its ground before taking a course which would run counter to the well-being of these Asian countries. On the political aspect, Powles considered New Zealand's views had, perhaps, been too naive in the past. 'Democracy and "left wingism" are no loner synonymous' he wrote, 'What we want in Japan is a non totalitarian system of government'. In this regard he thought the Americans had done 'fairly well' and the political framework was sound.[26] These comments demonstrated a more international outlook, greater political awareness and rather more humanity than was evident in the papers in Wellington, where, of course, the Department of External Affairs had to take into account New Zealand public and political opinion.

The reality was, that in spite of New Zealand's wish, on principle, to be one of the enforcing powers with a consequent right to participate in Allied policy, the government could not contemplate a policy which would involve them staying in Japan for a considerable length of time. New Zealand might exaggerate the security implications of every proposal in an attempt to 'pin the Allies down' and secure what were considered to be the 'minimum requirements' but ultimately was dependent on United States willingness to enforce any treaty. It was therefore questionable whether it was in fact in New Zealand's interests to insist on provisions to which the United States objected. Meekness was not a policy which at once commended itself to a small country demanding a 'voice' in international affairs but difficult choices might have to be made.[27]

. From New Zealand's point of view, the closeness of its relationship with Australia and the identification of the two countries together by outsiders, was something of a two-edged sword in delicate matters such as these. This was particularly the case while Evatt was Minister for External Affairs. Peter Fraser may have considered Evatt 'much maligned' but many New Zealand officials were less generous in their assessment of him. Displaying his well-known penchant for sporting metaphors, Berendsen, who was too egotistical himself to be an admirer of Evatt, wrote of Australian policy and the proposed Commonwealth conference in Canberra:

I have absolutely given the Australians up. They are completely incalculable and we find ourselves from time to time running happily alongside them and then, before we know where we are, they have turned and are streaking for the other goal-line. It is most embarrassing and I am firmly convinced that their object is to make sure that if there is a try to be scored or a goal to be kicked it will be done by Australia, and I think we run a serious risk of being left.[28]

While a joint approach with Australia might give New Zealand's voice more weight in the post-war discussions on the peace treaty, Australia's high hopes about what the Powers might be induced to do and Evatt's personal ambitions, were something of an embarrassment. Furthermore there was a certain amount of apprehension that Evatt's importunity might simply ensure that Australia was accorded a full voice and a vote in the Far Eastern settlement while New Zealand was not.[29] McIntosh wrote, 'I take it Evatt's main purpose is, as always, to enhance his prestige and, as a corollary, that of Australia'. For Evatt, McIntosh thought, the aim and best result of the conference would be the handing over, by Britain and the other members of the British Commonwealth, to Australia, the responsibility for negotiating with the Americans on the Japanese peace settlement and with the world in general on all matters relating to the Pacific.[30]

In the event, the memoranda on New Zealand's general attitude to the Japanese peace setlement, to the territorial clauses in the settlement and on the control of Japan, prepared by the Department in May and subsequently subjected to critical comment by Powles, seem to have been circulated largely unchanged to the Canberra conference in August. They are marked by suspicion of Japanese aggressive intentions and recommendations for the maintenance of disarmament, supervision and controls.[31] Long-term guarantees against the resumption of Japanese aggression were New Zealand's goal.

THE CANBERRA CONFERENCE

In fact, however, the line which New Zealand took in the discussions at Canberra was neither as hard nor as conservative as these papers suggested it might be. Powles had been brought from Washington as the expert adviser to the delegation led by Peter Fraser, Prime Minister and Minister of External Affairs. The Secretary of External Affairs, Alister McIntosh, also a member of the delegation, was a notoriously bad air traveller in those days of inadequately pressurized trans-Tasman flying boats. While McIntosh sat in a semi-conscious condition, Powles briefed Fraser as the party flew to Sydney.[32] The New Zealand Parliament was in session when the Prime Minister left. Fraser was preoccupied with domestic political problems, and in any case at the best of times, was notoriously dilatory. Furthermore, since his eyesight was bad and he had difficulty reading papers put up to him, a time had to be found when the most important could be read to him.[33] It seems doubtful whether he had given much consideration to the memoranda prepared in the Department of External Affairs. Before the conference McIntosh had written with weary cynicism to Berendsen, 'Our boys are working quite hard on the Japanese peace treaty and we should have a respectable body of paper material ready when the time comes. It is a pity nobody reads these things'.[34]

It seems most likely that Powles' briefing during their few hours in the air was the most extensive that Fraser had. Whatever was the case, Fraser made a lively contribution to the conference and, rather to the surprise of the New Zealand delegation and that of the United Kingdom, the conference was a very successful affair. Evatt proved to be an effective and genial chairman and the general tone of the conference was comparatively mild. McIntosh, who was a reluctant participant, described the conference as 'one of the easiest' he had attended. Nobody, he said, 'took the show seriously' and no decisions were made. Fraser's attempt to raise the important subject of Japanese whaling had been pushed aside by Evatt who was determined to stick strictly to the agenda. The delegates, said McIntosh, reminded him of 'a crowd of school-boys playing at conferences with one of the more callow masters in the Chair.' He described Fraser in this scene as 'a sort of benevolent but slightly testy uncle' somehow 'mixed up with the boys'.[35] The British were, however, more impressed with this conference, of which they had had some apprehension, than McIntosh. Fraser's presence was greatly appreciated and seen by them in a different light. Their delegation reported that, 'although Mr Fraser did not appear to be very thoroughly briefed on all the items' he radiated so much goodwill particularly towards the Indian, Pakistan and Burmese delegations – attending their first Commonwealth Conference – that 'his presence alone contributed enormously to the "family atmosphere"'. It was noted by the British, with apparent surprise that, Mr Fraser 'spoke often and took a vigorous and independent line which at times differed from Australia's'. Perhaps this was his 'slightly testy uncle' mood. Whatever the case, the British wanted to see Japan's economic development encouraged rather than hindered[36] and were pleased to record of Fraser:

> While stressing the importance of future security arrangements in the Pacific and recognising that New Zealand would have to play her part in them, he gave evidence throughout of an anxiety not to impose harsh terms on Japan, especially in the economic sphere. He showed particular interest in the political and social measures proposed and also in the relationship of the supervisory body to the UN.[37]

These were matters of particular interest to Powles. His mid-air briefing was evidently effective and the Prime Minister was a more sympathetic recipient of his line than the Department of External Affairs had been.

Fraser himself spoke warmly of the conference on his return claiming he had never been at a friendlier international conference. It was, he said, a 'family gathering' and 'most encouraging and inspiring'. The New Zealand delegation had had firmly in mind the primary importance of security but at the same time were conscious that to deprive Japan of her power of aggression was only half the task, and that for long-term security the Japanese must be encouraged to develop along peaceful and democratic lines.[38]

The Canberra conference was designed as an exchange of views and, as McIntosh had reported, no attempt was made to arrive at binding decisions or to draft a statement of policy about the Japanese peace settlement. The conference recorded its desire that there should be an early peace conference; that all members of the UN that had made a direct contribution to winning the Pacific war should be included at it; that voting on matters of substance should be on the basis of a two-thirds majority.[39] Departmental policy after Canberra seems to have remained unchanged, the primary emphasis being on security and the maintenance of a disarmed and demilitarized Japan. The External Affairs Committee of Parliament, however, which considered and endorsed the conference report felt constrained to stress the need for the peace settlement to reflect a proper balance between security against renewed aggression and the need to provide a framework which would allow the Japanese to develop a sound economy and a free and peaceful way of life.[40] Though Japan was still seen as the most likely disturber of the peace in the Pacific it is evident that the desire for a 'hard' treaty which would inhibit Japanese industrial rehabilitation had already vanished by the end of 1947 and emphasis on control had been toned down.

By the end of 1947, however, the prospects of an early peace conference had also vanished. Neither the USSR, which wanted matters left to a five power conference nor China, which wanted retention of the veto in peace conference procedure, was agreeable to the voting procedure by two-thirds majority so far proposed for any peace conference. It was clear that a stalemate existed. When Sir Carl Berendsen was in New Zealand for consultations in January 1948 he declared that 'matters were at a standstill' over the peace treaty and the position was 'most difficult'.[41] These comments 'nettled' Dr Evatt who with Australian officials, had had 'friendly' conversations on the peace treaty with the Russians in Moscow and in Canberra. They regarded themselves as 'keeping matters moving.'[42] Evidently they were mistaken. The procedural question could not be resolved and, as the Cold War developed in 1948, an election year when the United States was unlikely to take foreign policy initiatives, a peace treaty seemed as far away as ever.

The standstill was not altogether unsatisfactory from New Zealand's point of view. By now the Occupation was clearly such an American affair that plans for the final withdrawal of New Zealand troops from the BCOF could be made without the fear that, in so doing, the New Zealand government was failing to 'pull its weight' and consequently likely to lose its 'voice' at a peace conference.

THE ISSUES IN 1948

Although the prospects for an early peace conference seemed to have receded in 1948, debate about policies which might be adopted towards Japan went on. A meeting of Commonwealth prime ministers was to be held in October. Japanese problems and the future of the Pacific were on the agenda. A Departmental 'think piece' paper entitled 'Alternative Policies towards Japan' suggested there were two courses open. The first was a peace treaty accompanied by a defence pact between the United States and Japan for the defence of Japan; the second was a peace treaty accompanied by, or preferably including, a multilateral agreement delegating duties to the United States for defence against Japan i.e. for the enforcement of Japanese disarmament. Post-treaty control of Japan is seen here as an American responsibility, one of the functions of the peace treaty being to ensure this. A mutual defence pact between signatories guaranteeing each other against Japanese aggression was also seen as desirable.[43] New Zealand's assessment of the possibilities of the peace settlement, at least in the Department of External Affairs, seemed to be becoming more sophisticated, but the long term aim, New Zealand's security, had not changed.

At the Prime Minister's meeting in October 1948, British Foreign Secretary Ernest Bevin noted that the United States seemed no longer to regard Japan as a potential enemy but rather as a potential help against Russia. It seemed to Bevin that the tendency would be to withdraw MacArthur into the position of a purely supervisory power and to put the Japanese government back in Japanese hands. He suggested that new thinking on the Japanese settlement was required by members of the British Commonwealth.[44]

Both Evatt and Fraser expressed concern over this prospect of American withdrawal. Fraser deplored the possibility that the existing American administration of Japan might be 'pushed over' and replaced by chaos. No one need think that Japan would be grateful for her light treatment. The smaller nations of the Pacific still feared a recurrence of the 'Japanese menace'. What was being done to re-educate the Japanese people? Clearly Japan and its people could not be 'kept under' but was the building of Japan's war potential to be allowed? There was, he said, an urgent need for a conference on the future of Japan.[45] New Zealand's anxiety over what was seen as the United States 'policy of drift' was clear.

FRASER AND REGIONAL SECURITY PACTS

Although Fraser emphasized at the Prime Ministers' meeting and elsewhere the problems of the Pacific and the particular right of

New Zealand as a Pacific nation to be a party to the making of the Japanese peace settlement, his stand on the peace settlement was based at least as much on his belief in the right of small nations to be heard in international forums as on that 'Pacific consciousness' attributed to him in 1945 by the United Kingdom High Commissioner in Wellington. It is true that Fraser seems genuinely to have feared a recurrence of the 'Japanese menace' but he also believed that the events which determined the major issues of war or peace did not take place in the Pacific. Crises like the Berlin Blockade in 1948 seemed to confirm this thinking. In that case New Zealand gave Britain its support and contributed three RNZAF Dakota crews to the Berlin air-lift. At the same time it was expected that, in the event of a war, New Zealand would contribute forces in the Middle East to the defence of communications through the Indian Ocean.[46] Tradition, sentiment and economics made the security of the United Kingdom vital to New Zealand. Fraser therefore advocated the 'closest co-operation' with the United Kingdom on defence matters. He declared at the Prime Ministers meeting in October that, 'if Britain were defeated in war, it would only be a question of time before New Zealand fell too'.[47] It seemed by 1948, however, that Britain was moving closer to a European defence system and, with west European countries, into a regional security system which included the United States and Canada. Negotiations for what was to become the North Atlantic Treaty began in mid-1948. The anomaly of the New Zealand position was brought home. As a Pacific country she was not eligible to be a member of this new club. Nevertheless she was pledged to treat the Middle East, a strategic priority for this club, as her first obligation in the event of war. New Zealand consistently argued in the post-war years that peace was 'indivisible'; that security organized on a universal basis was the best option; that New Zealand should be involved in the forums where world problems were being discussed. New Zealand's voice in a regional body, a region in which decisive events did not take place, Fraser said, would be no voice at all. There were good practical reasons as well as ideological reasons for New Zealand's stand against regional security organizations.

Nevertheless the idea of regional security pacts kept recurring in the immediate post-war years. In July 1948 the New Zealand Prime Minister was informed by the United Kingdom about the security talks about to take place in Washington on a North Atlantic pact. The message stated:

> Our ultimate purpose is to establish under the UN charter a chain of regional pacts which will constitute a world-wide system of collective security.[48]

Subsequently Esler Dening, Assistant Under-Secretary of State at the Foreign Office, in the course of a Commonwealth tour, one aspect of which was the exchange of views on the Japanese peace settlement, visited Wellington.[49] He sketched a plan of a world-wide chain of pacts, the interesting feature of which, from New Zealand's point of view, was that New Zealand was to be included in a Pacific pact together with China and other Asiatic countries.[50] Fraser responded to these suggestions;

> I am by no means sure that the implications of this proposal have been fully appreciated, and I trust that we shall be fully informed before any suggestions are put forward by the United Kingdom to the United States and other third parties, even on a tentative basis, regarding any regional security pact affecting the Pacific area. In particular we consider that any regional association intended to include New Zealand should consist of countries having full confidence in one another. There are countries in Asia with which our relations, though we hope they will always be friendly, cannot be expected to have the intimate character necessary for a genuine security grouping.[51]

New Zealand's reservations about Asia and Asians are here delicately hinted at. Fraser thought that a regional organization such as had been suggested could have 'little reality' as a reinforcement of New Zealand's security. The only regional association likely to contribute effectively to New Zealand security should, he thought, comprise the United Kingdom, the United States, Australia, New Zealand and 'only such other countries having interests in the Pacific area as may seem to us (and we to them), deserving of full confidence'.[52].

In his reply to Fraser, Prime Minister Clement Attlee failed to deal with the essential objection to a Pacific pact. The United Kingdom, he stated, felt it was 'essential to build up *ad hoc* groups of peace-loving states' which all had the 'fullest confidence' in the good faith of every signatory and who would be prepared to act together under Article 52 of the United Nations Charter.'[53] But from New Zealand's point of view, the idea of a Pacific pact including New Zealand and Asiatic countries was 'insufficient, if not dangerous', from the point of view of New Zealand security. It flew in the face of both New Zealand's traditions and New Zealanders' prejudices. The Foreign Office was known, however, to be 'tenacious in such matters', and, as expected, Fraser had to make his points against regional pacts again at the meeting of the Commonwealth prime ministers in October.[54]

In Ottawa on his way home from this meeting Fraser was reported as saying that, if the need arose for democratic nations in the Pacific to stand together, he was sure that a Pacific pact would develop along the lines of the Atlantic pact. Such a pact, would, he said, include New Zealand, Australia, Britain, Canada, United States, Mexico and certain of the central and South American nations.[55] This statement expressed for the first time, publicly, the essence of New Zealand's position in regard to regional collective arrangements for New Zealand security. The tentative language used by the Prime Minister suggested that, in his view, the need had not yet arisen for the conclusion of a Pacific pact on the lines of an Atlantic pact. The immediate importance of the statement for New Zealand policy as the Department of External Affairs saw it, was negative. It conveyed a warning to the world that other kinds of Pacific pacts, and particularly pacts including New Zealand with Asiatic countries, were insufficient for New Zealand security.[56]

THE PEACE SETTLEMENT AND A PACIFIC PACT

Nevertheless discussion about a Pacific pact and about a Japanese peace treaty gained momentum and in 1949 two issues became intertwined as the United States reappraised its Far Eastern policy. The question of the security arrangements felt to be necessary if Japan was to be denied armed forces, and of the voting system to be employed at any peace conference were the chief questions to be settled. In the face of the Cold War the United States was coming to favour a peace treaty which was non-punitive and providing for the minimum post-treaty controls.

Such a treaty might be accompanied by a bilateral United States-Japan security arrangement which would deny Japan to a potential aggressor. The idea of an American guarantee in the Pacific similar to the guarantee contained in the Atlantic pact was also floated in preliminary studies as a means of making it possible for some Pacific countries to be less negative in their approach to the problem of Japan.[57] This tied up with queries about a Pacific pact, increasing pressure for which came from a variety of directions.[58] The balance of power in Asia was felt to be changing in the favour of the Soviet Union as the Communists marched to victory in China.

From the New Zealand point of view any regional grouping for self-defence in the Pacific which did not include one or more of the Great Powers, and specifically the United States, was seen to be 'unreal'.[59] The situation was difficult for New Zealand, anxious that discussions on a peace treaty with Japan should be resumed and fearful that delay would only work to its disadvantage.[60] As Peter Fraser told Parliament in September, however, New Zealand could not expect to compel a huge country like America to take action. The government, he said, were doing everything possible in connection with the Pacific pact but, in the Pacific, 'the United States felt that as they were in control in Japan, there was no hurry to force matters'. It would be a 'good thing' he said, if a peace treaty could be arranged so that all parties could 'know just where they stood'. Without the United States there could be no Pacific pact and no security.[61]

By the end of 1949 it was evident that the United States was determined on an early and 'soft' peace settlement with Japan even if the USSR and China refused to be parties to this. The United States also intended to negotiate a treaty providing for base facilities and the right to maintain forces in Japan. It was made clear to New Zealand officials that the interest of the United States in the stability of the Pacific should be accepted by New Zealand and Australia as a sufficient guarantee of their security without the conclusion of any formal arrangement.[62] New Zealand, in this scenario, had to decide whether it would commit an 'act of faith' and go forward with the United States even at the expense of a rupture with the Soviet Union and China in the belief that the Americans would support New Zealand if it should be menaced from Asia. By this time, New Zealand knew its chances of influencing the final settlement to be slim. There was to be a meeting of Commonwealth ministers at Colombo in January 1950. The matter of the peace treaty could be discussed there but, by that time, it seemed likely that the lines of the peace settlement would be fairly firmly settled.

6

The National Government and the Peace Treaty 1949–1950

As things transpired, it was a new Minister for External Affairs who spoke for New Zealand at the Colombo Conference in January 1950. After fourteen years, the last three of them with a four seat majority, the Labour government was defeated at the polls in November 1949. Sidney Holland led the newly-formed National Government. His Minister for External Affairs was Frederick Doidge.

Labour had come to office in 1935 with firmly held beliefs about the conduct of international affairs.[1] In wartime Fraser had had to temper ideology in practice; he had been forced by events to develop a 'Pacific consciousness'; he had presided over the expansion of New Zealand diplomatic posts beyond London to Washington, Canberra, Moscow and Ottawa; he had consulted in war and in peacetime with Commonwealth partners and Great Power allies. If New Zealand's approach to international affairs matured between 1940 and 1949[2] this had much to do with Fraser personally and little to do with public pressure or interest.

A NATIONAL GOVERNMENT

Inevitably the new team had less experience and different views. Prime Minister Sidney Holland, a shrewd politician, had hitherto shown little interest in international affairs. His subsequent grasp of them has been described as 'tenuous'.[3] He probably reflected the thoughts of many New Zealanders, however, when he referred to 'the dear old Empire', to hoisting the flag 'for Britain, the British Empire and Imperial Preference' and in his obvious pride in New Zealand's association with the British crown.[4] Frederick

Doidge, the Minister for External Affairs, started life as a journalis
in New Zealand. Between 1918 and 1935 he worked in variou
capacities in the Beaverbrook empire in London and took a
leading part in Beaverbrook's campaign for Empire Free Trade.
He had a wider knowledge of world affairs than Holland but hi
Beaverbrook experience left him with an equally 'Britain and
Empire' centred view. Indeed one observer in the Department o
External Affairs has described Doidge as 'mentally rebuilding the
British Empire when it had become obvious to everyone else tha
the Empire was fast disappearing'.[6] While the new government di
not seek to alter the main lines of New Zealand foreign policy, the
emphasis changed. By the time Fraser left office, the Cold Wa
was already an important factor in foreign policy considerations
and, for both Doidge and Holland, the 'red tidal wave' became a
very real threat.[8] In the National Party's period in office, there wa
to be less stress on collective security and the United Nations and
more on 'the march of communism'.[9] Defending New Zealand
against this march was a priority and, ironically, given thei
'Empire centred' view, Doidge and Holland found themselves, in
the interests of New Zealand security, looking to American
protection and leadership at least in Pacific and Asian affairs.

THE CHINA QUESTION

One of the problems for New Zealand foreign policy-makers in the
late 1940s and the 1950s was to avoid being caught in the cross-fire
of a deteriorating Anglo-American relationship. New Zealand's
economic and psychological ties with the United Kingdom were
demonstrably great but the felt need to secure United States
commitment to security in the Pacific was strong and, in the face of
the Communist successes in China by 1949, growing. The 'China
question' more than any other question was to expose rifts
between the United Kingdom and the United States. New Zealand
was then required to make difficult choices between the two
powers in whose good opinion it wished, and needed, to stand.
New Zealand's choice over the China question was much affected
by its attitude to the Japanese peace treaty and American policy in
Japan.

By 1949 New Zealand ministers and officials were conscious that a Communist victory in China was seemingly inevitable and would have implications for the United Nations, the Pacific region and the global power balance. From time to time through 1949 the British government invited the New Zealand government to comment on policy towards the Chinese Communists. The Labour Government's attitude to these approaches was consistently conservative. Peter Fraser had reservations about the principle of abandoning a wartime ally and the possibility of recognizing a government which had come to power by violence.[10] New Zealand had few direct dealings with China and had no wish to join the British-led debate on early recognition. New Zealand officials at a meeting with their Australian and British counterparts in Canberra in November 1949, and the New Zealand delegate at a meeting of Commonwealth representatives held in London later that month, were instructed to report that the New Zealand government proposed to take no action with regard to the recognition of the People's Republic of China. Personally, McIntosh would have followed the British line in favour of recognition[11] but the Prime Minister was against recognition because it would be seen as another Communist victory and the throwing over of old friends. He considered that the British were allowing commercial considerations to obscure long-term political issues. Recognition would encourage Communists in general and antagonize the United States in particular.[12] Underlying this last argument was the question of United States policy towards Japan. The situation in China might lead the United States to build up Japan's military strength. The possibility of a re-armed Japan was a New Zealand nightmare and from New Zealand's point of view could only add to insecurity in the Pacific as a whole. More than ever it was seen as important to retain American goodwill and encourage United States commitment in Japan and to the Pacific.

New Zealand and Australia urged the United Kingdom to delay recognition until after the Commonwealth Foreign Ministers meeting to be held in Colombo in January 1950. Elections would be held in New Zealand and in Australia before then and neither government wished to commit itself on the China question before the outcome of these elections was known.

In the meantime, however, the United Kingdom determined on recognition. In December 1949 New Zealand's support for this was sought. Doidge as a very new Minister of External Affairs, consulted Fraser about the British message and agreed that New Zealand should express its concern about the timing of the move and again ask the United Kingdom to delay action until after the Colombo meeting.[13] On 24 December the British decision to recognize was notified to New Zealand. Recognition took effect on 6 January 1950 a few days before the Colombo meeting opened. Berendsen, by now a renowned 'cold war warrior' writing to McIntosh commented, 'Britain did a very stupid and a very wrong thing in recognizing Communist China when they did and particularly it was wrong, stupid and indeed insulting to do it on the very eve of the Colombo conference'.[14]

Nevertheless it was done. New Zealand did not follow the British lead and this 'most striking and far-reaching divergence' from British foreign policy did not go unnoticed in the United States.[15] It was of course a British Labour government which had recognized China and the conservative National government in New Zealand might be expected to have less difficulty distancing itself from the actions of a socialist administration. Nevertheless the case demonstrated that New Zealand's loyalty was neither 'dumb nor blind'. Where New Zealand's interests in the Pacific were seen not to coincide with Britain's, even this new and most loyal National government would act independently.

THE COLOMBO CONFERENCE

In the shadow of these events Doidge went to Colombo, delighted to be present at an 'historic' gathering of that 'association that makes us great'.[16] Doidge declared to the assembled company that New Zealand was proud to think of itself as 'daughter in her mother's house, though mistress in her own'.[17] Such sentiments, pleasing as they may have been to the British delegation, suggested a more dutifully compliant attitude than had been characteristic of New Zealand generally since the war and most recently over the China question. Doidge's somewhat obsequious phraseology contrasts with Fraser's essential independence, notwithstanding his support at the same time for the links of the Commonwealth. In spite of Doidge's assertion that, in the view of the New Zealand government, the Japanese peace treaty was the most important issue before the conference, only half a day of what was described as 'brief and nebulous' discussion was devoted to the treaty.[18] Ernest Bevin, the British Foreign Secretary, reported that he had tried to find out current United States thinking on the treaty and had hoped that the United States might communicate its views to him before the Colombo Conference. This had not happened. The United Kingdom therefore submitted its own views to the conference as a basis for discussion.[19] Bevin suggested optimisticaly that it might be helpful to the United States government if the members of the Commonwealth were able to communicate to it their own agreed proposals. Here was a situation in which the Foreign Office could see advantage for its policies in the pursuit of Commonwealth solidarity. The British resented the assumption that the United States could dictate a peace on its own terms, which might ignore the views of its foremost ally. They saw in international discussions over the Japanese peace treaty an opportunity to regain lost prestige.[20] For Britain, the main interest in Japan was commercial. Growing American-Japanese trade ties had been observed with concern and the fear that the Americans would 'rig things to the advantage of United States business interests' was expressed.[21] In November 1949, however, a new Japan-Sterling Area agreement, to which New Zealand, Australia, India and South Africa were also parties, had been signed. This offered prospects for the expansion of non-American trade with Japan.[22] At Colombo, therefore, the British commercial fears had been somewhat mollified. They had not, however, gone away and were to have repercussions for New Zealand later.[23]

The British paper on the Japanese peace treaty circulated at the Colombo conference was generally moderate in tone. The broad objectives of disarmament, demilitarization, measures to obviate the possibility of renewed Japanese aggression and to encourage the development of a peace-loving Japan, remained. The need for an economicaly viable Japan was accepted.[24] Bevin reminded the Ministers that it would be unfortunate if the treaty-making powers were unduly influenced by feelings of hostility and imposed conditions which would create lasting resentment amongst the Japanese.[25] He impressed neither New Zealand or Australia.

In Australia, as in New Zealand, a conservative government had come to power in December 1949. The newly appointed Minister for External Affairs was Percy Spender. He made no bones about the Australian attitude. Australians, he said felt 'great bitterness' towards the Japanese and would not forget quickly Japanese wartime barbarism. Resurgence of Japanese militarism was a possibility 'within a generation'. Australia therefore called for safeguards against Japanese militarism and saw the conclusion of a peace treaty as a matter of urgency.[26] New Zealand's Frederick Doidge expressed himself in complete agreement with the Australian view. The only satisfactory solution he thought, would be a peace settlement which, while releasing Japan from the disabilities of the existing regime, would provide for long-term controls in substitution for those which were being relaxed. If an agreement could not be reached with Communist China and the Soviet Union, a settlement might have to be concluded without them.[27]

As the discussion continued, it was clear that New Zealand and Australia were on their own in taking a hard line. McIntosh reported:

> Australia and New Zealand said their piece which was the extreme view. The Asian countries made it quite clear they were all in favour of kissing and making friends and tossing hostages to fortune. The United Kingdom characteristically took a middle line and refused to show their hand. They distributed a paper which no-one read and Bevin didn't stick to it in his line either.[28]

The discussion isolated what were, at least on the surface, two fundamentally different approaches to the peace settlement problem. On the one hand New Zealand and Australia wanted an early treaty and long-term guarantees against a possible resurgence of Japanese aggression. On the other, the majority of Commonwealth members felt security against a resurgent Japan was only one, and perhaps not the most important, of the principles to be applied in the settlement. They saw the most immediate danger to Japan and other Pacific nations from the expansion of Soviet influence.

In view of the fact that the Americans had not given any indication of what the terms of their draft would be, the conference decided to refer detailed consideration of the terms of the peace settlement, the reconciliation of conflicting views and the seeking of a common line to a working party of officials in

London.[29] Bevin was to claim later that he had been 'forced to invent' this idea on the spot. He told the Americans that the Asiatic Dominions were 'really annoyed' at his inability to talk at all on the subject of the Japanese peace settlement and were 'pressing him for action'.[30] The discussion on the peace treaty was certainly unsatisfactory and McIntosh commented; 'We do miss Peter Fraser's far sightedness, astuteness, breadth and humanitarianism'.[31] In fact it was clear that, whatever the view of individual members of the Commonwealth, progress on the Japanese Peace Treaty was determined by the United States alone.

The subject of a Pacific pact which might enhance New Zealand and Australian security and calm their apprehension of Japan was not seriously canvassed at the Colombo conference. Later Doidge was to claim that he alone had advocated such a pact.[32] The record shows that, at the conference, Doidge said he did not think a Pacific pact would be of any value without the actual support of the United States, Canada and India. New Zealand was not anxious to proceed without them or to align herself with weaker powers.[33] Since both Canada and India made it abundantly clear they had no wish to be involved, the discussion of a Pacific security pact came to an end. Spender, whose advocacy of a Pacific pact on his return to Australia after the Colombo conference, caused Doidge to go on record as the 'sole advocate' of the pact at the conference, had apparently sounded out Bevin on this matter before the conference. He found the Foreign Secretary unresponsive to the idea of a Pacific pact. He believed, moreover, that Bevin deliberately raised the matter of a Pacific defence pact on the first day of the conference in order to have it dismissed. Thus Spender kept out of a discussion which might have been expected to be regarded as of vital interest to Australia. Spender claimed that he had already decided that the idea of a Pacific pact would have to be pursued elsewhere.[34]

THE LONDON WORKING PARTY

New Zealand had no great hopes of the proposed working Party in London. Berendsen protested against it on the grounds that it was 'wasteful of money' to hold such a meeting outside Washington where, in view of the activities of the FEC, so many of the officials concerned must be located. At best he thought it 'unwise' to hold a meeting in advance of knowing United States views on the Japanese treaty. He was not impressed by London's view that the formulation of Commonwealth views might help ensure co-ordination of United States views. While there might be something to be said for formulating Commonwealth views and informing the State Department before American views crystallized, it was at least as probable that the Americans would feel the Commonwealth was 'ganging up' on them.[35] Wellington agreed that the results achieved by the Working Party were likely to be limited but was not inclined to give up an opportunity to persuade other expected participants in the Japanese settlement that New Zealand's fears of renewed Japanese aggression had some justification.[36] McIntosh wrote privately to Berendsen, 'I regard the London Working Party as a completely footling affair.... All that New Zealand and Australia can do, I imagine, is to flag the old line and see what, if anything, can be salvaged.'[37] Conceding that it might be unrealistic to hope for the demilitarization of Japan, McIntosh nevertheless voiced fears that a rearmed Japan, would eventually use its arms against New Zealand. 'After all', he wrote, 'the essential point in New Zealand's long-term policy is safeguarding ourselves against the Asian countries.... More particularly our aim is to obtain a guarantee against Japanese aggression and I still feel if Japan is re-militarised to any extent it is merely an invitation to such aggression'.[38]

By this time New Zealand knew that it was a vain hope to expect any pervasive post-treaty control over Japan but felt, as McIntosh put it, 'We must try to get something and the essential point at this stage is not to show our hand or to indicate to what extent we will modify our attitude when it comes to the final conference'.[39]

The instructions to the New Zealand Working Party in London reflected this thinking. They reiterated New Zealand's desire for a speedy settlement, reaffirmed New Zealand's support for the basic Potsdam aims, particularly those relating to measures aimed at obviating the possibility of renewed Japanese aggression; accepted the procedural formula that all FEC nations should participate without a veto; recognized that it might be necessary to proceed without Russia and China; listed the security controls and machinery which ideally should be provided for, and accepted the American

position in regard to reparations and other claims against Japan.[40]
The line taken was similar to that outlined by Doidge at Colombo
but the pervasive controls demanded at Canberra were gone. It
was conceded that New Zealand would have to accept the American
assessment of the security position in the Pacific if it was to be a
party to any treaty at all. Further, it was recognized that insistence
upon controls felt to be designed against 'imaginary dangers' was
likely to provoke impatience. Nevertheless it was argued that
there was no reason why an attempt should not be made, while the
American attitude was still under consideration, to persuade
Washington that its fundamental requirements could be fully met
without relinquishing all effective control over the future policies
of the Japanese. Support for New Zealand's line was not expected
from Canada or the 'Asiatic Dominions' but it was hoped the
United Kingdom might view the New Zealand position sympathetically, if only because it would be hard to justify a less liberal
policy in relation to Germany.[41] Ironically, the British had similar
hopes of a sympathetic New Zealand hearing of the United
Kingdom position. It was reported to the Foreign Office that
Frank Corner, the principal official adviser to the New Zealand
delegation, 'ranges New Zealand with Europe and has no liking
for the Australasian position'.[42]

In the event, Corner fought vigorously for the New Zealand and
Australian line, but was aware from the beginning that this was
something of a lost cause. Before he left Washington (he was First
Secretary at the New Zealand Embassy), he called on Walton
Butterworth, Assistant Secretary of State, to learn the latest State
Department views on a Japanese peace settlement. The conversation revealed the 'extreme unlikelihood' of New Zealand obtaining a peace treaty which might advance its security interests.
Butterworth outlined the now familiar United States case for a
non-punitive treaty without security controls. He indicated that his
government was prepared to proceed without the Soviet Union or
China but was unwilling to sponsor a peace conference which
would have no veto, unless assured in advance of sufficient support
to out-vote proposals with which it disagreed. Butterworth was
unimpressed when his attention was drawn to public statements
indicating the continued concern of the New Zealand government
with the security aspects of a treaty. Doidge's public comment on
the possibility of a Pacific pact, left him equally unmoved. Corner

reported, 'He showed little appreciation of New Zealand's security apprehensions or, if he had considered them at all, regarded them as being without valid foundation'.[43] There seemed to be little advantage to New Zealand in the kind of treaty envisaged by the United States. Corner wrote privately:

> The United States attitude of no controls, no supervision, no sanctions . . . makes me quite depressed. There is nothing for New Zealand in such a treaty . . . I don't see that we are not justified in asking for a bare minimum of limitations and controls. If others don't agree (and everyone except Australia might be against us) I don't see much point in our interesting ourselves further in a treaty.[44]

There was not much point in spending money, time and energy on a treaty which ignored all the matters which concerned New Zealand. If, however, Corner went on, 'some general security arrangement for the Pacific could be engineered, we might have less cause to be apprehensive'. Butterworth, however, had held out no prospect of this. Corner ended gloomily:

> I think the United Kingdom will cave in on the Americans to avoid spoiling their overall relations with the United States. We have more balls to keep in the air simultaneously than the United Kingdom – stop Russian expansion, stop Japanese aggression and work for good relations with the United States; the United Kingdom and Canada are not so concerned with the second one or are prepared to let it drop for fear of hitting the other two.[45]

In response to these comments, Wellington warned, 'No indication should be given that we might be willing to consider any modification of our policy on the security aspects of the settlement'.[46]

Meetings of the Working Party began on 1 May. New Zealand and Australia insisted on the need for security safeguards and, as expected, found themselves in a minority. As time went on however, the New Zealanders had the impression that even the Australians were weakening; that rather than the close control advocated in the past they might accept remote controls, i.e controls over exports to Japan of certain materials, combined with a United States defence agreement.[47] Corner believed that, except for him, there was general agreement among officials, including the Australians, that nothing effective could be done to prevent Japan from rearming. He told Berendsen on his return to Washington that, despite all the vehement protestations of the Australians, 'they had authorised their officials at the Conference not to oppose rearmament in certain circumstances although Australian officials did not go so far as to say this publicly'.[48]

Detailed consideration of the terms of the Japanese settlement – the brief of the Working Party – could not of course be made while the attitude of the United States was unknown. The questions of procedure, security controls, economic and territorial provisions, were therefore all considered in general again.[49] The meeting if nothing else, confirmed that the unity of the Canberra conference of 1947 had gone, and with this any hopes the United Kingdom might have had of influencing United States thinking on the treaty through a united Commonwealth front. The New Zealanders felt that the meeting tended to exaggerate the danger of Soviet and Chinese expansionism in the Pacific but conceded that New Zealand's contention that Japan was a potential menace to the security of the Pacific could not be proved, or disproved, either. The indisputable evidence was, however, that there was no chance of New Zealand's policy towards Japan being achieved through a peace treaty. It was a question of what actions might now be taken by New Zealand to 'salvage something from the wreck'.[50]

Some ideas about 'remote controls' on Japan were canvassed at the conference, among them a guarantee, by the signatories of a peace treaty, of the security of Japan. The New Zealand delegation was unenthusiastic about a proposal which, while guaranteeing Japan's territorial integrity would leave New Zealand's own integrity undefended. It seemed likely to them, however, that this 'guarantee' proposal, in one form or another, would be raised again. They suggested, therefore, that it might be in New Zealand's interests to endeavour to turn the 'guarantee' idea out of the limited channel of a guarantee of Japan, into the broader stream of a mutual guarantee of the integrity of all participating countries. At this point the 'guarantee' idea would join up with the idea of a regional defence arrangement, or Pacific pact, to secure which, was a declared aim of New Zealand policy.[51] The New Zealand members of the Working Party did not have a brief to discuss a Pacific pact in relation to the Japanese peace settlement and noted the United Kingdom's reluctance to allow the introduction of this topic at the conference. Tactics had to be considered if a Pacific pact was to be promoted. It was suggested:

> To emphasise at every opportunity New Zealand's feeling of isolation and exposure and very real concern that an uncontrolled Japan may again threaten the security of the Pacific may well assist in the creation of an atmosphere favourable to the idea of a Pacific regional security arrangement.[52]

In the meantime, however, a peace conference still seemed far away.

7
Proposals for a Pacific Pact

Although the Japanese peace settlement was an issue in Commonwealth meetings at Colombo and London in early 1950, the true
preoccupations of Wellington were quite different. With enthusiasm
the new National government settled to the business of dismantling wartime controls on imports, ending rationing of petrol and
butter, and bracing itself for a confrontation with the unions.[1]
Foreign affairs had a low priority and, given the government's
domestic preoccupations and the limitations of their Minister, the
Department of External Affairs was concerned that the papers on
the Japanese peace settlement put up to Doidge and the cabinet,
should not be too complex.[2] Doidge was settling into his External
Affairs portfolio but, lacking his predecessor's background and
experience, found himself overwhelmed by the paper war. 'I just
seem never able to get through all that comes to my desk', he
moaned six months after taking office.[3]

Questions of foreign policy were, as the China question demonstrated, usually uncontroversial. The National government's
emphasis on Commonwealth ties and its anti-communism were
different only in degree from those of Labour and the National
government wished, like its predecessor, to maintain friendship
with the United States. Labour's defence policy, which pledged
New Zealand troops to the Middle East in the event of a 'hot war'
was endorsed by the National Government,[4] and the Cold War
scarcely impinged upon the lives of New Zealand's citizens.
Nevertheless, preoccupied though they were with domestic issues,
the New Zealand government and citizens could not ignore the
Communist victory in China. It added to fears, not untinged with
racism, about instability in the British and French colonial territories
of Malaya and Indo-China and the competence of governments in

the Philippines and Indonesia. New Zealand was particularly suspicious of the pretensions of the Philippines government. When a regional conference of 'democratic countries' to be held at Baguio was proposed in February 1950, New Zealand declined to attend, though under some pressure from the United States to do so.[5] The Baguio meeting, it was felt, would be attended by 'Governments of doubtful stability and minor importance' and New Zealand had no wish to be part of it or of any organization which might result from it.[6]

THE BERENDSEN PROPOSAL

Overwhelmed as he was with the papers on his desk, the Minister for External Affairs was in neither the mood nor the position to consider the implications for New Zealand's policy of the changing world scene. For Sir Carl Berendsen, New Zealand's experienced ambassador in Washington, however, the case was different. Berendsen had been in Washington since 1944 and was, in addition, New Zealand's principal delegate to the United Nations in New York. He had had high hopes of the United Nations and had fought vigorously in the hope that its members would give it more 'backbone' than the League of Nations had ever shown. Having always abhorred the veto, Berendsen watched with dismay and disillusionment as it became another Cold War weapon and the United Nations became another 'talking shop'. As early as 1947 Berendsen began making virulent anti-Communist speeches. By 1950 he had reached his most sulphurous anti-Communist phase. He was, therefore, outraged by British 'stupid and wrong' recognition of the People's Republic of China, took a 'dismal view of Asia' and described the proposed Baguio conference as 'baloney'.[7]

In March 1950 Berendsen recorded his views on the world situation and his recommendations for New Zealand policy in a dispatch to his new Minister, Doidge. It was enormously long and in characteristically purple prose. Berendsen had become convinced that society was moving towards a third world war which would be brought about by the machinations of the 'thugs and gangsters' of the Soviet Union assisted by the 'pestilential disease' of international Communism. Asia, he argued, was a 'boiling

cauldron' 'vibrant with resurgent nationalism', a situation ideally
adapted for Soviet 'fishing in muddy waters'[8] This state of mind
affected Berendsen's hitherto hard attitude to Japan and the
Japanese peace treaty. He feared that if Japan should decide to
join this 'communist conspiracy' the prospects for the Pacific
would be 'gloomy indeed'.[9] He became convinced that, on grounds
of 'equity, fairness and expediency', a generous and friendly peace
must be offered Japan. Meanwhile, New Zealand, without the
British navy to defend it, 'out on a limb', remote from help and
exposed to the potential impact of 'a thousand million depressed
people' must look for some alternative protection. Berendsen was
not a believer in regional arrangements for peace or defence but,
since the dangers were so great and a world system of collective
security still so distant, he was 'entirely ready' to accept a regional
system as the best compromise available.

A Pacific pact, as it had been spoken of so far, while 'superficially
attractive' was, he thought 'ambiguous, imprecise and completely
impracticable.' It was the old problem of the diversity of the
Pacific 'region'. 'Who would belong to the "Pacific Pact"?'
Berendsen asked. He thought a pact which included some or all of
the nations of the western Pacific, southern and eastern Asia,
could only result in New Zealand and Australia having to 'defend
the indefensible'. What New Zealand needed for its defence, he
concluded, was the assistance of the United States. Berendsen did
not think this could be expected automatically. To obtain it New
Zealand and Australia should be prepared to 'pay a fair price'.
This led Berendsen to suggest that the New Zealand government
should approach the United States government with a suggestion
for what Berendsen described as a limited Pacific pact. The United
States had already accepted the defence of a line running from,
and including Japan, down to and including the Philippines. Under
the terms of Berendsen's limited Pacific pact the United States
would undertake to extend the area of its responsibility for
defence to include New Zealand and Australia and in return New
Zealand and Australia would undertake to join the United States
in defending the northern line. The parties to such a pact might be
the United States, the United Kingdom, Australia, New Zealand,
Canada and, reluctantly, but inevitably because it was within the
United States defence area, the Philippines. Should the United
Kingdom be unwilling to take part in this pact, New Zealand

should still press for it. Under the arrangement, New Zealand would have to take its share in the defence of Japan, an ironic twist which Berendsen appreciated, but if Japan was, as he believed, to be demilitarized, some means had to be provided for its defence in Berendsen's dangerous world. Berendsen suggested it might do no harm to approach the United States along these lines.[10]

The response to this dispatch was disappointing to say the least. No doubt this was in part because it was so extraordinarily long. McIntosh reported to Berendsen a month after the dispatch was written, that Doidge had not yet discussed it with him. He commented; 'He [Doidge] is very Pact-minded but he has not thought the thing out, indeed none of them [the Cabinet] will'.[11] McIntosh himself was, he declared, 'appalled' by the prospect Berendsen held out of New Zealand having to take part in a guarantee of Japanese integrity.

Two months later Doidge confessed to Berendsen; 'I cannot give the consideration that I should and must to the important problems to which you refer in your valuable despatch'.[12] He agreed that there was no point in a Pacific pact which the United States did not underwrite. If there was any prospect of having a limited pact of the type Berendsen suggested, Doidge wrote, 'I wold be very happy to consider it, as I regard an American guarantee of our security as the richest prize of New Zealand diplomacy'.[13] Berendsen was therefore authorized to sound out the Americans if a suitable occasion presented itself.

It seems that it did not, nor did Berendsen try to make such an occasion. By the time he received Doidge's comments he had learned from Frank Corner of his impression, at the London conference of the Working Party on the Japanese settlement, that the rearmament of Japan was generally expected. Berendsen's thoughts on the limited Pacific pact were postulated on a demilitarized Japan. A rearmed Japan altered the situation. New Zealand would still need strong friends in the Pacific but Berendsen could not see New Zealand guaranteeing to defend a rearmed Japan except, perhaps, as part of a very wide system of collective security.[14] Berendsen felt he needed to think again about the effects of this possible development in Japan on his plan before attempting to get the views of the State Department. Within another month the Korean war had broken out and the situation had changed again. It seems an approach to the State Department was never made. Doidge, however, continued to speak in general terms about the desirability of a Pacific pact occasionally, as he admitted, borrowing a phrase or two from Berendsen.[15]

THE CHIEFS OF STAFF REPORT

The general talk in both New Zealand and Australia of a possible Pacific pact led the New Zealand Chiefs of Staff to anticipate that a statement of military considerations which might influence the government's decision about entering into, or pressing for such a pact, would eventualy be required. In April 1950, therefore they produced a report for the Minsiters of Defence and External Affairs.[16]

In these Cold War times the strategic thinking of the Chiefs of Staff was based on a war with the Soviet Union in which the Commonwealth and the United States would stand side by side. Given this framework, after examining the Soviet threat to world security and the likely pattern of a war between the Soviet Union and the Western Allies, the Chiefs of Staff could find no reason, on military grounds, for an approach to the United States for a Pacific pact. They could see no direct threat to New Zealand. Soviet operations in Asia and the Pacific could be adequately matched by American naval and air strength. It was assumed that the vital theatre of operations would continue to be Europe and in that case, it was argued, it would be a misdirection of New Zealand's military effort to assume obligations under a Pacific pact which might conflict with the commitment to assist in the Middle East. The United States, the Chiefs of Staff maintained, would certainly 'prefer to see a New Zealand Division and RNZAF tactical forces employed in the Middle East rather than tied down in the Far East in operations which would have no decisive effect on the ultimate outcome of the war'.[17]

Europe was seen as the area where the Cold War would be decided and the conclusion to be drawn from this paper was that, if a Pacific pact was justifiable, it might be justified on grounds other than strategic ones. Doidge's continued assertion, that the security of New Zealand and Australia could not be effectively ensured without a Pacific pact to 'wall in the tide of communism',[18] was not one which had the backing of the Chiefs of Staff.

THE APPOINTMENT OF DULLES

There was no sign up to 1950 that the talk of a Pacific pact had affected the thinking of the key player, the United States, or that the American administration was any further on in reconciling the various interests and departments concerned in the drawing up of the Japanese peace treaty. The treaty had been floundering on procedural questions for three years and by 1950 United States' planning was in any case deadlocked between the State Department, which favoured going forward with a peace treaty, and the Joint Chiefs of Staff who wanted no diminution of a 'regime of control' in Japan.[19]

In April 1950, John Foster Dulles was appointed consultant to the State Department with the task of breaking the deadlock. This proved to be a cruical appointment. President Truman had said that he wanted the best man for the job of treaty-making[20] and, although initially not enthusiastic about Dulles, the appointment of a Republican made possible the development of a bipartisan approah to the Japanese peace treaty in the key Foreign Relations Committee of Congress. The President could then afford to give the project of treaty-making his full and public backing.

Dulles energetically set about informing himself of the issues at stake, both domestic and international.[21] He favoured an economically prosperous Japan without 'unhealthy dependence' on the Asiatic mainland, and a security pact between the United States and Japan as the price of Japan's independence. He had no enthusiasm for a Pacific pact.

The outbreak of the Korean War in June 1950 found Dulles and John Allison, Deputy Director of Far Eastern Affairs, in Japan. Doubts the Japanese government may have had about the price of the peace treaty Dulles was offering were quickly quashed by the 'active war' in Korea. Dulles reported that events in Korea were 'awakening Japan out of its stupor'. He thought the Japanese mood for a long time might be determined by whether the United States took advantage of the situation to bring Japan into the free world. If matters were allowed to drift he feared more might be lost in Japan than could be gained in Korea.[22] In a speech delivered at San Franciso on 31 July he said:

The battle for Korea should not lead the free world to forget about Japan or to postpone dealing with its problems ... the Japanese nation should be given the opportunity to become equal partners in the community of free nations and to contribute to the peace and security, the economic prosperity and the cultural and spiritual life of the free world.[23]

Berendsen reported to Wellington that Dean Rusk, Assistant Secretary of State for Far Eastern Affairs, thought the Korean incident had increased the need for action on a Japanese Peace Treaty and that the Americans hoped to open talks very early as their further ideas crystallized.[24]

Nevertheless matters did not move ahead very rapidly, although the attitude of all parties was now coloured by events in Korea. Japan became an essential base for the Korean operation so that although it was politically desirable to show the Japanese people that the United States was moving towards a treaty, many in the American bureaucracy regarded such a treaty as 'militarily premature'.[25] Decisions were therefore delayed.

All the same New Zealand tried to prepare itself to consider whatever proposals the Americans might put forward. It was hoped in Wellington that Commonwealth representatives in Washington might 'consult closely' and jointly examine American proposals and it was suggested that Commonwealth ministers, meeting in London in September, might discuss developments. There was no great enthusiasm from other Commonwealth members for these suggestions.[26] In the Department of External Affairs a memorandum was prepared on the assumption that the State Department was on the point of opening talks about a treaty. It was noted that New Zealand's long-held view of the security requirements which should be built into a Japanese peace treaty was no longer shared by other Commonwealth governments. The United Kingdom and even Australia, it was thought, were increasingly ready to see Japan restored to full sovereignty without external control. The question of the extent to which New Zealand should continue to insist on what were considered to be its reasonable security requirements would have shortly to be faced when the American draft was presented.[27]

News of the American draft seemed likely to be obtained when the Australian Prime Minister, Robert Menzies, visited Wellington in August. Menzies was on an extensive tour and was expected to have had an opportunity to discuss the Japanese peace treaty with American officials in both Washington and Tokyo. In preparation for the informal talks which were to take place, the New Zealand Prime Minister, Sidney Holland, was briefed on the background to the policy New Zealand would like to see adopted towards Japan. New Zealand was in favour of an early treaty, he was told, especially since the Japanese appeared to be restive and further delay increased the danger that a separate treaty might be signed with Japan by the Soviet Union or China. The question of security in the Pacific was New Zealand's main concern. The country must be safeguarded from both renewed Japanese aggression and Russian imperialism.[28]

The Russian element, which was a new argument in New Zealand's case for security safeguards in the treaty, was one likely to be taken seriously by the Prime Minister. Russian imperialism had become a live issue in the light of events in Korea. In August 1950 the Russian imperialist threat in the Pacific was described as 'imminent'. Given this, it was suggested to the Prime Minister, New Zealand might have to be prepared to modify its attitude to the nature of the peace settlement with Japan. More than ever, American terms for a 'soft' peace with Japan would be difficult to resist.

RESPONSE TO THE KOREAN WAR

The Russian 'threat' was seen as more real by New Zealand once there was war in Korea. New Zealanders had had little interest in Korea before 1950, had accepted American post-war policy there, blamed the Soviet Union for failure to bring about reunification and regarded the North Korean regime as a Soviet puppet government.[29] When the North Koreans invaded the South in June 1950 the general view of the New Zealand press was that this was a war brought about by 'external influence'.[30] New Zealand's rather simplistic interpretation of events, its tradition of support for the idea of a universal and effective collective security system, the possibility that the fall of South Korea might set in action a series of events leading to the absorption of Japan into the Communist bloc and the eventual exclusion of the West from

Asia, leaving Australia and New Zealand exposed to 'hostile forces', disposed New Zealand to support action to halt aggression. Therefore when it was learned that the United States would act in Korea and that Britain would support this action, sentiment, custom, self-interest and a sense of obligation to the United States combined to bring about the announcement, on 1 July 1950, that HMNZS *Pukaki* and *Tutira* would be sent to the Korean area.[31] Both the realist and idealist elements of New Zealand's post-war policy were at work. Berendsen commented from Washington:

> We have got great kudos and widespread appreciation for this immediate indication that we are one of those who do not confine our support of the principles of freedom to words alone. We may have to do more yet – that of course is a matter for the government – but what we have done is so well-worth the doing and even from the last and most sordid point of view will return dividends in the future.[32]

As Berendsen predicted, more had to be done. When an appeal for ground forces was made, political considerations came into play. The United States indicated that New Zealand's contribution was regarded as of the 'utmost importance'.[33] The Americans wanted the public support of their allies. This factor played a part in the decision, announced on 26 July 1950, to offer a special New Zealand combat unit for service with other ground forces in Korea. Berendsen was sure that New Zealand's gesture would have a 'profound effect'.[34] He commented, 'I am certain that this renewed evidence of New Zealand's readiness to play its part will have widespread influence and will redound greatly to our credit and indeed ultimately to our practical advantage'.[35]

The evidence suggests that it is too much to claim, as it has been claimed, that New Zealand went into the Korean war to achieve an alliance with the United States.[36] The Korean war, however, was something of a turning point for both New Zealand and Australia, reminding the governments of both countries that their fundamental security concerns were focused on the Pacific, increasing their concern about their relations with the United States and consequently weakening their commitment to a co-operative security relationship with Britain in the Middle East and Southeast Asia.[37] Their participation in the war created goodwill and gave New Zealand and Australia some leverage with the United States in the matter of Pacific security.

At the time when both New Zealand and Australia had announced their commitment of ground troops to the war in Korea, the Australian Prime Minister was on his way from London to the United States. He was received there with considerable warmth and friendliness.[38] In Washington and in Tokyo which he visited subsequently, Menzies made it clear that he favoured proceeding promptly with a generous and non-punitive treaty with Japan, despite the fact that there would be problems 'selling' such a treaty at home.[39] The British embassy in Washington believed Menzies' co-operative attitude and the 'harmonious atmosphere' surrounding the visit were part of an Australian ploy to secure a United States guarantee for Australia's security.[40] While this guarantee was certainly the aim of Percy Spender, his Minister for External Affairs, the Australian Prime Minister was not persuaded of the need for it. From Washington he cabled Spender, 'a Pacific pact is not at present on the map because the Americans are uneasy about the stability of most Asiatic countries. We do not need a pact with America. They are already overwhelmingly friendly to us'.[41]

Menzies seems to have felt Pacific defence, including that of Australia and New Zealand, could be left to the Americans, and told the New Zealand Cabinet that the Americans regarded the Middle East as New Zealand's and Australia's 'proper theatre' in a 'hot war', and did not wish them to make any contribution to Pacific defence which would prejudice this.[42] He was not, at this stage at least, an advocate of either a peace treaty with security safeguards or a Pacific pact. His talks with Holland on 21 August centred on Korea, which was their immediate problem, but the news Menzies brought of American thinking on the Japanese peace treaty could bring little reassurance to the New Zealanders.

DOIDGE, SPENDER AND THE PACIFIC PACT

Although New Zealand had consistently maintained that guarantees of security were necessary against the possible resurgence of Japanese aggression, it was not altogether clear at the end of 1950 what was meant by security guarantees, in the face of a non-punitive Japanese peace treaty. It is true that Doidge had continued to talk about a Pacific pact during 1950 but he nowhere spelled out in detail what he meant by such a pact. The idea seems not to have made any real progress since Berendsen's shelved plan of March 1950. Furthermore events in Korea, and possibly Menzies' views as related by Holland, apparently removed such incentive as Doidge may have had to give the Pacific pact a New Zealand definition. In September 1950 Doidge said in Parliament:

> My own view now, and I think the view of the government, is that the pact is not as necessary as we thought it was six months ago. It is unnecessary now because of what is happening in Korea. Today the United States of America is in the Pacific. I think she is there now as a permanent partner in the policing of the Pacific. I feel certain the from now on that will be a matter of great concern to the United States of America.[43]

It was a different matter in Australia where Percy Spender, who had been a consistent advocate of a Pacific pact which included the United States as a guarantee of Australian security, was Minister of External Affairs. He had a clear idea of what a Pacific pact could be and was prepared to argue for it in detail.[44] He was determined to use the increased bargaining power generated by the war in Korea and the American desire for a quick and rehabilitating peace with Japan to further his purpose.[45]

Spender was a vigorous and opinionated minister who, the record shows, pursued his cause fearlessly in high places. By contrast Doidge appears to have been neither a persuasive nor particularly energetic advocate of New Zealand's policies. If he didn't actually collapse in a discussion, he certainly lacked Spender's drive and follow-through. As an old newspaperman he had a flair for ensuring his name appeared frequently in the press, but he has been described with careful neutrality by a leading historian and academic of the time, as 'rather an average sort of man of conservative persuasion who caused no disasters and did not try to prevent happening what was going to happen anyway'.[46] Not surprisingly Doidge and Spender did not get on[47] and this may have been one reason for New Zealand's low-key response to Spender's attempts to promote the Pacific pact as his idea. In addition New Zealand had, in any case, developed a certain low-key style. McIntosh, by now an experienced Secretary for External

Affairs, was a backroom man of high principles, not disposed to the striking dramatic poses and keenly aware of the realities of New Zealand's position in the world. He built up around him in his Department a small team of able men who shared his perception of New Zealand's role and diplomatic style. McIntosh was not an advocate of an 'ANZAC' front on this or any other question. Of this he wrote, 'In my view the New Zealand attitude towards so many of the external questions in this region and elsewhere should be that of a moderate and modest collaboration not necessarily taking any initiative but throwing in our support in accordance with the limitations of our resources and trying always to come down on the side of common sense and reasonableness'.[48]

In spite of Doidge's talk of a Pacific pact and Spender's ardent advocacy of it, there was no push from the Department of External Affairs to collaborate with Australia on the matter. It is not a surprise that Spender complained that 'even New Zealand' displayed little active interest in the Pacific pact proposals he made in August 1950.[49]

PRELIMINARY NEGOTIATIONS

In September 1950 the United States entered into discussions with other governments on the Far Eastern Commission about the possibility of a Japanese peace treaty and outlined to them the principles on which the treaty should be based. The approach had of course been anticipated in Wellington. Doidge had already been warned by his Department:

It seems likely that the United States, in order to secure Japan's voluntary cooperation in future with non-Communist powers, will wish the treaty to release Japan, within the limits of American strategic requirements, from the disabilities of the existing Occupation regime and restore her to a fully sovereign status. In the interests of Japan's economic viability it may be considered necessary to cut down industrial and other restrictions to a minimum. Since demilitarisation has been thoroughly carried out ... it will be a central aim of American policy to secure Japan's territorial integrity, either by securing bases in the four main islands or permitting the Japanese to rearm.[50]

This scenario was soon proved to be correct. It was reported from Washington that Dulles had made it clear, not only to members of the Far Eastern Commission but to members of the press, that the basic American aim was a treaty which would restore Japanese sovereignty and keep the Japanese on the side of the United States. Such a treaty would contain no restriction on Japanese rearmament, place no economic or other restrictions on Japan and would subject Japan to no further supervision or control. Pending completion of other security arrangements, Japanese security would be the responsibility of Japanese 'facilities' and the United States, and perhaps other forces to be stationed in Japan. This article was seen to be designed to avoid the impression that the United States was seeking bases, but rather, was entering into a mutually beneficial defence project.[51] Japan would recognize Korean independence and agree to United Nations Trusteeship of the Ryukyu and Bonin islands. Although any or all the nations at war with Japan could be a party to a treaty on this basis, if necessary, the United States indicated, it would be prepared to proceed alone with a bilateral treaty.

Clearly the terms as laid out, were widely different from the policy New Zealand had always advocated. Furthermore, since American views had been made known so publicly and so definitely there seemed, as New Zealand officials noted, very little chance of influencing them.[52] In Wellington the proposed treaty looked more like a treaty of friendship than a peace treaty[53] and as such met none of New Zealands security needs, but, as the New Zealand embassy in Washington noted, the choice for New Zealand and other governments appeared to be either this draft or no treaty.[54]

Given the world situation and particularly the situation in east Asia, however, a multilateral treaty in which, at the very least, most non-Communist members of the Far Eastern Commission participated, was highly desirable. This fact along with their contribution in Korea gave New Zealand and Australia their leverage with the United States. Although their chances of influencing the composition of the treaty were apparently nil, it was not pointless to continue to insist on what were considered to be New Zealand's and Australia's 'reasonable security requirements'. American desire for a multilateral peace treaty with Japan offered New Zealand and Australia an opportunity to achieve their own purposes - an American guarantee of their security. For Australia a Pacific pact was seen as the guarantee. New Zealand at this stage, in 1950, seems to have been less committed to the form such a guarantee should take.

When, in September, the Counsellor at the United States embassy in Wellington called to discuss with officials in the Department of External Affairs the likely New Zealand reaction to a Japanese peace treaty, which did not in itself prohibit Japanese rearmament, he was told that, notwithstanding the Korean crisis and other developments in Asia, the New Zealand position continued to be, that everything possible should be done to ensure that Japan would not again become an aggressor. While New Zealand recognized the need to keep Japan out of the Communist orbit she could only have the gravest anxiety for her long-term security if Japan were given full freedom to build up unlimited armed forces.[55] At the same time, this American official was told, New Zealand's apprehensions would be somewhat allayed if the security guarantee possible under a regional defence scheme in the Pacific could be obtained from the United States. It was pointed out that, if Japan were to become fully independent and strongly armed, she might consider her interests better served by making political concessions to Asian communism.[56] Wellington was making it clear that when Doidge arrived in Washington in October to discuss the peace settlement, New Zealand was likely to harp on Pacific security.

THE AUSTRALIAN STYLE

Doidge was due in Washington in October 1950. Spender was there in September busily pursuing his goal of a Pacific pact. He paid a formal call on President Truman on 13 September and, in an atmosphere of great goodwill, was able to make the case for a regional security arrangement in the Pacific. Truman declared his sympathy for Australia's case and promised to ask Secretary of State Dean Acheson to give consideration to Spender's views. Such a Presidential initiative was likely to lead to a less discouraging response from the State Department to the Pacific pact, and the conversation between Truman and Spender has therefore been identified as the turning point which led to the ANZUS treaty.[57] If this is so, a change in the American stance towards some kind of Pacific pact was not immediately apparent to the Australians or, later, to New Zealanders.

On 22 September Dulles discussed with Spender the proposed terms of the Japanese peace treaty. The American proposals can have been no surprise to Spender. He admitted later that he knew the line that Australia had taken in calling for restrictions on Japanese rearmament 'didn't have a chance', because the United States was not prepared to police the treaty. But his aim was to convey very directly, Australian opposition to the treaty which was being put forward.[58] He recalled that he was 'rather brusque' in his response to the terms outlined to him.[59] John Allison, Director of the State Department Office of North East Asian Affairs who was present at the interview, said, however, that he thought Spender was going to have apoplexy. He gave Allison the impression he thought everything was being given away to Japan.[60] It must have been an effective performance. Spender said his idea was to achieve as best he could the general framework of a reasonable peace and at the same time to make provisions for security in the Pacific from the Australian point of view.[61] He found Dulles and Dean Rusk anxious to find a means of bringing about security in the Pacific without committing themselves with great precision. Dulles said some 'compromise solution' would have to be found.[62]

In conversation with State Department officials Spender enlarged on his idea for a Pacific pact. It should, he explained, be along the lines of the Atlantic pact, particularly Article 5 of that pact, i.e. that an attack on any of the parties would affect all other parties to the pact. He thought the essential members were the United States, Australia and New Zealand and the United Kingdom with the Philippines as an Asian power. He doubted that the south Asian countries, India, Pakistan and Ceylon would want to join, although acknowledging their membership might be politically desirable. Spender made his case to the doubting American officials on the basis that Australia and New Zealand were expected, in the interests of global strategy, to send forces to the Middle East. This was hard to justify unless the public could be assured that, in the event of any attack, the United States could be relied upon to come immediately to their aid. Furthermore the existence of a Pacific treaty would make a 'soft' Japanese peace treaty more acceptable to Australians. Finally he argued that while

Australia and New Zealand were likely to be affected by decisions taken in western Europe they belonged to no organic body of nations dealing with global strategy or similar questions. A Pacific pact could be the vehicle to bring Australia and New Zealand into consultations.[63] As a result of Spender's efforts, American investigation of the Australian idea of a Pacific pact, of what precisely its membership should be, and what types of obligations Australia had in mind, began.[64]

In spite of all his efforts with Dulles and many others, however, Spender was not left with the impression that he would necessarily be successful. Allison told Australian officials that he appreciated the difficulty in which the United States proposal for a treaty placed Australia. But at the same time, he gave them the impression that he considered Australian security problems in relation to the proposed peace treaty with Japan as fundamentally a domestic political problem, and thus one with which the United States would not wish to be concerned.[65] Similarly Dean Rusk made it clear that he did not favour a Pacific pact. He spoke of the possibility of a Presidential statement affirming United States interest in the security of Australia and New Zealand, and of military consultations. There was no suggestion that a deal, which attracted officials in Canberra, of a United States commitment to come to Australian and New Zealand defence as a *quid pro quo* for the sort of Japanese peace treaty contemplated by the United States, might be feasible.[66] None of this was very encouraging. Nevertheless Spender was determined to fight on and so instructed Australian officials. They were to make it clear that, unless Australia was satisfied with the security position arising out of a Japanese peace settlement, Australia would not, under any circumstances, sign any peace treaty.

The Australian position was therefore widely known when Doidge arrived in Washington. The American position in spite of Spender's efforts seemed still to be that there was no need for a formal guarantee by the United States since it was a foregone conclusion that it would come to the aid of Australia if attacked.[67]

DOIDGE IN NEW YORK

External Affairs Minister Doidge met Dulles at Lake Success on 14 October 1950. Their conversation contained no reassurance for the New Zealand party which included Alister McIntosh who was travelling with Doidge, Sir Carl Berendsen and Frank Corner. Dulles at once made it quite clear that the peace treaty would not contain military clauses. It was essential, he argued, not to antagonize Japan and not to allow Japan to become a vacuum into which the Russians would certainly move if they had the opportunity. The aim of American policy was, he said, to make sure that the Russians 'didn't get Japan without having to fight for it'.[68] There was, of course, sympathy in the New Zealand Cabinet for this argument but this was not the New Zealand priority. Doidge reiterated that New Zealand's concern was for the effect of the treaty on its security, its fear was a resurgence of Japanese military strength, and its hope was for an adequate guarantee against possible Japanese aggresson. He raised again the question of a Pacific pact.

In response, Dulles made all the usual objections to a Pacific pact – the 'embarassing' question of membership and the lack of common civilization, community of interest and real trust between the diverse countries of the area. America, he said, did not want to give guarantees to governments which were likely to embark on 'questionable' policies. He made the point again, however, that he knew, and New Zealand knew, that America would come to the defence of New Zealand and Australia just as New Zealand and Australia would assist America in a similar plight. This was cold, and not alogether convincing, comfort to the New Zealanders. Berendsen in particular declared himself 'thoroughly sceptical' of these American promises.[69] It was clear that Japanese rearmament was going to be permitted without even the framework of a Pacific regional security guarantee and that United States policy was widely different from that of New Zealand.

At this stage New Zealand and Australian hopes of getting what they wanted looked slender. Doidge was reported as saying after the meeting, that New Zealand's attitude to Japan was 'live and let live', surely an exaggeration of the New Zealand position, and that New Zealand and Australia were 'more or less in harmony' with respect to a Japanese peace treaty. 'All we are asking', he said, 'are reasonable safeguards to protect peace and security in the Pacific. I think it perfectly logical there might be remaining in the Japanese mind some innate resentment over defeat and the germ of a desire for eventual revenge'.[70]

In these unpromising circumstances one option which had not been considered so far by New Zealand and Australia was some kind of closer association with the Atlantic pact. The idea, which may simply have been a kite flown by the Americans, was now floated. After the talks at Lake Success, Colonel C. Stanton Babcock, Dulles' military adviser, who travelled with the New Zealanders back to New York, said that if he were a New Zealander or an Australian thinking in terms of the security interests of his country, he would consider the possibility of seeking some closer association with the Atlantic pact powers. These powers might at the same time be asked to give some more definite indication of their interest in the security of New Zealand and Australia. Subsequently Dulles seemed to make a similar suggestion. At the United Nations, Berendsen pointed out to him, as Spender had done earlier, that New Zealand would inevitably be drawn into hostilities arising out of the Atlantic pact and would thus incur the obligations of that pact without any reciprocal undertaking from Atlantic pact members. Dulles said he saw no reason why, through American obligation to the United Kingdom under the Atlantic pact, some wider arrangement should not be worked out under which some kind of undertaking should be given to New Zealand in respect of the Pacific. Spender had not been impressed with this kind of possibility[71] but in Wellington it was thought to have perhaps some merit. Berendsen had always been sceptical of the efficacy of any American guarantee, such as Presidential announcement, that the United States would consider itself, in honour bound, to come to the aid of Australia and New Zealand if they were involved in hostilities. McIntosh was less pessimistic, believing New Zealand would be very lucky to get a general guarantee. He wrote, 'We canot even name the likely aggressor – some would say Russia, some Japan, some China. I can't help feeling that if the Americans can find a way, which I don't think they can – of singling us out for public embrace, let them do so'.[72]

All the same McIntosh did not really believe New Zealand was likely to get any such guarantee. In November 1950 he told Berendsen that he thought the most fruitful line for New Zealand was some sort of association, with its mutual guarantees, with the North Atlantic powers such as Colonel Babcock had suggested.[73] Berendsen agreed with him. Talk in Washington of an American guarantee to New Zealand and Australia was, he said, unofficial and likely to remain 'quite academic' until the situation in the Far East clarified itself. Association with the Atlantic Powers seemed to be the best line to follow.[74]

This line, however, was a difficult one to embark upon, and in fact, appears not to have been developed. In the meantime it seemed to McIntosh that Japan was engaged in the difficult acrobatic feat of getting as much out of the West as possible without destroying its chances of coming to terms with Asia. Always suspicious of the Japanese, he did not share the American feeling that they were likely to make trustworthy allies.[75] Doidge's message to Dulles, commenting on the United States attitude to the peace treaty and the princples on which the United States government believed it should be based, reflected this pessimism. He declared:

> it has been fundamental to New Zealand's approach to the settlement with Japan that the potential menace of Japan to the security of the Pacific should not be ignored. We recognise that the threat of military revival in Japan is a long-term one. Nevertheless we cannot help feeling that a treaty retaining no effective long-term control over Japan could result in a recurrence of the menace to which New Zealand and all Pacific nations were exposed in 1941. The New Zealand government have, therefore, maintained the view that the treaty should include adequate guarantees against possible Japanese aggression. We strongly feel that this aspect of the security problem should be given full weight in the preparation of the final settlement.[76]

New Zealand was still fighting to be heard, and, it would seem, in the matter of the specifics of the Japanese peace treaty and security guarantees, fighting a losing battle. The question of how far New Zealand was prepared to go in applying pressure for security guarantees was going to have to be decided in the very near future. Given New Zealand's need to maintain close relations with the United States, the Department of External Affairs argued that there was no advantage in asserting New Zealand's objections to the point of refusing to associate New Zealand with the American version of the Japanese peace treaty. As a matter of tactics, however, it seemed worthwhile to continue to express

doubts about whether it was worth signing a treaty which didn't go
some way towards meeting New Zealand's security requirements.
There was always the chance that this might help dispose the
United States to meet New Zealand's concerns by one means or
another.[77]

8
The Japanese Peace Treaty and the ANZUS Treaty: Final Negotiations

While Doidge and Spender put their case for security guarantees in the Japanese peace treaty, dramatic events were taking place in Korea. United Nations forces had reached the 38th parallel dividing North and South Korea by the end of September. On 1 October South Korean forces were sent across this line. American forward patrols followed on 7 October. These troops swept north. In early November they met stiff opposition from forces identified as Chinese, but the significance of this was discounted and victory seemed to be in sight when, on 24 November, the final advance towards the Yalu river, Korea's northern boundary, was resumed. At this point Chinese forces which had secretly moved into North Korea in strength during October and November, launched a major counter-attack. The United Nations faced an 'entirely new war'.[1] When the New Zealand ground force, known as Kayforce, arrived at Pusan on 31 December, the United Nations forces were in retreat. In this bleak situation the relatively small military commitment of New Zealand and Australia assumed a significance out of all proportion to its size. It was now urgent, from Washington's point of view, to obtain a peace settlement. Ironically, United States concern for the security of its area of first priority north of the equator, might be used to persuade the United States into participation in the maintenance of security in the south western Pacific.

REACTIONS IN NEW ZEALAND

Doidge returned to New Zealand at the end of October. Hardly dynamic at the best of times, he was, for much of the next two months, in indifferent health and left Wellington for his Tauranga constituency at the beginning of December.[2] Perhaps for this reason, the issues relating to the peace treaty and the various options, including a Pacific pact, which might be pursued in the search of New Zealand's security received little publicity from him. Furthermore, as far as a Pacific pact was concerned it was clear that Doidge's ideas had advanced no further. He said in Parliament on 2 November, 'a Pacific pact should be the natural corollary to an Atlantic Pact ... we have always been firm ... that there can be no satisfactory form of collective security in the Pacific unless the United States, Canada and India are parties to such a pact ... we are still exploring the possibilites of a regional agreement'.[3]

This was not the pact that Spender was suggesting. Moreover, Doidge appears to have forgotten that two months earlier he had said that a Pacific pact was 'unnecessary' since the United States had become a 'permanent partner' in policing the Pacific. On the peace treaty, Doidge reported that 'more definite progress' had ben made although he gave no evidence to support this assertion other than to indicate he had had 'valuable' discussions with Dulles' a 'brilliant man' and a 'most attractive personality'.

Doidge was absent when Parliament adjourned on 1 December and it was the Prime Minister who read a statement outlining the serious situation which had developed in Korea. He informed the House that the British Prime Minister, Clement Attlee, was going to Washington for discussions with President Truman.[4] To the tension which already existed between the United Kingdom and the United States over the recognition of the People's Republic of China, and the question of the Chinese seat in the United Nations, had been added concern that the United States might authorize the use of atomic weapons in Korea. Attlee sought to limit the area of conflict and to obtain assurances of more consultation between the United States and its allies.

In spite of the seriousness of the situation in global terms, McIntosh reported from Wellington, 'the whole atmosphere in relation to the Korean situation is unreal. No attention as such has been given to international problems'. Doidge, McIntosh wrote, had made 'a thorough mess' of matters in Cabinet and 'every damned thing in external affairs' had been passed to an already busy Prime Minister to discuss and decide.[5]

This did not augur well for the promotion of New Zealand's interests abroad in general or in relation to the Japanese peace treaty in particular. Furthermore the evident tensions between Britain and the United States presented New Zealand policy-makers with a dilemma between old loyalties and self-interest. In Washington where he continued to pursue an increasingly anti-Soviet, anti-Communist line, Berendsen viewed the British attitude to Far Eastern affairs as 'unwise in the extreme'. He believed New Zealand must stand with those whose continued support was essential to its survival. New Zealand must, he wrote, 'play the game with the Americans – we can play none without them'.[6] McIntosh replied:

> Mr Holland is all for sticking to the British through thick and thin and so is Mr Doidge. After all that is their traditional outlook. On the other hand they share your view that the US being in this to the extent that they are, means an enormous amount to us and we should therefore think twice before we line up against them.[7]

The Prime Minister's opinions were all the more important because a Commonwealth Prime Ministers' conference was to be held in London in January 1951. The British Prime Minister, Clement Attlee was concerned at the direction in which international affairs were moving. The main topics of the conference were bound to be the situation in Korea and the recognition of the Republic of China, but the Japanese peace treaty and the principle upon which the United States wanted a treaty based, were sure to be discussed in this context. It was necessary to persuade the New Zealand Prime Minister of the need to hold to the New Zealand stance on the treaty. This stance was now out of line with that of the United Kingdom, which had made it clear that it had no objection to a 'soft' treaty, and with all other members of the Commonwealth except Australia.

By way of a reminder to a Prime Minister with a limited interest in, and grasp of international affairs, and whose outlook was essentially centred on Britain and the 'Empire', the Departmental paper on the Japanese peace settlement drafted for the conference noted, 'New Zealand is a Pacific country. Our future is an inseparable part of the vast Pacific region in which Japan has played and is destined again to play a major role'.[8] On this basis New Zealand's case for protection against the possible resurgence of Japanese militarism was argued. The paper concludes:

> We strongly feel that while the settlement the United States has in mind may present no apparent threat to the United States whose economic and military resources are incomparably superior to those of Japan, its long-term implications are seriously disquieting ... New Zealand therefore feels bound to press for the security guarantees which we consider should be an essential part of the settlement with Japan.[9]

THE PRIME MINISTERS CONFERENCE

The Commonwealth Prime Ministers met in London from 4 to 11 January 1951. Commonwealth solidarity on the major issues – Korea; the recognition of the People's Republic of China; the Japanese peace treaty – if achieved, could of course have been a valuable lever in Anglo-American relations. That such a lever was needed was a reflection of Britain's inability to influence the United States especially in east Asian matters. That solidarity was not achieved reflected the growing diversity and independece of Commonwealth members.

The discussion on the Japanese peace treaty was typical. The United Kingdom circulated a paper, as a basis for discussion, on the attitude which should be adopted by Commonwealth governments towards the Japanese peace settlement in the light of developments in the Far East.[10] It was clear that the United Kingdom had no objection to Japanese rearmament or to a bilateral United States-Japan defence treaty. The essence of the United Kingdom proposals was that Japan should be restored to the status of a sovereign state and thereafter allowed to develop in her own way, in free association with the other nations of the world.

Australia was represented on 9 January by its High Commissioner in London, Sir Eric Harrison, the Prime Minister, Sir Robert Menzies having fallen ill. Harrison led off the discussion on the United Kingdom paper by expressing Australia's alarm at the 'tendency to slip into an easy treaty'. Australia objected to the military resurgence of Japan; she could not agree to unlimited Japanese rearmament; and she was not prepared to rely on keeping Japan as an ally of the democracies. Australia, he said, needed security against any future aggression by Japan.[11]

The statement which had been prepared for Holland in Wellington contained sentiments in the same tone. Nevertheless when Holland's turn to comment came, he took a much more flexible line than either his own brief, or Harrison. While he conceded that New Zealand's interests were 'much the same' as Australia's, her fear of Japanese resurgence was, he maintained, 'slightly less'. Japan, he felt, could not be left undefended and must therefore be defended either by occupation forces or allowed to arm and defend herself. There could be no certainty about the use to which Japan might put her armed forces, but Holland was not prepared 'to push this point too far.' He suggested that restrictions on Japan's naval and air forces might meet the case.[12] Holland's presentation contains none of the condemnation of the Japanese rearmament featured in the papers prepared for him and reads like a pale shadow of the Australian stance. Perhaps this was due to Holland's desire not to be too obviously out of line with Britain and other Commonwealth members. Certainly McIntosh commented at the time, that Frank Corner, who was a member of the New Zealand party, had done his 'noble best' to restrain the Prime Minister and McIntosh from becoming 'too British and less American'. McIntosh said that neither he nor the Prime Minister had taken much persuading but that unfortunately the Prime Minister was 'not quite confident in himself' and not clear as to the implications of various moves. The problem was, he complained (as officials dealing with politicians have frequently complained) that Holland didn't know or appreciate the background, and his officials could not get sufficient time with him to talk.[13]

In spite of Holland's lacklustre performance it was generally understood by the meeting that Australia and New Zealand required some form of guarantee against possible Japanese aggression. This guarantee, it was suggested, might take the form of a direct guarantee between Australia, New Zealand and the United States or it might be reached through some form of Pacific pact. It was suggested in the general discussion that New Zealand was already negotiating for a direct guarantee. On the basis of the evidence available this seems to be an exaggeration. In neither

Wellington nor Washington was there any enthusiasm for the idea and Berendsen was the greatest sceptic of a guarantee.

The only upshot of this discussion on the Japanese peace settlement was a statement to the effect that the Commonwealth prime ministers were in favour of the early conclusion of a peace treaty. Unanimity on the British paper had not been achieved because of the Australian and, to a lesser extent, the New Zealand stance. Nevertheless time was on the side of Australia and New Zealand in the matter of their security requirements. The Korean war dragged on and with it grew the American desire to keep Japan in the western camp and to strengthen the loyalty of American allies in the Pacific. In January 1951 Dulles informed the New Zealand government that the United States hoped to be able to devise 'some satisfactory means of reassuring the government and people of New Zealand'.[14] At the same time Spender was informed that the State Department was giving 'active consideration' to his proposals for a Pacific pact.[15]

DULLES' VISIT TO TOKYO

In fact the Americans were suspicious of the Commonwealth Prime Ministers' conference. Six of the thirteen members of the Far Eastern Commission were members of the Commonwealth. The nations represented in the Commission were those primarily concerned with the Japanese peace settlement and if Commonwealth solidarity was achieved, there was a danger that the treaty principles which Dulles had circulated to Far East Commission members in September might have to be negotiated. Dulles reported:

> The United Kingdom is seeking to gain the initiative and is itself drafting a Japanese peace treaty. This it seems is now being considered in London by the Commonwealth prime ministers who are also reported to be considering a Pacific Pact.[16]

Clearly delay in pushing through the Japanese peace settlement was not to the advantage of the United States. On 11 January 1951, it was announced that Dulles was going to Japan to conduct what further negotiations were necessary to bring the Japanese peace settlement to a satisfactory conclusion. Soon afterwards it was reported from Washington that the American party hoped to travel on from Japan to the Philippines and subsequently to Australia and New Zealand. Allison, Director of the Office of Far Eastern Affairs, who was to accompany Dulles told New Zealand officials in Washington that Dulles hoped to explore the possibility of a multilateral Pacific pact limited to the 'island nations of the Pacific', i.e. one which would avoid any commitment in respect of the mainland of Asia or Southeast Asia.[17]

Berendsen saw Dulles before his departure on 22 January. Dulles explained to him that, given the evidence of Communist intentions in Asia, the difficulties previously seen about a Pacific pact had disappeared. Although his ideas had not yet crystallized, Dulles was contemplating a multilateral arrangement less formal than the Atlantic pact, the signatories to be the United States, United Kingdom, Australia, New Zealand, the Philippines and Japan.[18] An attack on one of the parties would be regarded as an attack on all. Berendsen was delighted to observe, as he reported the details, that these suggestions were almost identical to those he had made a year earlier in his lengthy dispatch to Doidge. It seemed that Japan was intended to be an original signatory of the pact and that, until a binding agreement was concluded, Dulles expected Australia and New Zealand would be satisfied with a 'declaration of intent', possibly made concurrently with the Japanese peace settlement. This settlement, the principles of which were also outlined, would restore Japan to full sovereignty and be based on the assumption that Japan would progressivey assume a greater share of her defence.[19]

Dulles was in Japan for two weeks. In this time he obtained an understanding with the Japanese government about the nature of a peace treaty, and this became the basis of the draft settlement that was negotiated with the other signatories. Dulles did not persuade the Japanese Prime Minister to agree to rearmament, but arrangements were made for a United States-Japan bilateral security treaty which would allow for the maintenance of American armed forces in Japan and the leaving of bases in Japan.[20] Perhaps because of Japanese Prime Minister Yoshida's reluctance on the rearmament issue and because of the evident dislike of the British for a regional Pacific pact, the idea of an 'island chain' pact which would include Japan was not pursued with the Japanese.[21]

Dulles and his party went on to the Philippines and were expected to be in Canberra for talks on 15 February. It was not immediately known whether Dulles would travel on to New Zealand or whether he would insist on joint talks. Faced with this uncertainty, Wellington and Canberra made plans, and in so doing each exhibited a certain caution and suspicion about the other.

As the weaker party, New Zealand could see the value in joint talks and preliminary discussions to dispose of any major differences between Australia and New Zealand. Otherwise there was a danger of the Australians making 'impossible demands' in any joint discussions with Dulles. This would put New Zealand in the difficult position of arguing against them. If the discussions proceeded independently at Canberra and Wellington, New Zealand could be faced with an agreement it didn't like and which it would find difficulty in altering.[22]

The Australians, for their part, feared that the presence of the New Zealand representatives throughout the talks with Dulles would be inhibiting. It could prevent them from putting forward their point of view as forcefully as they might otherwise have done. The New Zealanders had not, after all, shown the same determination as the Australians with regard to the issue of Japanese rearmament at the recent Prime Minister's conference in London. Interest in the Japanese settlement did not seem, to the Australians, to be as deep in New Zealand as in Australia. Joint talks with the New Zealanders could, of course, provide an opportunity to draw up an agreed approach closer to the Australian point of view, and if the New Zealanders actively sought combined talks, these would be difficult for Australia to resist without creating misunderstanding. On the other hand, if Dulles was willing to hold talks both in Australia and New Zealand the best course seemed to be to inform New Zealand that a preliminary exchange of views would be welcomed and let the separate talks arrangement stand.[23] It is clear that New Zealand and Australia did not approach the talks with Dulles with the sense of solidarity and confidence in one another that might have been expected from two neighbouring countries importuning a distant Great Power. Nevertheless the Australians extended an invitation for preliminary talks which was accepted, and in the event combined discussions with Dulles also took place.[24]

NEW ZEALAND PREPARATIONS

In January 1951, the Department of External Affairs had to face up to shaping the recommendations for what looked as if it would be New Zealand's final stance on the peace treaty. Should New Zealand hold out against Japanese rearmament? What kind of a security guarantee might New Zealand most desire and realistically press for, in the face of the inevitable 'soft' treaty? Was the 'island chain' proposal feasible? There were plenty of ideas about, and Sir Carl Berendsen's proposal for a limited pact, outlined in his letter to Doidge of March 1950, at last received an airing and consideration, albeit in summarized form.[25] The Berendsen paper joined a number of others as a basis for discussion in the Department of External Affairs. One paper argued that New Zealand should agree to limited Japanese rearmament,[26] another, touching a well-known national nerve, argued that New Zealand's greatest vulnerability was to Asian racial aggression and that Dulles' proposals let two 'potential wolves', Japan and the Philippines, into the 'sheepfold'. Sentimental ties were also considered in a paper in which the Dulles proposals were seen to run counter to New Zealand's traditional and existing commitments to the Commonwealth, and to the requirements of British global strategy.[27]

A paper setting out the pros and cons of various security options was discussed with the Chiefs of Staff in early February. A direct United States-New Zealand treaty involving an American commitment to New Zealand security was dismissed as clearly unattainable; a comprehensive Pacific pact was felt to offer more disadvantages than advantages; a limited Pacific pact with Australia, New Zealand, the United States, the Philippines and Japan as members, was seen to have the advantage of excluding unstable countries on the Asian mainland, to act as a check on Japan and to be favoured by Australia. On the other hand there was felt to be a considerable public suspicion of Japan and the Philippines, and reluctance to make a firm commitment to the defence of either of them. It was agreed that further study of this option was needed. But all things considered, it was concluded, an informal guarantee of New Zealand security in the form of a Presidential announcement seemed to suit New Zealand interest best. The Chiefs of Staff thought this might be associated with the idea of recognition of New Zealand's part in Allied strateg' through her indirect assocation with NATO. This possibility, i was recommended, should be borne in mind in the forthcomin; discussions with Dulles.[28]

So far as the Dulles proposals for an 'island chain' pact wer' concerned, the debate had not advanced much further. Moreove the Chiefs of Staff reiterated their view, first stated a year earlie that, on military grounds, there were no reasons for an approach by New Zealand for a defence pact.[29] It was, it seemed, official and politicians with an eye on the political repercussions of a non punitive Japanese peace treaty, who pushed for some form of security guarantee. The determined attitude of Spender in Australia was no doubt also forcing them to make a stand for Nev Zealand.

Debate on New Zealand policy was also complicated b pressure coming from the United Kingdom, to which country Nev Zealand had passed on Dulles' proposals.[30] Whitehall was in fact informed of Dulles' proposals by both Wellington and b McIntosh, who was still in London after the Commonwealth Prime Ministers conference. McIntosh told the Deputy Under-Secretar of State at the Commonwealth Relations Office that the Nev Zealand Government was extremely interested in Dulles' idea and that one of the objects of Prime Minister Holland's impendin visit to Washington would be to discuss these ideas with th President and American officials. McIntosh commented on th irony of the prospect that New Zealand, having always bee nervous about Japanese rearmament and wishing for a guarante by the United States, might now get that guarantee at the price o agreeing to Japanese rearmament. Nevertheless, though its valu might now be rather less in New Zealand eyes, McIntosh though the guarantee would be helpful from the political point of view i getting the New Zealand public to accept the commitment to sen forces to the Middle East. This was, of course, what the Britis wanted to hear. McIntosh said he didn't think there was much i the security guarantee since he could not see any circumstances i which an enemy was likely to attack New Zealand. Anyway, ther could be 'no question', he said, of New Zealand accepting an agreement which didn't include Britain.[31]

McIntosh's line was reassuring to London, but as he was accompanying Holland to Washington, he was not going to be in Wellington or Canberra to influence matters. The United Kingdom comments on the Dulles proposals were therefore un-equivocal. Caution and further consultation were urged on New Zealand before any agreement was reached. New Zealand's commitment to send forces to the Middle East must not be compromised. A Pacific pact which did not include the United Kingdom as a full member would be regarded as unacceptable.[32] As one official put it, the main thing, from the point of view of the United Kingdom, was that 'Australia and New Zealand shouldn't commit themselves to something which affects them and us as well as the Middle East and Asia and that they should make this plain to Dulles.[33]

London wanted 'the mouth of the American gift horse' examined 'very closely'. The United Kingdom High Commissioner in Wellington saw Doidge who agreed to consider Whitehall's views 'carefully' and promised New Zealand's approach would be 'a cautious one', but to the irritation of the High Commissioner, did not promise further consultation.[34]

The final twist in the debate on a New Zealand policy, came in messages from the Prime Minister who was in Washington en route from the Prime Ministers conference in London. He reported positively on the chances of obtaining a Pacific pact but reminded Doidge that in the discussions with Dulles, New Zealand's responsibilites in the Middle East must not be forgotten. After a conversation with Dean Rusk he cabled that the idea of a tripartite pact made up of Australia, New Zealand and the United States had come up and that this seemed 'by far the best solution'. This would get over the problem of a commitment to defend regimes which New Zealand might find it morally and politically difficult to defend. Doidge was urged to keep in mind in the discussions with Dulles that it was its security that New Zealand wanted assured.[35]

On 9 February the Cabinet met to consider policy concerning the peace settlement and the proposed Pacific security arrange-ments. Doidge outlined the Dulles proposals and something of the history of Commonwealth debate on the peace treaty. In the discussions which followed, the traditional view of the conservative New Zealand politician was aired. It was suggested that it would be 'disastrous' to make a security arrangement which did not include Britain, whose active support would be essential if any economic or financial sanctions against Japan should become necessary. New Zealand should not be a party to a pact which, by excluding the United Kingdom, might apparently contribute to a weakening of her position in Asia and the Pacific. Any obligation towards the security of Japan was regarded as 'quite unacceptable' to New Zealand and, it was presumed, to Australia. But the general feeling was, that if New Zealand was not willing to come to the aid of Japan, it was not logical to deny Japan the right to rearm. She might otherwise be tempted by or fall into the hands of the Communists. It was agreed that New Zealand could not and would not object to a United States guarantee for Japan, but that New Zealand itself, should not guarantee Japan because of the New Zealand commitment in the Middle East. Such a guarantee would in any case be politically unacceptable in New Zealand.[36] Cabinet approved a statement of policy advocating a Presidential declaration as the best means of ensuring New Zealand security. Such a statement by the President would, it was noted, give expression to the 'natural identity of interests' between the United States and New Zealand and would be, in contemporary terms, 'the true Pacific pact'.[37] Doidge therefore went to Canberra with the proposal for a Presidential guarantee as his first preference.

There was no sense of urgency in New Zealand discussions, and New Zealand expectations were already different from those of Australia, where a Pacific pact of some kind remained the goal. In this difference, the excluded British whose 'feelers and probings' were causing considerable irritation in Canberra,[38] saw hope for an outcome not altogether unfavourable to United Kingdom interests. New Zealand was seen as likely to exercise a moderating influence. It was reported from Washington that McIntosh, evidently feeling since the Prime Minsters conference, 'more British and less American', and apparently low in 'Pacific consciousness', had told British officials there that despite the accident of geography, New Zealanders looked on themselves essentially as a Western power and believed that in a future war their survival would depend on an outcome in Europe and the Middle East. He contrasted this with the outlook of Australians who, he suggested, believed that in the last resort they could provide for their security by holding the territories in the Australian sphere. McIntosh felt that rapid progress would not be made on a security arrangement because there were too many viewpoints yet to be reconciled. The Japanese wanted to exact as high a price as possible for their co-operation; the Australians wanted a full-scale Pacific pact; the Americans looked on the question as a means of securing a quick and liberal Japanese peace treaty; the New Zealanders did not want a pact to which the United Kingdom was not a party. This was a satisfactory analysis as far as the British were concerned. It seemed to them that McIntosh's approach was 'essentially practical' and that his influence should be 'useful'.[39] He was not, however, free to go to Canberra where the atmosphere for the preliminary talks was not improved by reports, arising out of what appears to have been Holland's ineptitude at a press conference, that New Zealand thought Japan should be a member of a Pacific pact and that Holland might be making some kind of special deal in Washington.[40]

London discounted these press reports, but news that both McIntosh and the State Department had suggested that a tripartite Australia, New Zealand, United States pact might be the best solution to the security problem, did cause some anxiety in the Foreign Office. The idea was believed to be 'two or three days old' and 'not thought through' but the Foreign Office gave 'urgent consideration' to the new proposal in the light of Britain's global strategy and its interests in South-east Asia.[41] The British were also indignant to learn that General MacArthur appeared to be trying to influence proceedings. He told 'Bill' Challis, the New Zealand trade representative in Japan, that neither the Australian nor the New Zealand government was sufficiently Pacific-minded. What was wanted now, MacArthur said, was men who regarded themselves as 'denizens of the Pacific first and foremost' and who were not always thinking of the North Atlantic pact.[42] This was the kind of message likely to be received more sympathetically in Australian than in New Zealand government circles.

THE PRELIMINARY TALKS

The United States memorandum containing proposals for a Japanese peace settlement and the United States proposal for an 'island chain' pact which included Japan, Australia, New Zealand, the Philippines, the United States and possibly the United Kingdom, formed the basis of the preliminary talks which took place in Sydney and Canberra. The two proposals were recognized to be interrelated and the areas of agreement which existed between New Zealand and Australia were quickly established. It was clearly inevitable that Japan would be allowed some measure of rearmament. It was seen to be impossible to obtain explicit restrictions on this rearmament, but the best tactic for New Zealand and Australia seemed to be to continue to press for limitations on rearmament in the hope of obtaining a security arrangement which would give them a firm guarantee of United States protection.

The basis of those disagreements which occurred over the line to be taken, lay in different perceptions of the 'threat' from Japan, Asia in general, and international Communism. Australia's geographical position had given Australian politicians of both parties since 1941, an Asian and south west Pacific consciousness not parallelled in more isolated New Zealand. This difference in consciousness had brought Australian but not New Zealand troops home from the Middle East in 1943 and had been a factor in the Australian initiative for an Australian-New Zealand Agreement in 1944.[43] Now Australia wanted no part in promoting a mere Presidential statement such as New Zealand advocated. She wanted a formal and permanent association with the United States. Australia felt that in problems in the Pacific, her interests were not identical to those of the United Kingdom and she was not therefore prepared to commit herself exclusively to British global strategy. If no guarantee in the Pacific could be obtained Australia would be prepared to keep troops at home for local defence. In the long run, Australia was willing, if a United States guarantee could be obtained by no other means, to accept a security treaty which included both Japan and the Philippines. There was urgency in the Australian determination to seize what might be a 'last chance' to obtain a United States guarantee.

New Zealand's line was much more cautious. The prospect of a treaty which included the Philippines was disliked, and one which included Japan was described as 'highly unacceptable' to the New Zealand public. New Zealand's concern was with the long term risk of Asian aggression rather than any immediate threat from international Communism, and clearly the felt need for an immediate security guarantee in New Zealand was less than in Australia. New Zealand's military commitment to the Middle East and sensitivity to British opinion remained constant.

While the New Zealand and Australian views differed on these matters relating to the proposals before them, they were agreed that a tripartite Australia, New Zealand, United States treaty would solve many of their differences. It would be, as Holland had put it, 'by far the best solution'. It was not clear whether the kites flown in the United States just before the meeting really carried a substantive message but it was now resolved that Australia and New Zealand should jointly advocate a tripartite agreement when they met Dulles.[44] The result of the preliminary meetings was that Doidge had agreed to press for more than he and the Cabinet had originally advocated.

THE DULLES VISIT

The tripartite talks began in Canberra on 15 February 1951. Australia and New Zealand had agreed they would jointly advocate a tripartite pact over the 'island chain' proposal which was expected to be on the table along with the American proposals for a Japanese peace treaty. From the Australian and New Zealand point of view the question of Pacific security was so interrelated with the treaty that it was impossible to discuss one without the other. Dulles, however, having listened to the 'vigorous' objections of the United Kingdom to the 'island chain' proposal, chose to concentrate on the peace treaty, playing down the likely danger to Australia and New Zealand from a resurgent Japan.

This tactic placed Australia and New Zealand at a disadvantage, forcing Spender and Doidge to argue against the proposed peace terms and take the initiative on Pacific security. Spender said later, 'the labouring oar came upon me'.[45] Certainly the record shows Spender as the leading, and the tougher, more uncompromising negotiator, and Spender's claim that Doidge left the main argument to him, seems, from the record, to be a valid one. Doidge and Spender did not, according to McIntosh, get on well together[46] and Spender's annoyance when, in spite of their agreement to press for a tripartite pact, Doidge indicated on the first day that New Zealand would be satisfied with what the Australians regarded as a vague and undefined Presidential guarantee, (the stance on which the New Zealand Cabinet had agreed), is understandable. On the following day, when Doidge changed his line and made a clear statement of preference for a tripartite agreement, the Australians commented sourly that New Zealand had finally 'seen the light'.[47]

After the talks were over Doidge was to complain that the record gave too much emphasis to Spender's approach. McIntosh, explained, 'The difficulty was that Mr Spender said a number of things which Mr Doidge ought to have said but failed to do so'. Apparently when these things were, quite correctly, subsequently attributed to Spender, Doidge objected. McIntosh went on, 'Spender did make points for us, even though he did not believe them himself, but they had been put up to him in the officials talks earlier in the week and he had agreed not to dissent from our view'.[48]

Spender made it quite clear that Australia would be satisfied with nothing other than a formal guarantee and argued forcefully that Australia and New Zealand, countries which had obligations elsewhere in the world and traditional ties strengthened by the war, should be seen by the United States as a special case.

The sticking point in the peace proposals as far as Australia and New Zealand were concerned was the question of Japanese rearmament. There was no real objection to the territorial or political and economic clauses, although Spender sought clarification on a number of details. Dulles made it clear that the United States intended that Japan be given the capacity to defend herself and would not contemplate a treaty which imposed limitations on Japanese rearmament. He argued at length on the need to keep Japan out of Communist hands and to ensure Japan's voluntary co-operation with the United States and its allies. The United States, he reported, had made a provisional agreement with the Japanese government for American troops to remain in Japan although it was not prepared to give Japan a 'free ride'. In any case the requirement of the Vandenberg resolution[49] made it necessary for Japan to demonstrate a readiness to help herself if she expected protection from the United States. Dulles described Japan and the Philippines at that time as 'a screen' between

Australia and New Zealand, and the forces of the USSR and Communist China. The presence of American troops in Japan after the treaty was signed would, he said, be an assurance that there would be no aggression by Japan against the countries of the south Pacific.[50]

Dulles' emphasis on the imminent Soviet Communist menace did not strike a deeply responsive chord with either the New Zealand or Australian delegation and for that reason it was easier for them to make the case for limitations and controls on Japanese rearmament and/or security guarantees. New Zealand was genuinely less worried about any immediate Communist threat than with the possibility, in the long term, of Japanese remilitarization and Asian aggression in general. Though Australians took a less detached view of Asia, and their Pacific conciousness was undoubtedly higher than New Zealanders', the Australian government was also seeking protection from any quarter, including Japan.[51] Spender was adamant that the treaty proposed could not be accepted by the Australian government unless its objective and political disadvantages were offset by an acceptable security arrangement in the Pacific. In the end he evidently convinced the Americans.[52] His firm attitude and the doubts expressed by Doidge about the treaty proposals forced the discussion to the matter of a security treaty.

In spite of some pressure from the Americans, neither New Zealand nor Australia was prepared at that time to contemplate that Japan should be a party to a security treaty with them. Though Spender was prepared to accept the Philippines as a member, if that was the price to be paid for American participation, Doidge objected to the possibility throughout, the Philippines being regarded by New Zealand as an area 'morally and politically difficult to defend'. Of course the United Kingdom objections to a pact which included these countries but excluded the United Kingdom could also be used to bolster the argument that the most acceptable way to obtain the agreement to a peace treaty which the United States wanted, and a security treaty which Australia and New Zealand wanted, would be a tripartite pact. Such a pact would meet some of the United Kingdom objections to the offshore proposal and would not impair the ability of Australia and New Zealand to meet their Middle East commitments. As a result of this discussion, a joint committee of officials was set the task of drafting the tripartite treaty which was to become, with a few revisions, the ANZUS pact.

In reality the choice was either to go along with the kind of peace treaty on which the United States was clearly determined, or to go out on a dangerous limb and refuse to sign it. This problem had been looming from the moment it became clear that New Zealand and Australia were isolated in their objection to a 'soft' treaty. Neither the New Zealand nor the Australian government contemplated with any enthusiasm the heroics of a permanently isolated stand against the American plans. Each was painfully aware of the very real predicament with which they were now faced. According to Spender, he impressed on Doidge the importance of not revealing to the Americans their awareness of this predicament and of displaying a solid front in opposition to the treaty as the only card in their hand to win a firm security arrangement with the United States.[53]

In fact, when the draft tripartite agreement appeared it provoked very little debate. Doidge had some misgivings that the phrase, 'pending development of a more comprehensive system of regional security in the Pacific area', in the preamble, might imply commitment in the long run to a wider arrangement which included Japan and the Philippines and was reassured by Dulles and Spender that the ultimate goal of a wider agreement for Pacific security was a noble long-term aim.[54] There was little further discussion which Spender has explained was due to continuous consultation with the drafting committee.[55] The British thought, correctly, that the Australians must have been 'cooking up' the draft for days before the meeting and regarded their behaviour as 'unsatisfactory'.[56] Be that as it may, Doidge and Spender felt able, while reiterating their desire for limitations on Japanese rearmament, to declare themselves likely to be reassured should the proposed pact be concluded. Of course the United States Senate had yet to accept the draft agreement but, if it did, the problem the terms of the Japanese peace treaty presented Australia and New Zealand would be, if not solved, at least more manageable.

There were still people in New Zealand, including members of the New Zealand Cabinet, yet to be convinced that a treaty which included no restrictions on Japanese rearmament should be accepted. It was to these doubters that Dulles addressed most of his comments when he met the New Zealand Cabinet on

22 February 1951. At the Prime Minister's request he dealt particularly with the question of Japanese rearmament. Dulles dwelt on Japan's exposure to Soviet influence, and vulnerability to Soviet imperialism, and on the attraction for Japan of an alliance with China. He explained that in the short term the Japanese constitution would inhibit Japanese rearmament although in the long run the United States governmemt would expect Japan, in return for a security alliance with the United States, to contribute to its own defence. He argued that Japan's lack of raw materials would, however, act as a controlling factor in rearmament. Furthermore at that time, he said, the Japanese were in a passive mood and did not want to rearm. He stressed the need for an early settlement. Dulles explained to the Cabinet that the 'island chain' pact proposal, which had been approved before he left the United States, had been dropped because of United Kingdom objections, and sketched the possibility of a tripartite pact or possibly a quadruple pact with the Philippines as the fourth member. Cabinet members do not appear to have asked for details of pact proposals or to have queried Dulles' interpretation of the situation. Evidently they were suitably impressed with the force of Dulles' arguments.

DEBATE ON THE SECURITY TREATY

Nevertheless matters did not proceed entirely smoothly. Asked to comment on the draft security treaty, the United Kingdom put forward strong objections to the possible inclusion of the Philippines and expressed concern that the pact, particularly if it included the Philippines, might suggest that the United Kingdom was 'renouncing its proper share of responsibility in the area'.[57] These views were given to the Australians twelve hours before they reached New Zealand and were handed directly to the New Zealand Prime Minister, Holland, thus bypassing the Minister for External Affairs. Doidge, who had been under pressure from, and open with the United Kingdom's special observer in Canberra, was highly incensed on all counts.[58]

Doidge may have been incensed but the Australians, according to McIntosh, were 'ropable' about the British reaction.[59] Spender had already been enraged by the British unilateral undermining of the 'island chain' pact proposal and a stiff protest had been sent to the British Prime Minister.[60] The Commonwealth Relations Office had dismissed Spender's reaction as 'unreasonable'. He had, it was felt, given a 'lamentable' exhibition of Commonwealth co-operation. It was noted somewhat patronizingly that Spender seemed to feel a Pacific pact was 'a special baby of his own'.[61] It seemed to the Australians and the New Zealanders, however, that the British were doing their best to 'head the Americans off,' to 'torpedo' this latest version of a Pacific pact and substitute a Presidential guarantee.[62] The result was that, at Australian suggestion, joint talks with Australian officials were held in Wellington to determine a common response to British pressure.

It was not difficult for the officials, Alan Watt, Secretary of External Affairs in Australia and Alister McIntosh to reach agreement. The Prime Ministers of both countries had already indicated that, if a tripartite treaty could not be obtained, a quadruple arrangement including the Philippines would be an acceptable way of securing the 'vital American guarantee of security'. United Kingdom objections to the draft treaty were not thought to be well-founded and the greater importance of obtaining an American security guarantee against Asian expansion was generally affirmed. On the basis of the discussions a reply to the British was drafted.[63]

Up to that point the tripartite pact had not been discussed in the New Zealand Cabinet. This was partly because the government was preoccupied with a confrontation with the unions. A waterside workers strike began in February 1951 and on 28 February the Waterside Workers Union was deregistered. A bitter conflict developed and for the next five months this domestic problem overshadowed everything else. A further reason for delaying discussion was the known sympathy for the United Kingdom in the Cabinet and the dislike of its members for anything to do with the Philippines.[64] In the event, though a good deal of concern about the need to meet the United Kingdom objections was expressed on both sentimental and economic grounds in the Cabinet, Doidge's emphasis on the supreme importance on security grounds of a treaty with the United States now that 'Britannia no longer ruled the waves', carried the day and Cabinet approved the communication which had been drafted to the British Prime Minister, Attlee, and the Secretary of State for Commonwealth Affairs,

Patrick Gordon Walker.[65] This stressed New Zealand's continuing interest in the Commonwealth relationship, argued that the treaty proposed would not weaken that relationship and maintained that such a treaty was necessary to reassure the New Zealand public that in agreeing to a Japanese peace treaty without limitations on Japanese rearmament they were not exposing themselves to a repetition of the dangers of 1941 from a resurgent Japan. If the inclusion of the Philippines in the treaty was the price to be paid to obtain an American guarantee, New Zealand would accept this.[66]

READY FOR ACTION

New Zealand and Australia were now most anxious to conclude the negotiations with the United States and received with suspicion and anxiety the news that the United Kingdom intended to take its concern over the possible inclusion of the Philippines to the Americans. Their fear was, that if the discussion was further spun out, peace treaty proposals might solidify to such an extent that they would be forced to accept them without a security arrangement.[67]

In fact the United States administration accepted Australian and New Zealand preference for a tripartite pact as well as United Kingdom objections to the inclusions of the Philippines, and, after some negotiation on minor details, a Presidential statement foreshadowing a tripartite pact with Australia and New Zealand and bilateral security arrangements with Japan and the Phillipines was made. These arrangements would, Truman said, 'strengthen the fabric of peace in the whole Pacific ocean area' when peace with Japan was officially re-established[68] Berendsen cautioned against premature rejoicing until Senate approval of the security treaty had been obtained[69] but Doidge's public statement stressed the significance of a guarantee which would 'liberate New Zealand from the nightmare of a resurgence of Japanese militarism'[70] and Spender called Truman's statement 'a green light on the road to Pacific security'.[71] The United Kingdom High Commissioner commented that New Zealand public opinion 'though by no means well-informed' seemed to have moved some way to be ready to acquiesce in a generous treaty with Japan if New Zealand security could be safeguarded.[72] Press opinion seemed to be that a peace treaty must be made soon and must ensure that Japanese opinion was moulded so as to make Japan an ally.[73] Furthermore, although the publicity about the Dulles talks made foreign policy and the Japanese treaty something of a public issue, it was not a party political one. Walter Nash, Leader of the Opposition since Fraser's death in December 1950, in characteristic style and phraseology commented that, in his view, New Zealand could only 'adopt the Christian course' and hope that the policy of trusting Japan would bring its reward.[74]

It seemed that the government would have little difficulty obtaining public approval of a peace treaty along the lines proposed by the Americans provided the security treaty tentatively drawn up in Canberra proved acceptable to the United States government. Opposition to the proposals which allowed for Japanese rearmament could be withdrawn[75] and the major sticking point was thus disposed of. Such further queries as New Zealand had, relating to the possibility of a war guilt clause in the treaty, the future of Japanese stocks of gold and Japanese ship-building capacity, were minor by comparison and their dismissal by the United States was accepted without further objection.[76] When the text of the draft peace treaty was made known, Doidge announced that he was confident that a satisfactory peace, in conjunction with regional security arrangements, could soon be made and that these would lay the foundations for stable and peaceful arrangements between New Zealand and Japan.[77] New Zealand's concern now was to get the treaties, particularly the security treaty, signed.

THE FINAL PHASE

In correspondence with General MacArthur, Dulles wrote, 'The United States and Japan are the only significant sources of power in the Pacific, we actual, they potential. If we can work in accord, the lesser Pacific powers will get security and will sooner or later, formally or informally endorse that accord'.[78] New Zealand and Australia, who had been forced to recognize the limits of their leverage as small powers, were in no position to dispute actions taken on this assumption but the British were reluctant to accept that their views on the nature of the settlement could or should be ignored. They feared Japanese competition, particularly in

Southeast Asia, and wanted long-term economic controls on Japan, a stance with which Dulles was entirely unsympathetic.[79] The British nevertheless produced their own peace treaty draft in the spring of 1951 almost simultaneously with that of the United States.[80] It was June before a compromise was reached and a joint Anglo-American revised draft published.[81] The delay caused concern in the New Zealand and Australian camps since ther security arrangement was not yet formalized. In the end, few concessions were made to Britain, most of whose commercial demands had to be abandoned. Furthermore the British, who had wanted the People's Republic of China to sign the treaty, had finally to accept an American formula by which neither the People's Republic of China nor the Nationalist Government of China (Taiwan) was invited to sign.

While these negotiations went on the final details of the tripartite security treaty were worked out. The Americans asked for modifications to Article VII to streamline the proposal for a council on which members would be represented, and the Article VIII relating to the consultative relationship between this council and other states. Australia and New Zealand asked for additions to this Article in order to make clear the council's ability to consult with regional organizations such as NATO as well as states.[82] This change, about which Australia was more concerned than New Zealand,[83] was accepted after some confusion between New Zealand and Australia about the precise wording being sought. Such misunderstandings were too much for Berendsen in Washington whose store of patience tended always to be limited. He wrote:

> We are very much over-doing the business of looking a gift-horse in the mouth. Here we have been offered on a platter the greatest gift that the most powerful country in the world can offer a small and comparatively helpless group of people and we persist in niggling and naggling about what seem to me the most ridiculous trifles. We will be extremely lucky if we get the undertaking in the form which is now proposed and I wish to goodness you would stop what seems to me to be a sort of stupid pin-pricking which cannot help us and which may indeed cost us very dearly.[84]

Berendsen's mind was always on the Senate, whose approval of the Pacific pact he emphasized could not be taken for granted, particularly if the final text of the Japanese peace treaty had not been agreed. For this reason he and Spender, now Australian Ambassador in Washington, recommended acceptance of a last-minute qualification entered by the Americans in Article VIII that consultation should apply to states and authorities 'in the Pacific area', a qualification designed to restrict the field of action in which the treaty might apply. The Australians had hoped for a clear link between a Pacific security treaty and NATO. This the Americans wished to avoid but Dulles insisted that the restrictions of the security treaty to 'the Pacific area' did not preclude the establishment of a consultative relationship with NATO. Spender recognized it would be unwise to quibble on this point.[85]

In Wellington and Canberra it was recognized that the important thing now was to have the security treaty signed as quickly as possible lest any criticism of the terms of the Japanese peace treaty, which had not yet been published, might jeopardize the passage of the security arrangement through the Senate.[86]

Inevitably the preoccupation of the United States administration with the Korean war held things up, but the drafts of both the Japanese peace treaty and the security treaty were finally agreed upon. The draft peace treaty was released to the press on 12 July and the security treaty was initialled by Dulles, Spender and Berendsen later that day.

REACTION IN NEW ZEALAND

In Wellington the significance and drama of these events, which in retrospect may be seen as a landmark in New Zealand foreign policy, were rather overshadowed by the domestically more dramatic fact that the Prime Minster had, on 11 July, abruptly announced that Parliament was to be dissolved and a snap election called to test the country's support for the government's handling of the waterside workers' strike.[87] There was no debate and little comment when Doidge made his statement to the House on 13 July. He released the draft of the Japanese peace treaty and announced the initialling of the security treaty. The latter, he said, afforded New Zealand a 'firm security guarantee' and was an 'essential complement' to a 'liberal' Japanese peace treaty. New Zealand, he said, must face the fact that Japan, now 'exposed to the menace of Communist imperialism' like other free nations, should be able to contribute to her own defence.[88]

Press comment on the treaties, was on the whole, cautiously approving and more concerned with the security treaty than with the details of the Japanese peace treaty. The Christchurch *Press*, rather more enthusiastic than most, described the 'generous' treaty with Japan as 'probably the most enlightened settlement that has ever ended a war'.[89] This paper, the *New Zealand Herald* in Auckland and the *Otago Daily Times* in Dunedin all made the point that, since the New Zealand public was evidently not prepared to bear the cost of policing the terms of a 'hard' peace, New Zealand had little choice but to accept the principles outlined in the draft.[90] The tripartite pact was recognized as a concession to Australian and New Zealand misgivings and it was not, the *Otago Daily Times* assured its readers, a matter of 'selling out to the United States'.[91] The *New Zealand Herald* whose line was very cautious on the Japanese peace treaty nevertheless concluded a leading article:

> we should go with American in her effort to create a real peace with the east, not merely an armed one. This has been called 'the century of the Pacific'. It rests with us, as much as with the peoples of east Asia to determine whether the century will be Pacific in fact as well as in name.[92]

In reply to criticisms of the draft Japanese peace treaty, Doidge argued that restrictions of a permanent nature couldn't be put on Japan and that the peace treaty should be regarded as a 'treaty of reconciliation'. The danger for New Zealand he maintained, could well be not in Japanese rearmament but in the risk that Japan might refuse to rearm.[93] The *New Zealand Herald* commented cynically that a 'peace of reconcilliation' was not an exclusively philanthropic operation and that self-interest and the influence of Russian imperialism might well be seen as greater factors than alturism or faith in Japanese democracy.[94] While the government was prepared to accept the draft of the Japanese peace treaty, as time went on, a certain amount of public uneasiness about the treaty could be detected. Wellington was therefore anxious that both the peace treaty and the security treaty should be signed with the minimum delay and at about the same time.[95] Berendsen had reported in some alarm that Dulles had appeared 'uncertain and most unhappy' about initialling the security treaty in front of the television cameras in case the Senate Foreign Relations Committee might feel he was committing the United States to something without their knowledge and consent. He had warned that there was a long way to go before 'this fish' was 'in the bag'.[96] Russian attempts in August 1951 to initiate a detailed re-examination of the Japanese treaty were therefore regarded by New Zealand with the utmost concern.[97]

THE TREATIES SIGNED

In spite of the unresolved difficulties with the Russians, arrangements for the signing of both the security treaty and the Japanese treaty at meetings to be held in San Francisco from 1 to 7 September went ahead. Because the New Zealand election was to be held on 1 September it was decided that the ambassador in Washington, Sir Carl Berendsen, should sign on New Zealand's behalf. Berendsen, who had a great sense of drama and considerable flair, relished this task. Moreover the spotlight which he so enjoyed was thrown on him by the Americans who asked Berendsen to propose the adoption of Draconian rules of procedure in order to forestall any attempt by the Russians to sabotage the conference in the absence of accepted rules. The Americans were determined that the Russians should not be able to open up discussion on the peace treaty already negotiated and prevent there being the result they had planned, i.e. its acceptance by the conference. Dean Acheson, then Secretary of State, wrote later that, as Temporary President when the conference opened, he needed, 'like Horatius, two stout and reliable comrades', one to propose the rules of procedure, the other to second the motion. Berendsen and Oscar Gans, Minister of State of Cuba were the chosen ones.[98] The strategy was carefully planned. Berendsen asked for the floor immediately proceedings were opened. He then found himself in the aisle brushing shoulders with Gromyko who was intent upon reaching the podium before him. Berendsen wrote afterwards, 'I brushed better than he did, and I got there first without actually running or hurrying'.[99] Gromyko was forced to wait, the rules of procedure were adopted, and the possibility of

Russian obstruction of proceedings relating to the Japanese peace treaty was thwarted.

Berendsen generated a good deal of favourable publicity for New Zealand and himself at the conference where the circumstances combined to give him a high profile. He was a seasoned performer on radio and television, gave innumerable interviews in San Francisco and chose the time of his speech at the peace conference so that it gained the maximum television coverage nationwide.[100]

Berendsen's speeches at San Francisco reflected, as well as his own strong anti-Communist fears, New Zealand's growing effort to see itself as a Pacific nation. The security treaty he said, after signing for New Zealand, 'reflected the inescapable facts of geography on the one hand and on the other the especial perils to which the Pacific may be exposed in the course of the world-wide conflict between liberty and slavery with which the whole of mankind is today oppressed'.[101] The treaty would, he believed, 'create an area of stability' in the Pacific.

The signing of the security treaty was, however, a much more low-key affair than the meeting at which the peace treaty was signed. This began on 5 September. On this occasion Berendsen was at his most magisterial. Acknowledging that New Zealand would have welcomed some reasonable limitation of Japanese armaments his tone was, nevertheless magnanimous:

> For our part we wish the Japanese well; we have no desire to hold Japan in bondage nor reduce a proud, energetic and capable people to a status of inferiority. But geography has determined that Japan and New Zealand alike must live in the Pacific.[102]

Some of New Zealand's concern had, Berendsen admitted, been allayed by the tripartite security treaty, but in any case, he argued, taking a risk on a rearmed Japan, was preferable to leaving Japan an 'easy prey' to Communist aggression. If this was a risk, he said, 'it is a risk that we in New Zealand have taken with our eyes open as an earnest of the intention of our small country to play its part as a good neighbour in the Pacific. The onus is on Japan to fulfil this trust as we hope and believe Japan will fulfil it'.[103]

In its attitude to the making of the peace treaty and the ANZUS treaty, New Zealand seemed to be acknowledging the realities of its Pacific location and recognizing the importance of forging new relationships there after the war. The way was open for a new relationship between New Zealand and Japan. In 1951, however, there was no sense of urgency about this in New Zealand circles. For all the claims to Pacific status, New Zealand's strategic, commercial and sentimental priorities were still in Britain and Europe. Japan's potential as a trading partner had yet to be recognized or explored and she remained a distant, little-known Pacific 'neighbour' on whom lay the onus to earn New Zealand's confidence. As yet, New Zealanders did not see learning about Japan to be one of their responsibilities.

9
Establishing links

When Berendsen signed the Japanese Peace Treaty he had declared
that New Zealanders hoped and believed that Japan would fulfil the
trust being placed in her. Evidently he did not speak for all New
Zealanders. In 1952 the New Zealand Institute of International
Affairs published the pamphlet, *Must We Trust Japan?* If the eight
contributors to this pamphlet are in any way representative, it is
clear that many New Zealanders feared the worst and did not
believe Japan could or should be trusted. Democracy in Japan was
described as 'fragile', New Zealanders were reminded that their
first preoccupation in the Pacific should be their security and the
possibility of a recurrence of the Japanese threat was emphasized.
Dulles' alleged comment on his visit to Wellington in February
1951, that all Japanese were now pacifists, was dismissed sourly by
one contributor with, 'if you can believe that, you can believe
anything'.

But with the signing of the Peace Treaty New Zealand had to
face the prospect of dealing with Japan as an independent nation
and all that implied by way of the establishment of regular
diplomatic channels and commercial contacts. The formal end of
the Occupation was now a certainty. Once the treaty was ratified
by all signatories Japan could no longer be dealt with through the
structure imposed by SCAP.

New Zealand had had a man on the ground in Tokyo since May
1947. At that time R. L. G. 'Bill' Challis, an official of the
Department of Trade and Industry, had been appointed as trade
and reparations representative. New Zealand's interest in reparations was, as has been suggested, minimal, but it had been
announced that private trade with Japan would be permitted from
15 August 1947. The purpose of the United States in making this

announcement was to boost Japanese exports in order to reduce costs in Japan being borne by the United States Treasury. The development was seen as an opportunity for New Zealand, in association with Britain, to gain a foothold in Japan. There were, however, likely to be problems. New Zealand belonged to the Sterling Area a group of countries which settled their debts mainly through London. The Sterling Area arrangements were designed for the conservation of currency, in particular American dollars. As a whole the Sterling Area bought more from the United States than it sold there and, because of this dollar shortage, payments outside the Sterling Area were subjected to controls administered by the Bank of England.[2] The United States which in 1947 was in a position to control Japanese trade development was likely to insist on trade there on a dollar basis of which currency the Sterling Area was short. There were likely therefore to be problems regarding methods of exchange both in currency, currency values and in goods.

TRADE LINKS

Though the government seems to have been cautious on the issue of trade with Japan, a government-sponsored party of New Zealand business men took the opportunity to make an exploratory visit to Japan in August 1947 to discover whether goods suitable for New Zealand requirements might be available for export.[3] They returned disappointed with prospects and convinced that the United States was determined to dominate Japanese trade to the exclusion of all others. The United States, they reported, was using Japan to bolster and protect her own markets while making sure that Japan would never again compete in world trade. SCAP, they maintained, was setting prices and interpreting exchange rates to favour American traders.[4] Their impressions were not of course unfounded, furthermore New Zealand-Japan trade could be expected to be low on the agenda for both Japan and its banker, the United States.[5] There were, however, some hopes at the end of 1947 that Japan might be a market for the 'old wool' held by the Joint Organisation set up by the United Kingdom, Australian, New Zealand and South African governments' after the war to market surplus wool, but Japan had little to offer in exchange and it was not until the 1948–49 season that wool was shipped to Japan in any quantity.[6] By that time a Sterling Area Trade Agreement had been negotiated with Japan by the United Kingdom.

New Zealand-Japan trade finally became active in May 1948 and the first large purchase of wool was made in November.[7] With the prospect of continuing purchases of wool by Japan, New Zealand could expect both to be a net contributor to the Sterling Trade Area and to be able to buy more Japanese products. The £55,000,000 Sterling Area Trade Agreement signed with Japan in November provided a considerable increase in Japan's trade with the Sterling Area and was designed to avoid dollar expenditure on both sides. Under the agreement New Zealand expected to sell Japan goods to the value of $US2,500,000 – mainly wool but also hides and skins, casein and seeds – and to import textiles, oak timber and plywood to the same value.[8] This agreement was announced in the same week as the sentences at the IMFTE were pronounced in Tokyo. The irony was not lost on the leader writer at the *Otago Daily Times* who commented, 'Some may think the resumption of trade implies that Japan's treachery is being over-looked too easily and too soon ... but she must be permitted to find a livelihood for her people. This means that the resumption of foreign trade must be sanctioned, with protection against the unfair competition that marked Japan's pre-war trading'.[9] Japan's pivotal position in world trde was generally acknowledged by the government and the prospect of Japan's restoration as an economic power in the Pacific seems at that time to have been accepted in New Zealand without the hostility which became apparent in Australia.[10] In any case, in the early years the trade was heavily in New Zealand's favour. It was difficult, given the limited range of Japan's production, New Zealand's import restrictions and tariffs designed to protect New Zealand manufacturers, and an exchange rate fixed in April 1949 which undervalued the yen, to find goods to the value of the wool purchased. In 1950 therefore, Japan temporarily banned further purchases of New Zealand and Australian wool and Australian wheat claiming that the United Kingdom and its 'colonies' had failed to buy sufficient Japanese goods. The ban was to apply until Japan had Sterling in the bank to back her letters of credit.[11]

Japan's currency problems were somewhat alleviated and her industry greatly stimulated as a result of the outbreak of the war in

Korea later in 1950. Japan became a vital part of the United States effort in that war and, as an indication of Japan's increasing respectability, the question arose of her admission to the General Agreement on Tariffs and Trade (GATT), set up by the Western Allies in 1948 to ensure fairer trade practices in the post-war world. The United States pushed for Japanese membership but the countries of the Sterling Area found themselves torn. The question for them was whether it was more desirable to have Japan in GATT and thus oblige her to conform to the accepted norms of commercial behaviour even though this might oblige other members to give Japan most-favoured-nation treatment which could expose some of their industries to undesirable Japanese competition, than to risk keeping Japan out of GATT and face the possibility of unrestricted cut-throat competition and undesirable commercial practices like dumping, which had characterized Japanese trading before the war. The New Zealand government's stance was a cautious one. The prospect of Japanese competition with New Zealand's highly protected industries or with imports to New Zealand from other sources (the United Kingdom in particular), was not attractive. The margin between New Zealand's most-favoured-nation tariff and the preferential tariffs which, as a result of the 1932 Commonwealth tariff arrangements reached in Ottawa, New Zealand granted to British imports, was about 20 per cent. This it was felt would not be enough to forestall Japanese competition and could upset the trade with the United Kingdom, New Zealand's best customer. There were also domestic political implications to be feared. The strong United Kingdom manufacturers' agents in New Zealand were capable of causing political difficulties for the government[12] and it was also felt that the New Zealand public, uninterested as they had been hitherto, might be roused if the government actively supported the grant of most-favoured-nation treatment to Japan, or her admission to GATT. The Cabinet decided on the politically expedient course, of sitting on the fence and neither promoting nor actively opposing Japan's admission to GATT.[13]

In July 1952, Japan, supported by the United States, notified its wish to negotiate its accession to GATT and New Zealand was forced to take a position. When Japan was admitted to GATT in 1954, along with the United Kingdom and other Commonwealth countries except India and Ceylon, New Zealand invoked Article

35 of the GATT agreement which exempted them from granting Japan most-favoured-nation status.[14] They were thus insured for the time being, against the worst effects of possible Japanese competition.

Although in 1952 there was seen to be scope for increases in trade between New Zealand and Japan which would be 'mutually rewarding' and 'useful', Japan was not seen as a trading partner likely to be essential to New Zealand. Of New Zealand's major exports only wool was sold on the open market. The wartime Bulk Purchase Agreements under which the United Kingdom took all New Zealand surplus dairy produce and meat were still operating. In a promotional article in the Japanese press written in January 1952, Challis felt able to claim confidently that New Zealand's trading pattern with the United Kingdom was 'strong in tradition, sound in economics and tested in adversity and not likely to change greatly'.[15] Britain's entry into the European Community was not yet mooted and the bell had not yet tolled for New Zealand's farmers and exporters.

NEW ZEALAND POLITICAL REPRESENTATION IN JAPAN

While the development of trade links was not seen as a priority, the developments on the political front in Japan demanded more immediate action from the government. These had changed Challis's position in Tokyo and New Zealand's representational requirements there in general. When it was clear in 1951 that a peace treaty with Japan was soon to be signed McIntosh had urged that a diplomatic post should be set up there. The National government was reluctant to increase spending on diplomatic posts overseas and had in fact closed the New Zealand Legation in Moscow in 1950, so a good case had to be made.[16] The Japanese were, McIntosh told the Ministers of External Affairs and Industries and Commerce, 'very protocol minded' and for that reason representation by a consul who would not have political accreditation would be inadequate. He felt moreover that the United Kingom could not be asked to look after political matters for New Zealand because New Zealand's interests, 'both commercial an security', increasingly diverged from those of the United Kingdom in Japanese matters. The fact that the security agreement which

was to be signed with the United States and Australia would no
include the United Kingdom was a further reason for Nev
Zealand not depending on the United Kingdom. It would b
impossible to have the United Kingdom, which was outsid
the agreement, representing New Zealand in Japan. Anothe
possibility was to ask Australia to represent New Zealand'
interests. McIntosh dismissed this as likely to cause resentment i
the United Kingdom and too likely to give Australia, which Nev
Zealanders were wont to see in 'Big Brother' terms, a chance t
dominate in the Pacific. For all these reasons, he argued, Nev
Zealand must establish its own diplomatic post and raise Challis t
the status of minister. New Zealand would thus be in a position t
know what was happening, given there was to be a 'soft' treaty, t
watch Japan and to assess prospects for trade.[17]

There was no government reaction to McIntosh's memorandun
until September 1951, when Challis reported that since the signin;
of the peace treaty he had been unable to have any direc
contact with any officials on any matters whatsoever. SCAP ha
announced that, pending the ratification of the peace treaty
diplomatic relations would be conducted only with diplomati
missions accredited to SCAP. New Zealand was not on the lis
because Challis was a trade representative not a diplomat. Thi
meant that even the most routine matters had to go through th
United Kingdom Liaison Mission (UKLIM) where, Challis noted
the 'shades of Queen Victoria' lingered.[18] Challis urged his statu
be changed as soon as possible.[19] McIntosh agreed and hi
recommendation to the Minister that Challis become Acting Hea
of Mission and Charge d'Affaires was accepted. Cabinet decide
that when the peace treaty came into force the New Zealan
mission should become a Legation and at that time approva
should be given to the establishment of a Japanese Legation i
New Zealand.[20] SCAP approved the establishment of a Nev
Zealand mission and Challis became Head of Mission. Th
changes were announced in New Zealand on 3 January 1952.[21] I
April 1952 when the peace treaty was finally ratified and SCAI
withdrew, the New Zealand mission became a Legation an
Challis's title became Charge d'Affaires.

When in December 1951 he was informed of the Cabinet'
decision to establish a diplomatic post in Japan Challis wrote, 'It i
heartening to have this indication that the cabinet realises th

importance to our future of events in the Far East and south east Asia. It is time we grew up and accepted the fact that if we are to have the privilege of a voice and a vote in international affairs, there is some responsibility on us to keep ourselves informed'.[22]

In the immediate post-war period Fraser and Berendsen had been concerned that New Zealand should have a 'voice' in the world. But the function of a diplomatic representative is also to act as his or her country's ears and eyes and to report events from the perspective of his or her own country's interests. With representation in Japan, New Zealand could for the first time begin to build its own body of political information on that country and its own contacts in it. Furthermore the proposed establishment of a Japanese Legation in New Zealand was likely to promote New Zealand-Japan ties.[23] Two New Zealanders with Japanese language skills had been recruited by the Department of External Affairs and one of these, R. M. Miller, who had served with the BCOF in the Combined Services Detailed Interrogation Centre (CSDIC) became Second Secretary in the New Zealand Legation in 1952.[24]

Keeping the New Zealand government informed was one aspect of Challis's work as Charge d'Affaires. He also had the task of making New Zealand known in Japan. This was, and probably remains, the more daunting side of the work for, as Challis wrote, the people of New Zealand and Japan 'know too little about each other'.[25] In 1952, however, there seemed to be time to remedy this situation and New Zealand's representatives in Japan saw their primary function as political reporting and the cultivation of a political relationship. This was difficult enough. In 1950 Challis had commented, 'To work for the New Zealand government in a place such as this is first to give one a sobering realization of the relatively small role New Zealand fills in the scheme of world affairs'.[26] Of course New Zealanders knew they came from a small nation but in world forums such as the League of Nations and the United Nations the reality of this was disguised by the fact that, in adopting a high moral tone, New Zealand saw itself in a leadership role, as a small nation speaking out impartially on the issues of the day and trying to keep the bigger powers honest. It was in this role that New Zealand took its stand against the League of Nations appeasement' and general lack of backbone over the crises in Abyssinia, Spain and China in the late 1930s;[27] it was in this role that Berendsen, for example, as New Zealand's representative,

with fine disregard for Great Power status, declared he would not
be admonished by the American chairman of the FEC. Furthermore as a Commonwealth member, New Zealand saw itself as part
of an influential team, a team moreover in which the opinions of
the 'old white Dominions' carried weight. If a New Zealand
representative like Berendsen appeared less deferential than
might have been expected of a representative from a small and
distant country, and if New Zealand policy appeared to inhabit 'an
idealistic world, a little detached from harsh diplomatic realities',[28]
this background helps explain why.

During the war New Zealand had established diplomatic posts
with allies in Washington, Canberra and Moscow. In 1949 a post
had been opened in Paris, France being not simply a former ally
but also a south Pacific power. In 1950, after the government
in New Zealand changed and as the international situation deter-
iorated, the post in Moscow was closed. The basis on which New
Zealand's sparse diplomatic network had been built before 1951
was therefore quite straightforward.

The post which was now being opened in Japan, however
opened on a different basis from any previously established by
New Zealand. Japan had very recently been an enemy. New
Zealand had no cultural or comradely links, no trading relationships of value and long-standing, and no links of old friendship
with her. New Zealand had no constituency in Japan

New Zealand diplomacy therefore faced a new kind of challenge
Japan had many fences to mend and new trading patterns to establish
but in this process New Zealand and the south Pacific had at best a
very low priority. The United States was the main focus of
Japanese diplomatic and commercial interest and given Japan's
preoccupation with reconstruction, and the United States preoccupation with the Korean war and the intensifying Cold War, hard
work by New Zealanders would be required if New Zealand was to
make any impression on the Japanese government at all. In Japan
New Zealand, fighter for small nation's rights, with or without the
Commonwealth connection, could expect to count for little.

The forging of ties with Japan therefore was likely to be more
difficult diplomatic work than any undertaken so far by New
Zealand's small Department of External Affairs. The prospect
was not too discouraging in 1952 partly because New Zealand's
diplomatic priorities were still elsewhere. Relations with Britain

and the United States and membership of the Commonwealth and
the United Nations were matters of primary concern. This meant
in practice that the New Zealand representatives in Japan were
seen as having a watching brief. They were seen as being in Japan
to check on the operation of the Peace Treaty and the development of 'democratic tendencies' there. There was no pressure
from Wellington in 1952 or thereafter in the 1950s for the very
active promotion of the New Zealand-Japan relationship in Japan.
In 1952 New Zealand was in the happy, if insecurely-based
position, of believing Japan needed New Zealand more than New
Zealand needed Japan. Good relations were expected to develop
slowly and, far from being pressured to promote New Zealand's
interests in and understanding of Japan, New Zealand diplomats
there often had the feeling that Wellington was little interested in
their work or developments in Japan.[29]

NEW ZEALAND AND JAPAN IN 1952

Both American and British historians have commented on the lack
of interest among the public of those countries towards post-war
Japan.[30] Similarly there had been no sustained interest in the
Occupation or the treaty-making in New Zealand. It is doubtful
whether New Zealanders' view of Japan was much more positive
or much better informed in 1952 after the Occupation than it had
been in 1945. It is true that several thousand New Zealanders had
now served in Japan in the BCOF but neither New Zealand nor
any other participant in the BCOF contributed much to the
Occupation of Japan and, if the press is any guide, public interest
in Japan was little higher in consequence. Nor had the FEC,
of which New Zealand had initially high hopes, been able to
influence the Occupation or events in Japan. The fact of New
Zealand's representation in this organization did not therefore
become a means of publicizing in New Zealand post-war progress
in the rehabilitation and development of Japan. New Zealanders
had made a very positive contribution to the work of the IMTFE
but the New Zealand public had shown little interest in the
Tribunal and its work.

Nor, in spite of ANZUS, could the public generally be described
as more 'Pacific minded' and in 1951 MacArthur complained,

no doubt not disinterestedly, to Challis, that neither the Australian nor the New Zealand governments was sufficiently Pacific minded.[31] Pacific minded or not, however, Pacific considerations were now entering foreign policy in a new way. In 1951 when MacArthur made his comment, the New Zealand government had already sent men and ships to support United Nations forces in Korea. New Zealand's response to the Korean situation arose not simply out of a desire to support the principle of collective security but was in part a response to the call of the United States with which it wished to 'show solidarity'. To that extent there was somthing of a new element in this foreign policy decision. As a Pacific power, New Zealand had to be concerned for the good opinion of the United States, the dominant power in the Pacific.

Although in 1952 the New Zealand government and the New Zealand public still gave priority to the British and Commonwealth connection, the realities of power in the post-war Pacific world which had led Australia and New Zealand to press for an alliance with the United States to confirm their security from a possible resurgence of Japanese militarism, were such as bring about a change in those priorities in the long run. Officially, New Zealand's defence priorities remained in the Middle East but the talk after 1952 of New Zealand's primary defence contribution being in the Middle East is, in retrospect, scarcely credible unless the British training of New Zealand's senior officers and the mindset of New Zealand's senior politicians is taken into account. In the next decade the drama of the Suez crisis, instability in Southeast Asia, British gradual withdrawal from that area and the British decision to join the European Community forced New Zealanders to recognize the realities of power in the Pacific world which in fact the Japanese peace settlement and ANZUS, which was historically part of that settlement, represented.

After 1947, there was no Commonwealth solidarity on the issue of the Japanese peace treaty, and the debates only served to illustrate the growing divergence between the United Kingdom's interests in the Pacific and Asia and those of New Zealand and Australia. The historian of British Occupation diplomacy has suggested that the Occupation years can be seen in retrospect as the last opportunity to arrest a growing British feebleness in the region.[32] New Zealand recognized this growing feebleness only reluctantly but had accepted by 1950 that in their view of Japan and their security requrirements in the Pacific, New Zealand and Australia were on their own. The reality of this divergence of interests forced New Zealand to stick to an independent line although, with Australia, New Zealand was informed 'convincingly' by the United Kingdom, that their fears of Japan as the main potential aggressor in the Pacific were outdated'.[33]

By reiterating at all times its specifically south Pacific view of Japan as a potential threat to security, New Zealand had, with Australia, emphasized in an international context, an identity and interests which were separate and different from those of the United Kingdom. Indeed the establishment of a New Zealand Legation in Japan implied an acknowledgement of a growing divergence of interests with the United Kingdom. As a distinct New Zealand view emerged in matters relating to Japan, confusion in the minds of Americans and others about the nature of the Commonwealth relationship became less relevant. Besides, that relationship was changing as the Commonwealth became more diverse after 1947. New Zealand, as one of the 'old white Dominions', could expect to be less influential in this increasingly multi-racial grouping and in any case, as one of the 'old white Dominions', New Zealand saw the enlarged team as a less significant team in world affairs.

The Occupation and the peace treaty were essentially 'American shows' and New Zealand's part in the drama was very small. All the same it can be argued that against all probability, the small powers, New Zealand and Australia, had made their voices heard and, by holding the line in the matter of their security concerns about Japan had forced the Americans to look south when making policy choices. This alone was something of a triumph for their diplomacy. For all its vague wording and reference to 'constitutional processess'[34] the security treaty between Australia, New Zealand and the United States in 1951 represented American underwriting of New Zealand and Australian security at that time and, although it evoked little public interest then, should surely be regarded as a significant product of the early post-war diplomacy of New Zealand and Australia.

A New Zealand relationship of any significance with Japan itself had yet to be forged in 1952. But New Zealand and Japan now had an ally in common, the United States, under whose security umbrella in the Pacific, both might expect to shelter. From the point of view of the Japanese this was a more important link between them than it was for New Zealand. New Zealand politicians and the New Zealand public, relatively unsophisticated in matters of foreign relations, were unaccustomed to making connections between their relationship with one country and its connection with another. But to the Japanese in 1952, as in the years since 1952, their relationship with the United States was more important than any other. Broadly speaking, a good friend and ally of the United States, one of whom the United States indicated approval, could expect to be regarded as a good friend by Japan. Moreover the Japanese were disposed to notice the extent to which America's allies and friends cultivated and valued their relationship with the United States. This reality, which was constantly reiterated by New Zealand ministers and ambassadors when New Zealand came to try to cultivate closer relationship with Japan from the 1960s, had yet to be learned by New Zealand.[35] Meantime, in 1952, having obtained, through the security treaty, protection from possible Japanese aggression and having established a watching post in and commercial connection with Japan, New Zealanders expected, and found, their relationship with that country to be, if not close, cordial. Progress had been made, the groundwork for future development had been laid. It was in fact a far cry from the situation in 1945.

Notes

INTRODUCTION

1 See F. L. W. Wood, 'The Anzac Dilemma', *International Affairs* (1953) XXIX. p. 183 and F. L. W. Wood, *This New Zealand*, Hamilton, 1952, pp. 152–61.
2 See Robin Kay (ed.), *Documents on New Zealand External Relations Volume II: The Surrender and Occupation of Japan* Wellington, 1982, No. 1 p. 3.
3 See Robin Kay (ed.), *Documents on New Zealand External Relations Volume III: The ANZUS pact and the Treaty of Peace with Japan* Wellington, 1985, No. 1, pp. 3–4.
4 Roger Buckley, *Occupation Diplomacy*, Cambridge, 1982, p. 1.

CHAPTER 1

1 Keith Sinclair, *A Destiny Apart: New Zealand's Search for a National Identity*, Wellington 1986, p. 107.
2 F. L. W. Wood, *New Zealand in the World*, Wellington, 1940, p. 110.
3 See Angus Ross, *New Zealand Aspirations in the Pacific*, Oxford 1964, pp. 4–9.
4 Ross, above, pp. 234–44, 252–70.
5 Ross, above, p. 267.
6 See J. W. Davidson, *Samoa mo Samoa: the Emergence of the Independent State of Western Samoa*, Oxford 1967, pp. 97–8.
7 See W. David McIntyre, *New Zealand Prepares for War*, Christchurch, 1988, pp. 14–26.
8 Sinclair, *A Destiny Apart*, p. 251.
9 *The Press* (Christchurch), 23 October 1941.
10 *Auckland Star*, 31 January 1942.
11 This correspondent was H. G. W. Woodhead, a long-time resident of China, founder and editor of the *China Yearbook*, editor of the

Peking and Tientsin Times who was subsequently interned by the Japanese.

12 See James Bertram, *The Shadow of a War*, London 1947, p. 66–7, and *NZ Listener* 16 November 1945, pp. 9–10. See also *Evening Post* (Wellington), 22 October 1940, report of speech by Frank Milner to British-American Cooperative Movement, NZ Section.

13 Sir Carl Berendsen, 'Memoirs' (unpublished, in possession of the family), Book II, Chapter XIX.

14 *The Press*, 11 May 1942.

15 *Round Table* (London) (1942), XXX, p. 95

16 See H. Witheford, 'War Narrative: Censorship of the Press', NZ National Archives, WA II/21.

17 *The Press,* 6 April 1942.

18 *The Auckland Star*, 31 October 1942.

19 New Zealand Army Board, *Pacific Story: A Survey of the early history of the Third New Zealand Division*, Wellington, 1945 p. 27.

20 Oliver O. Gillespie, *The Pacific: New Zealand in the Second World War*, Wellington, 1952, p. 324; McIntyre, *New Zealand Prepares for War*, p. 252.

21 J. M. S. Ross, *Royal New Zealand Airforce*, Wellington, 1955, p. 134; Geoffrey Bentley, *RNZAF, A Short Story*, Wellington, 1969, p 97–139; Charles Darby, *RNZAF; The First Decade*, Melbourne, 1978, p. 5–7; Kenneth R. Hancock, *New Zealand at War*, Wellington, 1946, p. 142.

22 Sir Harry Batterbee (UKHC to NZ) to Secretary of State, 22 February 1944, PRO, DO 35/1119 G5801.

23 *Round Table*, (1944) XXXIV, 179–84.

24 *NZ Listener*, 11 August 1944, pp. 12–13.

25 *NZ Listener*, 21 September 1945, p. 5.

26 Batterbee to Dominions Office, 26 September 1945, PRO, DO 35/2011.

27 Dominions Office note to Sir John Stephenson, 25 January 1944, PRO, DO 35/1214.

28 Wood, *New Zealand in the World*, p. 110.

29 *Census New Zealand* 1936, Wellington, 1945, 'Race', vol. X p. 1. The census in 1945 recorded 11 full blooded Japanese and 12 of mixed race. See *Census New Zealand* 1945, 'Race', vol. VIII p. 1.

30 See Ian F. G. Milner, *New Zealand's Interests and Policies in the Far East*, New York, 1940, pp. 57–76 for a more detailed discussion of pre war economic relations.

31 *Statistical Report on Trade and Shipping of the Dominion of New Zealand 1942*, Part 2, Wellington, 1946, p. 7.

32 See P. S. O'Connor, 'Keeping New Zealand White 1908–1920' *NZ Journal of History*, (1968) II. 41–65.

33 Quoted in Richard Thompson, *Race Relations in New Zealand* Christchurch, 1963, p. 15.

34 Quoted by O'Connor, 'Keeping New Zealand White' p. 58. The words are those of P. H. Hickey.

35 Barry Gustafson, *From the Cradle to the Grave*, Auckland, 1986, pp. 117–18.

36 Bruce S. Bennett, *New Zealand's Moral Foreign Policy 1935–1939*, Wellington, 1988, pp. 57–64; M. P. Lissington, *New Zealand and Japan 1900–1941*, Wellington, 1972, pp. 93–110.

37 See Christopher Thorne, 'Racial Aspects of the Far Eastern War of 1941–1945', *Proceedings of the British Academy*, (1980) LXVI. 342ff. for a discussion of this type of development.

38 See Thorne, above p. 332. The issue of racism and the response of societies to the Far Eastern war 1941–1945 is dealt with in detail in Christopher Thorne, *The Issue of War: States, Societies and the Far Eastern Conflict of 1941–1945*, London, 1985.

39 *NZ Listener* 2 April 1942, p. 7. The rules of thumb were quoted from *Time* and the *Listener* warned readers that they were not always reliable; there was no infallible way of telling the Japanese and Chinese apart.

40 *NZ Listener*, 10 December 1943, pp. 4–6.

41 Nancy M. Taylor, *The New Zealand People at War: The Home Front*, Wellington, 1986 vol. I pp. 344–6.

42 *Auckland Star*, 12 March 1942; see also Taylor, above, p. 346.

43 *Standard* (Wellington), 7 May 1942.

44 *NZ Listener* 13 April 1945. p. 7.

45 Quoted by Thorne, *Issue of War* p. 129 from I. Mclaine, *Ministry of Morale; Home Front Morale and the Ministry of Information in World War II*, London, 1979, pp. 158–9.

46 'Memorandum on Australia-New Zealand Cooperation', Sir Carl Berendsen, 10 December 1943. Sir Alister McIntosh-Sir Carl Berendsen correspondence held in Ministry of Foreign Affairs. Correspondence used by permission.

47 Robin Kay (ed.), *Documents on New Zealand External Relations Volume I. The Australian New Zealand Agreement 1944*, Wellington, 1972, Nos. 32–40, pp. 41–53.

48 W. J. Hudson and H. J. W. Stokes (eds), *Documents on Australian Foreign Policy*, Canberra, 1983 Vol. VI, p. 614 fn. 1.

49 McIntosh to Berendsen, 21 December 1944.

50 McIntosh to Berendsen, 21 December 1944; McIntosh to Berendsen, 29 May 1950.

51 Kay, *Documents 1*, No. 43, pp. 65–73, No. 53, pp. 140–8, No. 57, pp. 151–6.

52 Dominions Office note to Sir J. Stephenson, 25 January 1944, PRO DO 35/1214.

53 'Australian-New Zealand Agreement', Memorandum by the Secretary of State for Dominion Affairs, 2 February 1944, PRO, DO 35/1989.

54 McIntosh to Berendsen 16 February 1944. For the British reply, 12 February 1944 see Kay, *Documents I*, No. 58, pp. 156–9.

55 Kay, *Documents I*, Appendices 8 & 9 pp. 273–7.

56 Berendsen to McIntosh, 21 February 1944.

57 See *New Zealand Foreign Policy: Statements and Documents 1943–5* (hereafter cited as *NZ Statements and Documents*), Wellington, 197. No. 7, pp. 81–6.
58 Berendsen, 'Memoirs', Book III, Chapter I.
59 'Memorandum', Sir Carl Berendsen, 10 December 1943, McIntosh t Berendsen, 20 December 1943.
60 Robin Kay (ed.), *Documents on New Zealand External Relations, Vo III: The Anzus Pact and the Treaty of Peace with Japan*, Wellingto 1985, No. 94, p. 267.
61 Kay, *Documents III*, No. 163, p. 477.
62 Kay, *Documents I*, No. 91, p. 214.
63 *NZ Statements and Documents*, No. 5, p. 71.
64 McIntosh to Berendsen, 18 November 1949.
65 Kay, *Documents II*, No. 6 pp. 11–13; Roger Bell, 'Australiar American Disagreement over the Peace Settlement with Japan, 1944 1946' *Australian Outlook*, (1976) XXX p. 247.
66 Kay, *Documents II*, Nos. 12, 13, p. 27.
67 Kay, *Documents II*, No. 32 pp. 50–1; also No. 9, pp. 18–21, No. 1 p. 28.
68 Kay, *Documents II*, No. 35 p. 54; Nos. 38 and 39 pp. 56–7.
69 Bell, 'Australian-American Disagreement over the Peace Settlemer with Japan', pp. 248–51; Kay, *Documents II*, No. 43, p. 63; Nos. 50–2 pp. 74–7; No. 69, p. 98 fn. 3, No. 70, p. 102 fn. 3.
70 *NZ Statements and Documents*, No. 5, pp. 77–8.
71 This subject is dealt with more fully by W. D. McIntyre, 'Pet Fraser's Commonwealth', in NZ Institute of International Affair *New Zealand in World Affairs*, vol. I, Wellington, 1977, pp. 48–55.
72 Fraser to Evatt (draft telegram), 23 April 1947, NZ National Archive EA 102/9/3. See also McIntyre, 'Peter Fraser's Commonwealth' pr 49–50.
73 Summary of remarks by Dr Evatt, 23 December 1945, NZ Ministry c Foreign Affairs Archives, 268/9/9 Pt. 1.
74 McIntosh to Berendsen, 21 December 1944.
75 See Bell, 'Australian-American Disagreement over the Peace Settle ment with Japan' p. 240.
76 Fraser to Evatt, draft telegram, 23 April 1947.
77 A. W. Snelling to the Right Hon. Viscount Addison, 31 August 194 PRO DO 35/3761.
78 Snelling to Addison, above.
79 Snelling to Hon. F. E. Cumming Bruce, 13 May 1949, PRO DO 35/279 {
80 Hon. F. E. Cumming Bruce to Snelling, 13 June 1949, PRO DO 3: 2798.
81 Berendsen, 'Memoirs', section on 'Personalities: Fraser'. They di not always agree. See fn.87 below.
82 This fact accounts for the great consistency of the New Zealand stanc in these bodies despite the fact that the government changed thre times in the period. Professor Angus Ross, Department of History University of Otago, commented on this consistency when interviewin

Berendsen. Berendsen said, 'The same hand wrote the speeches. I wrote them'. Interview with Emeritus Professor Angus Ross, Dunedin, October 1985.

3 Berendsen to Campbell, 1 February 1938, NZ National Archives EA 264/2/7 pt 13.

4 Interviews with Messrs Frank Corner, Charles Craw, Sir George Laking, Tom Larkin, James Weir, October 1985. Berendsen said if a thing was fifty-one per cent white and forty-nine per cent black, it was white!

5 Snelling to Addison, 13 May 1949.

6 Snelling to Cumming Bruce 13 May 1949.

7 Berendsen, 'Memoirs': Book II 1929–1944. McIntosh is reputed to have said at the time that he was afraid Berendsen would kill the Prime Minister.

8 See Malcolm Templeton, 'Notes on the Development of the Prime Minister's Department', 1946, NZ National Archives WAII 21/47B. A list drawn up for the author by Malcolm Templeton contained 15 names including some clerical staff. Templeton to author, 11 April 1988.

9 Alister McIntosh, 'The Origins of the Department of External Affairs', NZ Institute of International Affairs, *New Zealand in World Affairs* vol. I, Wellington, 1977, pp. 12–21; Sir Alister McIntosh, 'Working with Peter Fraser in Wartime' *NZ Journal of History* (1976) X. 2–4; Templeton, 'Notes on the Development of the Prime Minister's Department', 1946.

10 Snelling to Addison 31 August 1949.

11 Gordon Daniels, 'New Zealand and Occupied Japan, 1945–48', in Ian Nish (ed.), *The British Commonwealth and the Occupation of Japan*, London, 1983.

CHAPTER 2

1 *Documents II*, No. 106, pp. 155–7; Roger Buckley, *Occupation Diplomacy*, Cambridge 1982, p. 71.

2 Kay, *Documents II*, No. 204, p. 402.

3 Berendsen, 'Memoirs', Chapter V; Kay, *Documents II*, No. 177, pp. 295–314.

4 Interview with Sir Guy Powles, Wellington, October 1985. Powles had been active in the Labour Party before the war. Sir Guy Richardson Powles, KBE CMG, ED; Born NZ 5 April 1905; First Secretary and Counsellor NZ Legation and Embassy, Washington, 1946–8; High Commissioner in Western Samoa, 1949–60, in India, 1960–2, in Ceylon, 1961–2; Ambassador to Nepal, 1961–2, Ombudsman (Parliamentary Commissioner for Investigations), 1962–75; Chief Ombudsman, 1975–7.

5 Kay, *Documents II*, No. 114, p. 165–6; No. 125, pp. 210–11; Nos. 173–6, pp. 288–91; George Blakeslee, *The Far Eastern Commission*, Department of State publication 5138, Washington, 1953, pp. 12–15.

6 Kay, *Documents II*, No. 580, p. 1358. Broadcast by Walter Nash.
7 On Berendsen's skill as a draftsman see Alister McIntosh, 'The Origins of the Department', in NZ Institute of International Affairs *New Zealand in World Affairs* Vol. I pp. 21–2; Blakeslee, *The Far East Commission*, p. 16.
8 Kay, *Documents II*, No. 136, p. 225; No. 140, p. 234–5; No. 157, pp 262–4; Buckley, *Occupation Diplomacy*, p. 73.
9 Kay, *Documents II*, No. 145, pp. 246–7; No. 215, pp. 453–4.
10 Kay, *Documents II*, No. 136, p. 226.
11 Kay, *Documents II*, No. 140, p. 237.
12 Kay, *Documents II*, No. 146, p. 249.
13 Blakeslee, *The Far East Commission*, p. 16.
14 See Berendsen on this, Kay, *Documents II*, No. 314, p. 720.
15 Kay, *Documents II*, No. 145, p. 247.
16 Blakeslee, *The Far East Commission*, p. 32.
17 Kay, *Documents II*, No. 158, p. 265.
18 Kay, *Documents II*, No. 177, p. 308.
19 Kay, *Documents II*, No. 180, pp. 330–1; Interview with C. Craw Wellington, October 1986.
20 See Blakeslee, *The Far East Commission*, pp. 194–211; Kay, *Documents II*, No. 318 pp. 724–34 for Basic Post-Surrender Policy for Japan.
21 Blakeslee, *The Far East Commission*, p. 34; Kay, *Documents II*, No 179, p. 328.
22 Kay, *Documents II*, No. 181, p. 333–4.
23 Kay, *Documents II*, No. 181, p. 333; No. 186, p. 343; No. 206, fn. 3 p 418–19.
24 Blakeslee, *The Far East Commission*, p. 48–58; Kay, *Documents II*, No. 197, pp. 376–9; No. 214 pp. 442–6.
25 Kay, *Documents II*, No. 231, p. 492.
26 Blakeslee, *The Far East Commission*, p. 58.
27 Blakeslee, above, pp. 59–65.
28 *Documents II*, No. 196, pp. 371–3.
29 Kay, *Documents II*, No. 274, pp. 628–9.
30 Blakeslee, *The Far East Commission*, pp. 175–82.
31 Kay, *Documents II*, No. 348, p. 822, p. 824 fn. 1; No. 349, pp 825–9.
32 Kay, *Documents II*, No. 221, p. 467; No. 223, p. 470; Blakeslee, *The Far East Commission*, above, p. 105–7.
33 Kay, *Documents II*, No. 234, pp. 506–9.
34 Kay, *Documents II*, No. 289, p. 665.
35 Kay, *Documents II*, No. 295, pp. 680–1.
36 Blakeslee, *The Far East Commission*, p. 111.
37 Kay, *Documents II*, No. 304, p. 701–3; No. 306, p. 709; No. 325 pp. 746–7.
38 Kay, *Documents II*, No. 360, p. 857; No. 374, p. 902; No. 456 and 457 pp. 1137–9.
39 Kay, *Documents II*, No. 373, pp. 900–1.

40 Berendsen to McIntosh, 22 September 1947, Berendsen, 'Memoirs', Book III 1944–1952, Chapter V.
41 Kay, *Documents II*, No. 206, p. 417; No. 210, p. 429.
42 Berendsen to McIntosh, 4 June 1946.
43 Berendsen to McIntosh, 27 June 1947.
44 Berendsen to McIntosh, 27 June 1947, above; Kay, *Documents II*, No. 205, pp. 409–11, No. 263, pp. 599–600, No. 266, p. 607.
45 Kay, *Documents II*, No. 332, p. 777.
46 Kay, *Documents II*, No. 228, p. 487; No. 231, p. 498; See Buckley, *Occupation for Diplomacy*, p. 76 for other criticisms of McCoy.
47 See Berendsen, 'Memoirs', Book III, 1944–1952, Chap. XVI.
48 Kay, *Documents II*, No. 231, pp. 495–8.
49 Kay, *Documents II*, No. 269, p. 619.
50 For a detailed account see George Blakeslee, 'Negotiating to Establish the Far Eastern Commission' in R. Dennett and J. E. Johnson (eds), *Negotiating with the Russians*, Boston 1951; See also Kay, *Documents II*, Part II, 'The Machinery of Control' pp. 229–90.
51 Kay, *Documents II*, No. 464, p. 1155.
52 Kay, *Documents II*, No. 170 p. 283–4.
53 Kay, *Documents II*, No. 149, p. 253; No. 159, p. 266; No. 163, p. 271–2.
54 Alan Rix (ed.), *Intermittent Diplomat: The Japan and Batavia Diaries of W. Macmahon Ball*, Melbourne, 1988, pp. 7–9; Buckley *Occupation Diplomacy*, pp. 80–1; Bevin to Addison, 26 January 1946, PRO DO 35/2038, UK Liaison Mission to Foreign Office, 27 February 1946, PRO DO 35/2038.
55 Kay, *Documents II*, No. 470, pp. 1159–61.
56 Rix, *Intermittent Diplomat*, p. 13, pp. 65–9, 75 (and note), 78–9; Buckley, *Occupation Diplomacy*, p. 83; Kay, *Documents II*, No. 482, pp. 1184–7.
57 Rix, above, pp. 12–13, 231–4.
58 See for example Kay, *Documents II*, No. 496, p. 1221.
59 Kay, *Documents II*, No. 507 p. 1244.
60 Buckley, *Occupation Diplomacy*, p. 81.
61 Kay, *Documents II*, No. 471, p. 1162.
62 J. V. Wilson, 'Memo for Mr McIntosh', 18 April 1946, NZ National Archives EA 268/9/4.
63 Kay, *Documents II*, No. 473, p. 1164.
64 , See Wilson, 'Memo for Mr McIntosh', for draft; Kay, *Documents II*, No. 474, p. 1165.
65 Kay, *Documents II*, Nos. 507–10, pp. 1244–9.
66 Kay, *Documents II*, No. 513, pp. 2151–2. Harold Evans, Associate to the New Zealand judge at the IMTFE described a meeting of the ACJ.
67 Kay, *Documents II*, No. 514, p. 1252.
68 McIntosh to Challis, 21 September 1949, NZ National Archives EA 268/9/4.

CHAPTER 3

1 Buckley, *Occupation Diplomacy*, p. 86.
2 *Official History of New Zealand in the Second World War 1939–1945: Documents Relating to New Zealand's Participation*, Wellington 1963, Vol. III No. 442, p. 465.
3 Above, No. 458, pp. 488–9. Nos. 442–58 cover the discussion of the problem before the war in Europe ended.
4 *Official History* III, No. 459, pp. 489–90, No. 468, pp. 499–502; Buckley, *Occupation Diplomacy*, p. 87.
5 *Official History* III, No. 459, p. 490.
6 *Official History* III, No. 464, pp. 494–5.
7 *Official History* III, No. 476, pp. 510–11.
8 Kay, *Documents II*, No. 523, pp. 1264–5.
9 Kay, *Documents II*, No. 524, p. 1266.
10 Kay, *Documents II*, p. 1268 fn 3; *Official History* III, No. 445, p. 469. Those who had served in the 3rd NZ Division would qualify for replacement before the rest of their draft and this was seen as likely to cause some logistical problems.
11 *Official History* III, No. 482, p. 514.
12 Kay, *Documents II*, Nos. 527 and 528, pp. 1269–70.
13 Kay, *Documents II*, No. 529, p. 1271 and fn. 1.
14 Kay, *Documents II*, No. 534, pp. 1275–8.
15 Kay, *Documents II*, No. 537, p. 1280 and fn 3; *Otago Daily Times* (Dunedin) 15 November 1945, 4 January 1946, 9 January 1946.
16 Kay, *Documents II*, Nos. 531–3, pp. 1272–5; Buckley, *Occupation Diplomacy*, p. 89.
17 Kay, *Documents II*, No. 540, pp. 1282–4.
18 Kay, *Documents II*, No. 540, pp. 1282–4, No. 544 pp. 1291–3, No. 546, p. 1295, No. 550 p. 1299.
19 Kay, *Documents II*, No. 542, pp. 1285–8.
20 *Dominion* (Wellington), 1 October 1945.
21 Kay, *Documents II*, No. 543, pp. 1289–90.
22 R. Singh, *Official History of the Indian Armed Forces in the Second World War, 1939–1945: post-war occupation forces: Japan and South-East Asia*, Kanpur 1958 p. 14: Buckley, *Occupation Diplomacy*, p. 88.
23 Kay, *Documents II*, No. 551, pp. 1300–2.
24 Kay, *Documents II*, Nos. 557 and 558, pp. 1309–12.
25 Kay, *Documents II*, No. 561, p. 1319.
26 Kay, *Documents II*, Nos. 559 and 560, pp. 1312–17.
27 Kay, *Documents II*, No. 562, pp. 1320–1, No. 566, pp. 1328–35.
28 Kay, *Documents II*, No. 563, pp. 1322–3. This scepticism was shared in informed British circles. See Buckley, *Occupation Diplomacy*, p. 90.
29 Kay, *Documents II*, Nos. 568–71, pp. 1337–40, No. 574, pp. 1347–8; *Otago Daily Times*, 4 February 1946.
30 See Singh, *Official History of the Indian Armed Forces*, p. 23.
31 Kay, *Documents II*, No. 542, p. 1287.
32 *Dominion* 1 October 1945.

33 Kay, *Documents II*, No. 580, pp. 1357–61.
34 Kay, *Documents II*, No. 581, pp. 1361–4.
35 Kay, *Documents II* No. 572, pp. 1341–6.
36 Kay, *Documents II*, Nos. 580 and 581, pp. 1357–64.
37 Kay, *Documents II*, No. 592, p. 1385; Singh, *Official History of The Indian Armed Forces*, pp. 19–20.
38 Singh, above, pp. 47–48.
39 Kay, *Documents II*, No. 592, p. 1387.
40 *NZ Parliamentary Debates* vol. 276, pp. 318–19.
41 Interview with M. Findlater, August 1988; Interview with C. Irwin, January 1989.
42 Historical Narrative of 2NZEF October 1945–March 1946, NZ National Archives WA-J 67/3 Box 113; HQ BCOF Staff Course 10 August 1946, WA-J 67/11 Box 113.
43 War Diary 2NZEF (Japan) March 1946, NZ National Archives WA-J 1/5 Box 1. At one stage on the voyage there were 227 patients in hospital, 87 of them with measles. 119 patients were discharged at Singapore because of the limited hospital accommodation available in Japan.
44 See Frank Rennie, *Regular Soldier*, Auckland 1986, pp. 97–8.
45 Kay, *Documents II* No. 591, p. 1388.
46 Interview with C. Irwin, January 1989. Evidence to Board of Enquiry, NZ National Archives WA-J 67/16 Box 113.
47 Kay, *Documents II*, No. 591, p. 1395; Historical Narrative of 2NZEF October 1945–March 1946, NZ National Archives WA-J 67/3 Box 113; Interview with C. Irwin, January 1989.
48 Kay, *Documents II*, No. 591, p. 1397, No. 600, p. 1420, No. 614, p. 1449.
49 Kay, *Documents II*, No. 600, p. 1417; Evidence to Board of Enquiry, NZ National Archives WA-J 67/16 Box 113; Interview C. Irwin; Rennie, *Regular Soldier*, pp. 98–99.
50 *Otago Daily Times*, 4 April 1946, 12 June 1946.
51 'Home was never like this' (Journal prepared by NZAES), undated NZ National Archives WA-J 75/3 Box 129.
52 Kay, *Documents II*, No. 583, pp. 1366–7, No. 585, pp. 1368–9.
53 See Rennie, *Regular Soldier*, p. 101.
54 Kay, *Documents II*, No. 591, p. 1379.
55 R. Cunninghame, Memo for Mr Wilson, no date August 1946, NZ National Archives, EA 87/11/16. Cunninghame had been in the RNZ Navy during the war where he was one of those who learned Japanese in preparation for the expected invasion of Japan. He was a member of the NZ FEAC delegation to Japan in January 1946 and joined the Department of External Affairs thereafter.
56 Kay, *Documents II*, No. 589, pp. 1375–6.
57 Kay, *Documents II*, No. 590, pp. 1376–8, No. 600, p. 1423.
58 Kay, *Documents II*, No. 600, p. 1423.
59 Kay, *Documents II*, No. 581, p. 1362.
60 See Bryan Cox, *Too Young to Die*, Auckland 1987. p. 250.

61 Kay, *Documents II*, No. 591, p. 1388.
62 Kay, *Documents II*, No. 579, p. 1355, No. 596, 1407–9.
63 Rennie, *Regular Soldier*, p. 99.
64 Kay, *Documents II*, No. 621, p. 1457.
65 Ian Nish, Britain and the Occupation of Japan – Some Personal Recollections' in Gordon Daniels (ed.), *Proceedings of the British Association of Japanese Studies*, Sheffield, 1979, pp. 150–9; Interview with R. Miller, Wellington, February 1989.
66 Kay, *Documents II*, No. 600, p. 1418.
67 Documents II, No. 676, p. 1595; Ronald Henry Quilliam 'Diary', unpublished, in possession of the family) 21 October 1946.
68 Singh, *Official History of The Indian Armed Forces*, p. 36.
69 Kay, *Documents II*, No. 589, p. 1375.
70 Kay, *Documents II*, No. 606, p. 1435.
71 Kay, *Documents II*, No. 540, pp. 1282–4; Singh, *Official History of The Indian Armed Forces*, pp. 35–40.
72 Kay, *Documents II*, No. 592, p. 1394; Buckley, *Occupation Diplomacy*, p. 93.
73 Kay, *Documents II*, No. 587, p. 1372, No. 587, p. 1394. Lieutenant-General Sir Leonard Thornton was Commander, BC Sub-Area Tokyo briefly in 1946.
74 Kay, *Documents II*, No. 552, pp. 1302–4.
75 Kay, *Documents II*, No. 587, p. 1370, No. 599, p. 1411.
76 Kay, *Documents II*, No. 599, p. 1411.
77 Kay, *Documents II*, No. 587, p. 1374 fn. 7.
78 Kay, *Documents II*, No. 592, p. 1394.
79 Kay, *Documents II*, No. 600, p. 1421.
80 Kay, *Documents II*, No. 552, p. 1304 fn. 1, No. 596 p. 1406–9.
81 Singh, above *Official History of The Indian Armed Forces*, pp. 51–5.
82 Kay, *Documents II*, No. 635, p. 1473–4.
83 Kay, *Documents II*, Nos. 601–3 pp. 1427–32.
84 Kay, *Documents IIDominion*, 7 and 8 February 1947.
85 See Buckley, *Occupation Diplomacy*, p. 100 fn. 59.
86 *Dominion* 7 February 1947, 27 March 1947, *Star Sun* (Christchurch), 15 April 1947, *Evening Post*, 2 May 1947.
87 Kay, *Documents II*, No. 608, pp. 1439–40, No. 610, p. 1442.
88 Kay, *Documents II*, No. 608, p. 1440.
89 *Dominion*, 7 February 1947.
90 *Kay, Documents II*, No. 609, p. 1440–1.
91 Kay, *Documents II* No. 613, pp. 1446–7.
92 Kay, *Documents II*, No. 615, p. 1449.
93 Kay, *Documents II*, No. 628, p. 1464.
94 Kay, *Documents II*, No. 624, p. 1460.
95 Kay, *Documents II*, Nos. 626 and 627, pp. 1461–3.
96 Kay, *Documents II*, Nos. 634 and 635, pp. 1472–3.
97 Kay, *Documents II*, No. 636, p. 1476.
98 Kay, *Documents II*, No. 632, p. 1470.

99 Kay, *Documents II*, No. 636, p. 1477, No. 637, pp. 1481–4.
100 Kay, *Documents II*, No. 637, p. 1484 fn. 3.
101 Singh, *Official History of The Indian Armed Forces*, p. 37.
102 Quoted by Singh, above p. 41.
103 See Buckley, *Occupation Diplomacy*, p. 102 fn. 66.
104 R. L. G. Challis from the Department of Industries and Commerce went to Japan in May 1947 as New Zealand's representative in matters relating to reparations. This was not a diplomatic post but related to the Occupation. In 1951 he became the head of New Zealand's Diplomatic Mission to SCAP and in 1952 Charge d'Affaires, New Zealand Legation, Japan.
105 Buckley, *Occupation Diplomacy*, p. 102.

CHAPTER 4

1 Memorandum to President Roosevelt from the Secretaries of State and War and the Attorney General, 22 January 1945. Quoted in Richard Minear, *Victor's Justice*, Princeton, 1971 pp. 9–10.
2 Kay, *Documents II*, No. 648, p. 1504.
3 Kay, *Documents II*, No. 6, pp. 11–12.
4 Kay, *Documents II*, Nos. 653, 654, pp. 1511–18.
5 Kay, *Documents II*, No. 649, pp. 1505–6.
6 Memo for the Acting Prime Minister, 4 January 1946, NZ Ministry of Foreign Affairs Archives, 59/2/49 Pt. 1.
7 Speech at farewell to Brigadier Ronald Quilliam, *New Zealand Law Journal*, (1946) XXII 40.
8 Hon. Sir Erima Harvey Northcroft, Kt, DSO, VD 1884–1953. Appointed Justice of the Supreme Court 1935.
9 Ronald Henry Quilliam, CBE, 1891–1972. Crown Solicitor 1931–1955.
10 Kay, *Documents II*, No. 650, pp. 1507–8.
11 Speech at farewell to Brigadier Quilliam.
12 Above.
13 See Buckley, *Occupation Diplomacy*, p. 108; Minear, *Victors' Justice*, pp. 8–9.
14 See Bradley F. Smith, *Reaching Judgment at Nuremberg*, London, 1977, pp. 46–58.
15 See Smith, above, p. 18–19; Buckley, *Occupation Diplomacy*, pp. 112–13; Minear, *Victor's Justice*, pp. 37–9, pp. 13–14, 58–9.
16 See Smith, above, pp. 13–14, 58–9.
17 See Smith, above, pp. 13–14, 75.
18 Kay, *Documents II*, No. 654, pp. 1513–18; Buckley *Occupation Diplomacy*, p. 119 fn. 54.
19 *Foreign Relations of the United States*, vol. VIII, 1946, pp. 390, 418–20.
20 Kay, *Documents II* No. 652, p. 1510.

21 In September 1945 the *Otago Daily Times* suggested that, by way of punishment the Emperor's fortune should be confiscated and in January 1946 reported with approval that the Emperor was to pay taxes but also noted the importance of the throne in giving the Japanese a sense of unity. See *Otago Daily Times*, 24 September 1945, 3 January 1946.

22 *Foreign Relations of the United States*, vol. VI 1945, pp. 646–7, 782–3.

23 R. R. Cunninghame, newly recruited to the Department of External Affairs at the time recalls writing a note one weekend in response to a casual request from Frank Corner on the pros and cons of trying the Emperor. Cunninghame decided the Emperor should the tried. As far as he is aware nothing came of his note. Interview with R. R. Cunninghame, 15 September 1989.

24 *Otago Daily Times* 18 January 1946.

25 Kay, *Documents II*, No. 652 pp. 1509–1510.

26 Kay, *Documents II* No. 178 p. 325.

27 *Foreign Relations of the United States*, vol. VIII 1946, pp. 395–97; Buckley *Occupation Diplomacy*, pp. 60–2.

28 *Otago Daily Times*, 29 January 1946, 3 February 1950.

29 *Dominion* 18 January 1946; interview with Hon. Sir Peter Quilliam, Wellington, 7 December 1988.

30 See Rix *Intermittent Diplomat*, p. 132.

31 Interview with Harold Evans, Christchurch, 24 August 1988.

32 Kay, *Documents II*, No. 658, p. 1527.

33 Quilliam to Shanahan, 20 February 1946, NZ Ministry of Foreign Affairs Archives, 59/2/49 pt. 1; interview with Harold Evans, Christchurch, 24 August 1988. Later Northcroft asked for a copy of Shakespeare printed 'large enough to be read by an elderly judge's ageing eyes'. Northcroft to Shanahan 24 October 1946, 59/2/49 Pt. 2.

34 Kay, *Documents II*, No. 660, pp. 1529–31, No. 663, pp. 1541–2.

35 Quilliam to Nash, 20 February 1946, NZ Ministry of Foreign Affairs Archives, 59/2/49.

36 Arnold Brackman, *The Other Nuremberg*, New York, 1987, p. 64.

37 Quilliam, 'Diary', 10 March 1946.

38 Kay, *Documents II*. Nos, 661, 662, pp. 1532–41, No. 664, pp. 1543–5, No. 666, pp. 1551–3; Quilliam, 'Diary' 12, 14 March 1946.

39 Quilliam, 'Diary' 18, 19 April 1946; Kay, *Documents II*, No. 669, pp. 1560–1; For comments on Comyns Carr and his draft of the indictment see alse Meirion and Susie Harries, *Sheathing the Sword*, London, 1987, pp. 118–24.

40 Kay, *Documents II*, No. 668, p. 1557–9, No. 681, p. 1613.

41 See Brackman, *The Other Nuremberg*, p. 71 on the view of the judge from the Netherlands. For more recent criticism see Minear, *Victor's Justice*, p. 81–3.

42 See Minear, above pp. 108–9.

43 Kay, *Documents II*, No. 667, p. 1554, No. 669, p. 1559–60.

44 Northcroft to Shanahan, 13 August 1947, NZ Ministry of Foreign Affairs Archives, 59/2/49.

45 Kay, *Documents II*, No. 681, pp. 1610–15.
46 Northcroft to Shanahan, 13 August 1947.
47 See Brackman, *The Other Nuremberg*, pps. 24, 61, 70–1.
48 Kay, *Documents II*, No. 676, p. 1594, No. 681, p. 1613. Quilliam and Evans received the pay prescribed for officers of their rank. As a Brigadier, Quilliam received 66 shillings per day. By contrast the UK prosecutor received £52.10. per day plus expenses plus £26.5. per day when in court. See Kay, *Documents II*, pp. 1638–9 and fn. 1.
49 Kay, *Documents II*, No. 710, pp. 1675–6, No. 713, p. 1685.
50 Northcroft to Shanahan, 28 August 1946, NZ Ministry of Foreign Affairs Archives, 59/2/49 Pt. 2.
51 Northcroft to Sir Michael Myers, 18 May 1947, NZ Ministry of Foreign Affairs Archives, 59/2/4 Pt. 3.
52 Interview with Harold Evans, Christchurch, August 1988.
53 Kay, *Documents II*, p. 1668 fn. 2. The dissatisfaction of Lord Patrick, the British judge is clear from the British files. See for example material cited by Harries, *Sheathing the Sword*, pp. 166–7.
54 The original American judge resigned after less than two months and this had already caused the court some embarrassment.
55 Kay, *Documents II*, No. 707, pp. 1667–8.
56 Harries, *Sheathing the Sword*, p. 168.
57 Quilliam, 'Diary' 20 June 1946.
58 Kay, *Documents II*, No. 678, 1601–4, No. 680, pp. 1606–9.
59 Kay, *Documents II*, No. 666, p. 1552, No. 677, p. 1599, No. 695, p. 1646.
60 Kay, *Documents II*, No. 696, p. 1647. Northcroft to Quilliam, 21 October 1946, (private letter in possession of the family) Kay, *Documents II*, No. 696, p. 1647.
61 Quilliam, 'Diary', 14 October 1947; Quilliam to Shanahan, 20 January 1948, NZ Ministry of Foreign Affairs Archives, 59/2/49 pt. 3.
62 Northcroft to MacIntosh, 16 July 1946, NZ Ministry of Foreign Affairs Archives, 59/2/49 pt. 2.
63 Shanahan to Northcroft, 1 April 1947, Shanahan to Quilliam 9 April 1947, NZ Ministry of Foreign Affairs Archives, 59/2/49. Quentin-Baxter (b. 1922) became one of New Zealand's leading experts in international and constitutional law. He joined the Department of External Affairs in 1949 and in the next twenty years represented New Zealand at a series of international conferences. In 1968 he was appointed Professor of Jurisprudence and Constitutional Law at Victoria University of Wellington, a post which he held at the time of his death in 1984. From 1966–1969 he represented New Zealand on the United Nations Commission on Human Rights and was its chairman in 1969. In 1971 he was elected to the International Law Commission and remained a member until the time of his death. In 1973 and 1974 he headed the New Zealand team to the International Court of Justice to present the case against France in respect of its atmospheric testing of nuclear weapons in the South Pacific. For his many other contributions in this field see Christopher Beeby, 'Obituary' *New Zealand Law Journal*, December 1984, pp. 390–1.

64 Quentin-Baxter to Registrar, Victoria University of Wellington, 13 June 1968. (Letter in possession of Alison Quentin-Baxter); interview with Alison Quentin-Baxter, Wellington, August 1988.

65 Northcroft to Shanahan, 13 August 1947, 18 March 1948, 21 May 1948, NZ Ministry of Foreign Affairs Archives, 59/2/49 Pt. 3.

66 See R. Pal, *International Military Tribunal for the Far East*, Calcutta 1953.

67 Northcroft makes this point in Northcroft to Shanahan 16 July 1946. Of the 28 persons charged, two had died and one had been declared unfit to plead.

68 Northcroft to Shanahan, 21 May 1948, NZ Ministry of Foreign Affairs Archives, 52/2/49.

69 Northcroft to Shanahan, 22 June 1948.

70 See Brackman, *The Other Nuremberg*, p. 365.

71 Interview with Alison Quentin-Baxter Wellington August 1948. This is apparently especially evident in the case of Count 1, the conspiracy charge.

72 Justice Northcroft to Dr Quentin-Baxter, 27 September 1948 (letter in possession of Alison Quentin-Baxter).

73 See Quentin Quentin-Baxter, Curriculum Vitae, 17 January 1949. (In possession of Alison Quentin-Baxter) Quentin-Baxter cited Lord Patrick, the British judge, and Northcroft as the judges to whom he was closest and as his preferred referees. He stated that Cramer, the American judge, and McDougall, the Canadian judge would also be willing to act as referees. These seem likely to have been the 'active group'. In a letter to Quilliam dated 27 April 1948, Evans enclosed a copy of a memorandum in three parts on Preparations for War which Quentin-Baxter had prepared for Northcroft. (Copy of letter in possession of Harold Evans). Quentin-Baxter told his wife, who is a lawyer, that Northcroft for the most part accepted his work and did not change it before sending it on to the other judges. Interview with Alison Quentin-Baxter, Wellington, August 1988.

74 Minear, *Victor's Justice*, pp. 31–2, 160–3; Harries, *Sheathing the Sword*, pp. 164–170. The judgement and separate opinions are part of the complete collection of papers of the International Military Tribunal for the Far East held at the University of Canterbury, Christchurch.

75 Northcroft, Memorandum for the Prime Minister, 17 March 1949, Papers of the IMTFE, University of Canterbury.

76 See for example Minear, *Victor's Justice* and Brackman, *The Other Nuremberg*.

77 Kay, *Documents II*, No. 739, p. 1736–7. The complete document of which No. 739 is a part is to be found in the IMFTE papers held at the University of Canterbury.

78 Kay, *Documents II*, No. 272, pp. 1702–7.

79 Kay, *Documents II*, No. 740, pp. 1745–7. The speech is also reported in the *New Zealand Law Journal*, 1949, XXV, pp. 133–8.

80 MacIntosh to Quilliam, 13 May 1946, NZ Ministry of Foreign Affairs Archives, 59/2/49 Pt. 1.

81 Shanahan to Quilliam, 25 October 1946, NZ Ministry of Foreign Affairs Archives, 59/2/49 Pt. 1.
82 *Otago Daily Times* 9, 11, 12, 13, 15, 23 November 1948.
83 Kay, *Documents II*, No. 729, pp. 1720–1.
84 Kay, *Documents II*, Nos. 452 and 453, pp. 1124–35.

CHAPTER 5

1 Interview with Frank Corner, 8 October 1985. New Zealand's lack of experts and resources is explained in Day to Sterndale Bennett, 17 February 1945, FO 371/46324.
2 Buckley, *Occupation Diplomacy*, pp. 7–9.
3 Kay (ed.), *Documents II*, Nos. 136, 137, pp. 224–9.
4 Kay, *Documents II*, No. 28, p. 44.
5 Summary of remarks by Dr Evatt, 23 December 1945, note by Frank Corner, NZ Minister of Foreign Affairs Archives, 268/9/9 Pt. 1.
6 Minister of External Affairs Canberra to Secretary of State Dominion Affairs, 26 October 1946, Memorandum for Mr Shanahan, 'Disposal of Japanese Fleet', 30 October 1946; Minister of External Affairs to Secretary of State, Dominion Affairs, 6 November 1946, NZ Ministry of Foreign Affairs Archives, 268/6/2 Pt. 1.
7 F. E. Cumming Bruce to P. J. Dixon, 27 January 1947, FO minute, 6 February 1947, PRO FO 371/63766.
8 Summary of remarks by Dr Evatt, 23 December 1945.
9 McIntosh to External Affairs, 7 March 1947, NZ National Archives, EA 102/9/4 Pt. 1.
10 Kay, *Documents III*, No. 5, pp. 12–13.
11 Kay, *Documents III*, Nos. 8, 9, pp. 16–21; No. 12, pp. 24–5.
12 Bernard Kuskie (Australian HC Wellington) to Secretary, Preparatory Committee for the Peace Settlement (PCPS), 5 May 1947, Commonwealth Archives Canberra, A1838 536/2B.
13 Evatt also sought United States support for this scheme. See Buckley, *Occupation Diplomacy*, p. 155.
14 Fraser to Evatt, 23 April 1947, NZ National Archives, EA 102/9/3.
15 On paradox in the Commonwealth relationship see McIntyre, 'Peter Fraser's Commonwealth, pp. 39–88.
16 Sir Orme Sargent to Secretary of State (Bevin), 29 March 1947, PRO FO 371/63766; Dominions Office to Canada, Australia, New Zealand, 11 April 1947, FO 371/63767.
17 Kuskie to Secretary PCPS, 16 May 1945 Commonwealth Archives Canberra A1838 536/2B.
18 Cecil Day to McIntosh, 24 April 1947, NZ National Archives, EA 102/9/1.
19 R. R. Cunninghame to G. R. Powles, 24 April 1947, NZ National Archives, EA 102/9/1.
20 'New Zealand's Strategic Interests in the Pacific and Far East: An

appreciation by the Joint Planning Committee', 27 May 1947, NZ National Archives 102/9/7 Pt. 1.

21 Kay, *Documents III*, No. 58, pp. 94–103. This paper was first drafted 12 May 1947, see NZ Ministry of Foreign Affairs Archives 102/9/38.

22 Draft memorandum, 'General Attitude to Japanese Settlement', 12 May 1947, NZ Ministry of Foreign Affairs Archives, 102/9/38.

23 'General attitude to Japanese Settlement', Comment by G. R. P., 2 June 1947, NZ Ministry of Foreign Affairs Archives, 102/9/38.

24 Kay, *Documents III*, No. 25, p. 44.

25 Draft memorandum, 'General Attitude to Japanese Settlement', 12 May 1947.

26 'General Attitude to Peace Settlement', 2 June 1947.

27 This point is strongly made in a memorandum 'The enforcement of the Peace Treaty' by J. V. W. (J. V. Wilson), 21 May 1947, NZ Ministry of Foreign Affairs Archives 102/9/1. Wilson, a New Zealander who had worked at the League of Nations, Geneva, before the war had accompanied the Lytton Commission to Manchuria in 1931. He was suspicious of Japan and a more experienced officer than most in the Department. Interview with R. R. Cunninghame, Wellington, 15 September 1989.

28 Berendsen to McIntosh, 9 June 1947.

29 Kay, *Documents III*, No. 31, p. 53.

30 McIntosh to Berendsen, 10 June 1947.

31 Kay, *Documents III*, Nos. 58 to 60, pp. 94–127.

32 Interview with Sir Guy Powles, Wellington, 8 October 1985.

33 McIntosh, 'Working with Peter Fraser in Wartime', p. 5.

34 McIntosh to Berendsen, 7 June 1947. R. R. Cunninghame recalled getting 'bogged down' preparing the papers in Wellington and felt sure they were not read by or to the the Prime Minister before he left. R. R. Cunninghame interview, 15 September 1989.

35 McIntosh to Berendsen, 12 September 1947.

36 See Buckley, *Occupation Diplomacy* pp. 153–4.

37 J. M. C. James (CRO) to Mr Price, 10 September 1947 PRO FO 371/53779; Report on British Commonwealth Meeting at Canberra 26 August – 2 September 1947, 29 September 1947. PRO FO 371/63781.

38 *Otago Daily Times*, 6 September 1947.

39 Kay, *Documents III*, No. 66, pp. 174–94.

40 Kay, *Documents III*, No. 67, pp. 195–7.

41 *Dominion*, 28 January 1948.

42 Kay, *Documents III*, No. 90, p. 256.

43 Memorandum, 'Alternative policies towards Japan', 28 July 1948, NZ Ministry of Foreign Affairs Archives, 102/9/4 Pt. 2.

44 Kay, *Documents III*, No. 94, p. 265.

45 Kay, *Documents III*, No. 94, p. 268.

46 *NZ Parliamentary Debates* 28 September 1948, vol. 283, pp. 2590–2600.

47 Meeting of prime ministers 20 October and 21 October 1948, PMM

(48) 11th meeting and PMM (48) 13th meeting, NZ Ministry of Foreign Affairs Archives, 153/26/4 Pt. 1.

48 Sir Patrick Duff (UKHC in NZ) to Prime Minister, 2 July 1948, quoted in memorandum, 'Pacific Pact', by J. V. W. (?), 11 January 1949, NZ National Archives, EA 102/9/4 pt. 3.

49 Buckley, *Occupation Diplomacy*, pp. 163–4.

50 Memorandum, 'Pacific Pact', 11 January 1949. Presumably Dening visited Wellington in either December 1948 or early January 1949. In the copy of the memorandum held in the National Archives, the words 'together with China and other Asiatic countries' have been underlined.

51 Kay, *Documents III*, No. 163, p. 477.

52 Above.

53 Sir Patrick Duff to Prime Minister, 20 July 1948.

54 Memorandum, 'Pacific Pact', 11 January 1949.

55 Kay, *Documents III*, No. 164, p. 478.

56 Memorandum 'Pacific Pact', 11 January 1949.

57 Kay, *Documents III*, Nos. 97, 98, pp. 274–7.

58 Kay, *Documents III*, Nos. 169–171, pp. 485–8.

59 Kay, *Documents III*, No. 173, p. 490.

60 Kay, *Documents III*, No. 105, pp. 285–6.

61 Kay, *Documents III* No. 184, p. 506.

62 Kay, *Documents III*, No. 108, pp. 291–7.

CHAPTER 6

1 See W. David McIntyre, 'Labour Experience in Foreign Policy' in Hyam Gold (ed.) *New Directions in New Zealand Foreign Policy*, Auckland, 1985, pp. 11–14.

2 See above pp. 14–17.

3 R. M. Miller to author, 10 August 1989. McIntosh once told Miller to keep briefings for the Prime Minister simple enough to be read by an 11 year old boy riding past them on a bicycle.

4 *NZ Parliamentary Debates* 2 November 1950, vol. 292 p. 3956; *NZ Statements and Documents*, No. 38, p. 206.

5 A. H. McLintock (ed.), *Encyclopedia of New Zealand* Wellington, 196, vol. I p. 494.

6 R. M. Miller to author, 10 August 1989.

7 See McIntyre, 'Labour Experience in Foreign Policy', pp. 18–19.

8 *NZ Statements and Documents*, No. 40, p. 208.

9 *NZ Statements and Documents*, No. 38, p. 206.

10 C. J. Elder and M. F. Green, 'New Zealand and China' in Ann Trotter (ed.) *New Zealand and China*, Dunedin, 1986, pp. 44–5.

11 McIntosh to Berendsen, 18 November 1949.

12 Elder and Green, 'New Zealand and China', pp. 45–6.

13 Elder and Green, above, pp. 47–8.

14 Berendsen to McIntosh, 14 February 1950.

15 *Foreign Relations of the United States*, vol. VI 1951, p. 1488 fn 2.
16 *NZ Statements and Documents*, No. 38, p. 206.
17 Colombo Conference, 1st Meeting FMM (50), 9 January 1950 PRO CAB 133/178.
18 Kay, *Documents III*, No. 109, p. 301; McIntosh to Berendsen February 1950, Wellington to Washington, 5 April 1950, NZ National Archives, EA 102/9/4.
19 Kay, *Documents III*, No. 109, pp. 297–8. For the UK paper, FMM (50) 2, see no. 110, pp. 311–29.
20 Buckley, *Occupation Diplomacy*, pp. 172–3, p. 193.
21 Above pp. 163–5.
22 Above, pp. 166–70.
23 Above, pp. 173–4.
24 Kay, *Documents III*, No. 110, pp. 331–29.
25 Kay, *Documents III*, No. 109, pp. 298–9.
26 Kay, *Documents III*, No. 109, pp. 299–300.
27 Kay, *Documents III*, 109, pp. 301–2.
28 McIntosh to Berendsen, 1 February 1950.
29 Japanese Peace Treaty. FMM (50) 10th meeting 13 January 1950 PRO CAB 133/78.
30 *Foreign Relations of the United States*, vol. VI 1950, pp. 1198–9.
31 MacIntosh to Berendsen, 1 February 1950.
32 *NZ Statements and Documents*, No. 40, p. 208.
33 Colombo Conference FMM (50) 2nd meeting 9 January 1950, PRO CAB 133/78.
34 Sir Percy Spender, *Exercises in Diplomacy*, Sydney 1969, pp. 13–14.
35 Kay, *Documents III*, No. 114, pp. 335–7.
36 Kay, Documents III, No. 115, pp. 337–8.
37 MacIntosh to Berendsen, 12 April 1950.
38 Above.
39 Above.
40 Kay, *Documents III*, No. 118, pp. 340–8.
41 Memorandum for Wade and Shanahan: 'Working Party on Japanese Peace Settlement', 6 April 1950, NZ National Archives, EA 102/9/4.
42 H. A. Graves (Washington) to F. S. Tomlinson, 18 April 1950, PRO FO 371/83829.
43 Kay, *Documents III*, No. 120, pp. 350–2.
44 Corner to Shanahan, 29 April 1950, NZ National Archives, EA 102/9/4.
45 Above.
46 Minister for External Affairs to NZ High Commission London, 30 April 1950, NZ National Archives, EA 102/9/4.
47 Kay, *Documents III*, No. 125, p. 358.
48 Berendsen to McIntosh, 23 May 1950.
49 Kay, *Documents III*, No. 126, pp. 259–79.
50 Kay, *Documents III*, No. 127, pp. 380–2.
51 Kay, *Documents III*, No. 127, p. 383.
52 Kay, *Documents III*, No. 127, p. 384.

CHAPTER 7

1 See Robert Chapman, 'From National to Labour' in W. H. Oliver (ed.), *The Oxford History of New Zealand*, Wellington, 1981, pp. 357–8.
2 McIntosh to Berendsen, 12 April 1950.
3 Kay, *Documents III*, No. 200, p. 545.
4 This endorsement came on 23 June 1950, two days before war erupted in Korea. Cabinet minute (CM(50)37, 26 June 1950, PRO CAB 222/ 2/2.
5 Kay, *Documents III*, Nos. 185–90, 192–7, pp. 507–22.
6 Kay, *Documents III*, No. 188, p. 511. Burma, India, Pakistan, Thailand, and Indonesia were, presumably, these countries. Subsequently both New Zealand and Australia came under pressure from the United States to participate but resisted this. See Kay, *Documents III*, Nos. 190, 192–4, pp. 514–19.
7 Berendsen to McIntosh, 23 May 1950.
8 Kay, *Documents III*, No. 198, pp. 522–32.
9 Berendsen, 'Memoirs', Book III, Chapter XV.
10 Kay, *Documents III*, No. 198, pp. 522–32.
11 McIntosh to Berendsen, 12 April 1950.
12 Kay, *Documents III*, No. 200, p. 545.
13 Kay, *Documents III*, No. 200, p. 546.
14 Berendsen to McIntosh, 23 May 1950.
15 Kay, *Documents III*, No. 200, p. 546, No. 201 p. 547; *Dominion*, 16 June 1950.
16 Kay, *Documents III*, No. 199, pp. 536–45.
17 Kay, *Documents III*, No. 199, p. 537.
18 Kay, *Documents III*, No. 201, p. 547.
19 *Foreign Relations of the United States*, vol. VI, 1950, pp. 1113–15; 1117–29.
20 Above, pp. 1160–1.
21 Above, pp. 1161–6, 1175–82.
22 Above, pp. 1228–9, 1243.
23 Quoted in Sir Oliver Franks (Washington) to Secretary of State for Foreign Affairs (Bevin), 11 August 1950, NZ National Archives EA 102/9/4. A note dated 21 September 1950 attached to this dispatch states that it was obtained from the UK High Commission in Wellington on a confidential basis.
24 Kay, *Documents III*, No. 129, p. 390.
25 Summary of Anglo-American discussions on Japan, 8 August 1950, PRO FO 371/83832.
26 Kay, *Documents III*, No. 131, pp. 391–2, Nos. 133, pp. 394–6.
27 'Japanese Peace Treaty', memo written on the assumption that within a fortnight the State Department will be ready to talk about a treaty, 1 September 1950, NZ National Archives EA, 102/9/4.
28 'Japanese peace treaty and security in the Pacific'. Notes for Mr Holland for informal discussions with Mr Menzies, 16 August 1950 NZ National Archives, EA 102/9/4.

29 See I. C. McGibbon, 'New Zealand's Intervention in the Korean War, June–July 1950', *The International History Review*, (1989) XI 273–5; Robert R. Eaddy, 'New Zealand and the Korean War: The First Year, unpublished M.A. thesis, University of Otago, 1983.

30 *Evening Post* 25 June 1950.

31 See Eaddy, 'New Zealand and the Korean War'.

32 Berendsen to McIntosh, 14 July 1950.

33 Berendsen to Doidge, 17 July 1950, quoted by McGibbon, 'New Zealand's Intervention in the Korean War' p. 283.

34 Berendsen to McIntosh, 26 July 1950.

35 Quoted in F. L. W. Wood, 'Foreign Policy 1945–1951' in NZ Institute of International Affairs *New Zealand in World Affairs* vol. I, p. 106.

36 See Nigel S. Roberts 'New Zealand, Denmark and Norway: Foreign Policy and National Character' in John Henderson, K. Jackson and R. Kennaway, (eds), *Beyond New Zealand: The Foreign Policy of a Small State*. Auckland, 1980, p. 31.

37 See Wood, 'Foreign Policy 1945–1951' p. 106; Robert O'Neill *Australia and the Korean War* vol. I, Canberra, 1981, p. 96.

38 O'Neill, above, pp. 77–87.

39 *Foreign Relations of the United States*, vol. VI 1950 pp. 1261–2.

40 Sir Oliver Franks to Secretary of State, 11 August 1950, NZ National Archives, EA 102/9/4.

41 Quoted in O'Neill, *Australia and the Korean War*, vol. I, p. 87. See also Spender, *Exercises in Diplomacy*, p. 39.

42 Record of a discussion at a meeting of Cabinet, 22 Auguust 1950, with Rt. Hon. R. G. Menzies, Prime Minister of Australia, CM (50) 59, Quoted by Eaddy, 'New Zealand and the Korean War', p. 35.

43 *NZ Parliamentary Debates*, vol. 291, p. 2142, 5 September 1950.

44 Spender, *Exercises in Diplomacy*, pp. 34–9.

45 Spender, above, p. 47.

46 Interview with Emiritus Professor F. L. W. Wood, Dunedin, 18 November 1987. On the other hand, R. M. Miller who was an officer in the Department of External Affairs described Doidge as 'totally unencumbered by an original thought or a generous impulse', Miller to author, 10 August 1989.

47 McIntosh to Berendsen, 29 May 1950.

48 Above.

49 Spender, *Exercises in Diplomacy*, p. 35.

50 Japanese Peace Settlement (paper prepared for London talks) 11 September 1950, NZ National Archives, EA 102/9/4.

51 Kay, *Documents III*, No. 137, pp. 397–9; No. 139, pp. 401–2.

52 Corner to Laking, 25 September 1950, Kay, *Documents III*, p. 405 fn. 2.

53 Note to Mr Shanahan on memorandum on Japanese Peace Settlement, 11 October 1950, NZ National Archives, EA 102/9/4.

54 Extract from *Current Events* from Washington, 29 September 1950, NZ National Archives, EA 102/9/4.

55 Note for file. Call of Mr Sidney Browne, Counsellor, United States

Embassy Wellinton, 21 September 1950, NZ National Archives, EA 102/9/4.
56 Above, 21 September 1950.
57 This is the view of Robert O'Neill in *Australia and the Korean War* vol. I p. 111. See also Spender, *Exercises in Diplomacy*, pp. 40–1 for an account of Spender's activities.
58 See interview with Sir Percy Spender, 20 June 1964, Dulles Oral Archive, Mudd Library, Princeton University; Spender, *Exercises in Diplomacy*, p. 45.
59 See Interview with Sir Percy Spender, 20 June 1964.
60 See Interview with John Allison, 20 April 1969, Dulles Oral Archive, Mudd Library, Princeton University.
61 Interview with Spender, 20 June 1964.
62 Spender, *Exercises in Diplomacy*, p. 48; Kay, *Documents III*, No. 202, p. 548.
63 Record of talks concerning the Pacific Pact, 13 October 1950, Commonwealth Archives Canberra, A1838 535/6 Pt 1; Kay, *Documents III*, No. 202, pp. 548–50.
64 Australian Mission to U.N. to Minister External Affairs, 11 October 1950, Commonwealt Archives Canberra, A1838, 535/6 Part 1; Kay, *Documents II*, No. 202, 548–51; Spender, *Exercises in Diplomacy*, p. 56.
65 D. W. Nicol to A. H. Tanqe, 18 October 1950, Commonwealth Archives Canberra, A1838, 535/6 Part 1; Spender above, p. 60.
66 Japanese Peace Settlement and Pacific Pact, 27 October 1950, Commonwealth Archives Canberra, A1838 536/6 Pt. 1; Spender to Watt, 31 October 1950, A1838 536/6 Pt. 1.
67 Kay, *Documents III*, No. 202, pp. 548–9.
68 Kay, *Documents III*, No. 140, pp. 406–7.
69 Kay, *Documents III*, above, pp. 409–10; No. 203 and 204, pp. 551–4.
70 *Japan News*, 25 October 1950.
71 Kay, *Documents III*, Nos. 203 and 204, pp. 551–4.
72 McIntosh to Berendsen, 24 November 1950.
73 McIntosh to Berendsen, above.
74 Kay, *Documents III*, p. 417 fn 3; Berendsen to McIntosh, 12 December 1950.
75 McIntosh to Challis (Tokyo), 7 December 1950, NZ National Archives EA 102/9/4.
76 Kay, *Documents III*, No. 143, pp. 416–17.
77 Memorandum, 'Japanese Peace Settlement', 15 December 1950, NZ National Archives EA 102/9/4.

CHAPTER 8

1 See O'Neill, *Australia and the Korean War*, vol. I, pp. 140–2.
2 McIntosh to Berendsen 24 November 1950; McIntosh to Berendsen, 15 December 1950.

3   *NZ Parliamentary Debates* vol. 292, pp. 3940–2, 2 November 1950.
4   Above vol. 293, pp. 4848–9, 1 December 1950.
5   McIntosh to Berendsen, 15 December 1950.
6   Berendsen to McIntosh, 25 November 1950.
7   McIntosh to Berendsen, 15 December 1950.
8   Memorandum, 'Japan' (prepared for P.M.'s Conference London 1951), December 1950, NZ National Archives EA 102/9/4 Pt. 5.
9   Above.
10 Kay, *Documents III*, No. 147, pp. 425–31.
11 Kay, *Documents III*, No. 148, pp. 432–3.
12 Kay, *Documents III*, No. 148, pp. 433–4.
13 McIntosh to Berendsen, 10 January 1951.
14 Kay, *Documents III*, No. 146, p. 425.
15 O'Neill, *Australia and the Korean War*, vol. I, p. 177.
16 *Foreign Relations of the United States*, vol. VI, Pt. 1, 1951, p. 782.
17 Kay, *Documents III*, No. 149, pp. 438–41.
18 Kay, *Documents III*, No. 151, pp. 444–5, No. 205, pp. 554–5.
19 Kay, *Documents III*, No. 150, pp. 441–3.
20 Kay, *Documents III*, No. 157 pp. 451–3, No. 159 pp. 458–62, *Foreign Relations of the United States* vol. VI Pt. 1, 1951, pp. 810–11, 827–30, 849–57ff.
21 See Hosoya Chichiro, 'Dulles-Yoshida talks 1950–1951', in Ian Nish (ed.), *The East Asian Crisis, 1945–1951: the Problem of China, Korea and Japan*, London, 1982; *Foreign Relations of the United States*, vol. VI Pt 1, 1951 p. 831. Kay, *Documents III*, No. 216, pp. 578–81.
22 Shanahan to McIntosh, 26 January 1951, NZ National Archives EA 102/9/4.
23 For the Secretary: Visit to Australia by Dulles, 30 January 1951, Commonwealth Archives Canberra, A1838 535/6 Pt 2.
24 Kay, *Documents III*, No. 211, p. 571.
25 Summary of Sir Carl Berendsen's proposal for an alliance with the United States, 9 February 1951, NZ Ministry of Foreign Affairs Archives, EA 102/9/46.
26 Memorandum, 'Security Provisions', 5 Febuary 1951, NZ Ministry of Foreign Affairs Archives, 102/9/46.
27 Draft paper on Dulles proposals, undated, probably 7 February 1951, NZ Ministry of Foreign Affairs Archives, 102/9/46.
28 Kay, *Documents III*, Nos. 208, 209, pp. 558–68.
29 Kay, *Documents III*, No. 209 above, p. 568.
30 Kay, *Documents III*, No. 207, p. 557.
31 J. J. S. Garner (Commonwealth Relations Office) to Sir Percival Liesching, 29 January 1951, PRO DO 35/2927.
32 Kay, *Documents III*, No. 210, pp. 569–70, Nos. 215, 216 pp. 575–81, Commonwealth Relations Office to High Commissioners Australia and New Zealand, 6 February 1951, PRO FO 371/92531.
33 Sir Esler Dening to Commonwealth Relations Office, 4 February 1951, PRO DO 35/2927.

34 United Kingdom High Commissioner NZ to Commonwealth Relations Office, 7 February 1951, PRO DO 35/2927.
35 Kay, *Documents III*, Nos. 213, 214, pp. 573–4, No. 218, pp. 582–4, No. 220, p. 586.
36 Japanese Peace Settlement, Cabinet Meeting, 9 February 1941, NZ National Archives EA 102/9/4.
37 Kay, *Documents III*, No. 222, pp. 587–8.
38 Kay, *Documents III*, No. 212, pp. 572–3.
39 British Embassy Washington to Foreign Office, 9 February 1951, PRO, FO 371/92071.
40 Kay, *Documents III*, No. 219, p. 585; Washington to Foreign Office, 9 February 1951, above.
41 British Embassy Washington to Foreign Office, 9 February 1951; Foreign Office to British Embassy Washington, 10 February 1951, PRO FO 371/92071.
42 Clutton to Johnston, 12 February 1951, PRO FO 371/92071.
43 See Geoffrey Blainey 'Two Countries: the Same but Very Different' in Keith Sinclair (ed.), *Tasman Relations*, Auckland 1987, pp. 317–324.
44 Kay, *Documents III*, Nos. 224, 225, pp. 590–2, No. 231, pp. 625–34; Spender, *Exercises in Diplomacy*, pp. 103–11.
45 See Spender, above p. 129. See 'Interview with Sir Percy Spender', 22 June 1964, Dulles Oral Archive, Mudd Library, Princeton.
46 McIntosh to Berendsen, 29 May 1950.
47 See Spender, *Exercise in Diplomacy*, p. 124.
48 McIntosh to Berendsen 16 March 1951. R. M. Miller who was in the New Zealand party in Canberra described Doidge's performance as 'inept'. Miller to author, 10 August 1989.
49 The Vandenberg Resolution of 11 June 1948 called for United States association with regional and other collective security arrangements to be based on 'continuous and effective self help and mutual aid'. See Kay, *Documents III*, p. 453, fn. 3.
50 Kay, *Documents III*, No. 226, pp. 593–613; No. 231, pp. 634–41.
51 Spender, *Exercises in Diplomacy*, pp. 104, 110.
52 Allison and Babcock who accompanied Dulles certainly felt Australia and New Zealand would not have signed the peace treaty without security guarantees. See interview with John Allison, 20 April 1969 and Major General C. Stanton Babcock, 23 July 1964, Dulles Oral Archive, Mudd Library, Princeton.
53 Spender, *Exercises in Diplomacy*, p. 147.
54 Kay, *Documents III*, No. 226, pp. 606–13, No. 231, pp. 641–53.
55 Spender, *Exercises in Diplomacy*, p. 149.
56 Sir Percival Liesching to Secretary of State, 21 February 1951, PRO DO 35/2927; Spender, *Exercises in Diplomacy*, p. 130. R. M. Miller recalled vividly Sir Esler Dening's obvious irritation at having to wait around in the Canberra Hotel while New Zealanders and Australians were discussing an ANZUS treaty with Dulles.
57 Kay, *Documents III*, No. 235, pp. 658–60.
58 McIntosh to Berendsen, 16 March 1951; UK High Commissioner to

Australia to Commonwealth Relations Office, 22 February 1951, PRO DO 35/2927.

59 McIntosh to Berendsen, 16 March 1951.

60 Memorandum left by Australians with the Prime Minister, 22 February 1951, PRO FO 371/92072. Spender also expressed his indignation at the United Kingdom actions at the time of the Dulles talks see Kay, *Documents III*, No. 226, p. 604.

61 Footnote, Johnston, 23 February 1951, PRO FO 371/92072; UK High Commissioner in Australia to Commonwealth Relations OFfice, 22 February 1951; PRO DO 35/2927.

62 McIntosh to Berendsen, 16 March 1951. In fact the British had toned down their comments and Patrick Gordon Walker consciously tried to avoid giving offence. See Gordon Walker to Bevin, 9 March 1951, PRO FO 371/92072 and CP(51)76, Pacific Defence, 9 March 1951, PRO CAB 129/45.

63 Kay, *Documents III*, No. 237, pp. 662–5.

64 McIntosh to Berendsen, 16 March 1951.

65 Kay, *Documents III*, No. 240, pp. 673–4.

66 Kay, *Documents III*, No. 241, pp. 674–9.

67 Kay, *Documents III*, Nos. 245 and 246, pp. 685–7.

68 Kay, *Documents III*, No. 258, p. 701 fn. 1.

69 Kay, *Documents III*, No. 254, p. 697, No. 257, pp. 699–70.

70 Kay, *Documents III*, No. 259, pp. 702–3.

71 Kay, *Documents III*, No. 260, pp. 703–5.

72 U.K. High Commissioner to Commonwealth Relations Office, 'Japanese Peace Treaty' 6 April 1951, PRO FO 371/92539.

73 See for example *Otago Daily Times* leading article, 21 February 1951.

74 U.K. Commissioner to Commonwealth Relations Office, 'Japanese Peace Treaty', 6 April 1951, PRO FO 371/92539.

75 Kay, *Documents III*, No. 235, pp. 835-8.

76 Kay, *Documents III*, No. 347, pp. 921–3.

77 Kay, *Documents III*, No. 332, pp. 859–60.

78 *Foreign Relations of the United States*, vol. VI Pt. 1 1951, p. 931.

79 See John W. Dower, *Empire and Aftermath: Yoshida Shigeru and the Japanese experience 1878-1954*, Cambridge Mass. 1979, p. 571 n. 76.

80 Kay, *Documents III* No. 327, pp. 841-6; No. 338, pp. 869–901.

81 *Foreign Relations of the United States*, vol. VI Pt. 1, 1951, pp. 1119–33; Kay, *Documents III*, No. 387, pp. 1027–44.

82 Kay, *Documents III*, Nos. 266–72, pp. 725–32.

83 Note of telephone conversation with McIntosh, 18 June 1951, Commonwealth Archives Canberra A1838 532/11 Pt. 2.

84 Berendsen to McIntosh, 25 June 1951.

85 Kay, *Documents III*, No. 278, pp. 737–9. For the Australian view see Kay, *Documents III*, No. 226 p. 601, Nos 267, 268 pp. 725–7.

86 Casey to Doidge, 30 June 1951, Commonwealth Archives Canberra, A1838 532/11 Pt. 4; Doidge to Casey, 4 July 1951, Commonwealth Archives Canberra, A1838 535/6 Pt. 7.

87 Robert Chapman, 'From Labour to National' in W. H. Oliver (ed.), *The Oxford History of New Zealand*, Wellington 1981, p. 358.
88 *NZ Parliamentary Debates*, vol. 294, 13 July 1951, pp. 318–20; Kay, *Documents III*, No. 392, pp. 1050–2.
89 *The Press*, 14 July 1951.
90 *The Press*, 14 July 1951, *New Zealand Herald* (Auckland), 14 July 1951, *Otago Daily Times*, 17 July 1951.
91 *Otago Daily Times*, 17 July 1951.
92 *New Zealand Herald*, 14 July 1951.
93 *Evening Post*, 31 July 1951.
94 *New Zealand Herald*, 16 August 1951.
95 Kay, *Documents III*, No. 395, p. 1057; No. 419, p. 1112.
96 Berendsen to McIntosh, 13 July 1951.
97 Kay, *Documents III*, No. 412, pp. 1088–1189, No. 419, p. 1112.
98 Dean Acheson, *Present at the Creation*, New York, 1969, pp. 542–3.
99 Berendsen, 'Memoirs', Book III, Chapter XVI.
100 See Ann Trotter, 'Personality in Foreign Policy: Sir Carl Berendsen in Washington', *New Zealand Journal of History*, 1986, XX 167–80.
101 Kay, *Documents III*, No. 299, Annex 2 pp. 767–9.
102 Kay, *Documents III*, No. 434, pp. 1162–8. Much of this speech, for which Berendsen received high praise was written by Frank Corner, First Secretary at the New Zealand Embassy in Washington. Interview with Frank Corner, Wellington, October 1985; Berendsen, 'Memoirs', Book III, Chapter XVI.
103 Kay, *Documents III*, No. 434, pp. 1162–8.

CHAPTER 9

1 See J. W. Winchester in, NZ Institute of International Affairs, *Must We Trust Japan?*, Wellington, 1952, p. 18.
2 G. R. Hawke, 'The Growth of the Economy', in W. H. Oliver (ed.), *The Oxford History of New Zealand*, Wellington 1981, p. 373.
3 *Otago Daily Times*, 21 August 1947.
4 *Otago Daily Times*, 16 October 1947.
5 See W. S. Borden, 'The Pacific Alliance: The United States and Japanese Trade Recovery 1947–1954', unpublished Ph.D thesis, University of Wisconsin, Madison, 1981; Michael Schaller, 'Securing the great Crescent: Occupied Japan and the Origins of Containment in South East Asia', *Journal of American History* 1969, LXIX, No. 2 pp. 392–99.
6 See Edwin McArthy, *Wool Disposals 1945–52: The Joint Organisation*, Canberra 1967, pp. 26–7, 93–4.
7 *Otago Daily Times*, 10 June 1948, 14 July 1948.
8 *Otago Daily Times*, 10 November 1948.
9 *Otago Daily Times*, 15 November 1948.
10 *Otago Daily Times*, 29 November 1949.

11 *Otago Daily Times*, 13 March 1950.
12 Summary of Discussion between New Zealand and Japanese Officials, June-July 1954, NZ National Archives EA 58/12/2 Pts. 6, 7.
13 Memo for the Counsellor NZ Embassy (Washington), 25 September 1950, NZ National Archives EA 102/9/4.
14 *Dominion* 6 January 1954. New Zealand revoked Article 35 with regard to Japan in 1962.
15 *Japan News* (Tokyo) Trade Supplement, 26 January 1952.
16 The Legation in Moscow closed on 13 June 1950. See Malcolm Templeton, *Top Hats Are Not Being Taken*, Wellington, 1989, p. 70.
17 McIntosh to Ministers of External Relations and Industries and Commerce, 16 May 1951, NZ National Archives EA 14/2/2 Pt. 2. McIntosh's paper is based on an earlier paper, 'New Zealand Representation in Asia, 9 May 1950', EA 64/14/2 Pt. 2.
18 UKLIM, The United Kingdom political mission to SCAP. Challis to McIntosh, 22 March 1950, NZ National Archives EA 268/9/4.
19 Challis to Shanahan, 14 September 1951, NZ National Archives EA 14/2/2 Pt. 2.
20 Memorandum (McIntosh) for the Minister for External Affairs, 27 September 1951, NZ National Archives EA 14/2/2 Pt. 2; Cabinet paper, CP(51)796, by Minister for External Affairs, 15 November 1951, EA 62/14/2 Pt. 2; Memo for the Minister of External Affairs, 22 November 1951, EA 62/14/2 Pt. 2.
21 External Affairs to all NZ High Commissioners, 7 December 1951, NZ National Archives EA 62/14/2 Pt. 2; Tokyo to Wellington, 15 December 1951, EA 62/14/2 Pt. 2; *Japan News* (Tokyo), 3 January 1952.
22 Extract from General Report from Tokyo by Challis, 15 December 1951, NZ National Archives EA 62/14/2 Pt. 2.
23 A Japanese Legation was opened in Wellington in March 1953.
24 Interview with R. M. Miller, Waikanae, 1989. The other Japanese linguist was R. R. Cunninghame who learned Japanese when in the RN.
25 *Japan News* 26 January 1952 above.
26 Challis to McIntosh, 22 March 1950, NZ National Archive EA 268/9/4.
27 See J. V. Wilson, 'New Zealand's Participation in International Organisations', in (ed.), T. C. Larkin, *New Zealand's External Relations*, Wellington 1962, pp. 67–71.
28 Gordon Daniels, 'New Zealand and Occupied Japan 1945–48', p. 35.
29 Interviews with R. R. Cunninghame, 15 September 1989, J. V. Scott, 16 September 1988.
30 See Roger Buckley, 'Working with MacArthur; Sir Alvary Gasgoigne, UKLIM and British Policy towards Occupied Japan, 1945–52', in Ian Nish, (ed.), *Aspects of Occupied Japan*, London 1986, p. 8; Grant Goodman, 'MacArthurian Japan; Remembered and Revised', in Ian Nish, (ed.), *The British Commonwealth and the Occupation of Japan*, London 1983, p. 13.

31 Clutton (UKLIM Tokyo) to Johnston (Japanese and Pacific Department FO), 12 February 1951, PRO FO 371/92071.
32 Buckley, *Occupation Diplomacy*, p. 201.
33 UK High Commissioner (Australia) to Patrick Gordon Walker, 9 March 1951, PRO DO 35/2928.
34 For the ANZUS Treaty see Kay, *Documents III*, No. 283, pp. 744–7.
35 See for example H. Wade (Tokyo) to Prime Minister, 3 December 1971, NZ Ministry of Foreign Affairs Archives, 40/12/1 Pt. 17a. Tension between New Zealand and the United States in 1984 over New Zealand's anti-nuclear policy and the United States subsequent declaration in 1985 that ANZUS was 'inoperable' caused some problems for Japan in its relationship with New Zealand both on the grounds of its wider foreign policy and because of a certain embarrassment about Japan's policy in relation to nuclear powered and armed ships and the American policy of 'neither confirm nor deny'.

Bibliography

UNPUBLISHED PRIMARY SOURCES

(i) Official Records: held by –

Commonwealth Archives, Canberra, Australia.
New Zealand Ministry of Foreign Affairs (now Ministry of External Relations and Trade), Wellington, NZ.
New Zealand National Archives, Wellington, NZ.
Public Record Office, London.

(ii) Private papers, Correspondence and Oral History Records

Sir Carl Berendsen papers – 'Memoirs', in possession of the family.
Columbia University Oral History Series on the Occupation of Japan, New York.
J. F. Dulles Oral History Project, Mudd Library, Princeton.
J. F. Dulles papers – Mudd Library, Princeton.
International Military Tribunal for the Far East proceedings and judgment – University of Canterbury, Christchurch, NZ.
General D. MacArthur papers – MacArthur Memorial, Norfolk, Va.
Sir Alister McIntosh correspondence (restricted) – NZ Ministry of Foreign Affairs Archives, Wellington, NZ.
Sir Erima Harvey Northcroft papers relating to the International Military Tribunal of the Far East – Canterbury University, Christchurch, NZ.
Quentin Quentin-Baxter letters and papers – in possession of Alison Quentin-Baxter, Wellington, NZ.

Ronald Henry Quilliam diaries – in possession of Sir Peter Quilliam, Wellington, NZ.

PUBLISHED PRIMARY SOURCES

(i) Official Documents:

Appendices to the Journals of the New Zealand House of Representatives, 1939–1952.

Butler, Rohan and Pelley, M. A., *Documents on British Policy Overseas*, Series 1, London, 1984. vol. 1 1945.

Census New Zealand 1936, Wellington, 1945. vol. IX.

Census New Zealand 1945, Wellington, 1951. vol. VIII.

Foreign Relations of the United States,

1945, Washington, 1969. vol. VI.

1946, Washington, 1971. vol. VIII

1947, Washington, 1972. vol. VI.

1948, Washington, 1974. vol. VI.

1949, Washington, 1976. vol. VII, Pts. 1 and 2.

1950, Washington, 1976. vol. 1976.

1951, Washington, 1977. vol. VI.

Hudson, W, J. and Stokes, H. J. W. (eds.), *Documents on Australian Foreign Policy 1937–1949*, Canberra 1983. vol. VI.

Kay, Robin, (ed.), *Documents on New Zealand's External Relations*:

The Australian New Zealand Agreement 1944, Wellington, 1972. vol. 1.

The Surrender and Occupation of Japan, Wellington, 1982. vol. II.

The ANZUS Pact and the Treaty of Peace with Japan, Wellington, 1985. vol. III.

Neale, R. G. (ed.), *Documents on Australian Foreign Policy 1937–1949*, Canberra, 1975. vol. 1.

New Zealand Department of External Affairs Publications:

No. 11. *United Nation Conference on International Organization*. Report on Conference held at San Francisco 25 April–26 June 1945 by Rt. Hon. Peter Fraser, Chairman of New Zealand Delegation, Wellington 1945.

No. 29. *Select Documents on the Surrender and Control of Japan*, Wellington, 1946.

No. 33. *United Nations*, Report of the New Zealand Delegation to the second part of the first regular session of the General Assembly held at New York, 23 October–15 December 1946, Wellington, 1947.

No. 38. *Japanese Peace Settlement*, Wellington, 1947.

No. 60. *The United Nations*, Report of the New Zealand Delegation on the second session of the General Assembly held at New York 16 September–29 November 1947, Wellington, 1948.

No. 61. *The United Nations*, Report of the New Zealand Delegation to the second session of the General Assembly held at New York 16 April–14 May 1948, Wellington, 1948.

No. 82. *The United Nations*, Report of the New Zealand Delegation on the second part of the third regular session of the General Assembly held at New York 5 April–8 May 1949, Wellington 1949.

No. 89. *The United Nations*, Report of the New Zealand Delegation on the fourth regular session of the General Assembly held at New York, 20 September–10 December 1949, Wellington, 1950.

No. 101. *The United Nations*, Summary of the report of the New Zealand Delegation to the fifth regular session of the General Assembly held at New York, 19 September 1950, Wellington, 1951.

No. 106. *Japanese Peace Settlement*, Wellington, 1951.

No. 121.*Treaty of Peace with Japan and Related Documents*, Wellington, 1952.

New Zealand Foreign Policy: Statements and Documents 1943–1957, Wellington, 1972.

New Zealand Official Yearbook 1941, Wellington, 1941.

New Zealand Parliamentary Debates, vols. 268–297.

Official History of New Zealand in the Second World War 1939–1945: Documents Relating to New Zealand's Participation, Wellington, 1963, vol. III.

Statistical Report on Trade and Shipping of New Zealand 1942, Wellington, 1946, Part 2.

(ii) Newspapers

Auckland Star, Christchurch Star-Sun, Dominion (Wellington), *Evening Post* (Wellington), *Japan News* (Tokyo), *New Zealand Herald* (Auckland), *Otago Daily Times* (Dunedin), *Standard* (Wellington), *The Press* (Christchurch).

(iii) Journals and Periodicals:

Australian Outlook (Sydney), *Free Lance* (Wellington), *New Zealand External Affairs Review*, later *New Zealand Foreign Affairs Review* (Wellington), *New Zealand Law Journal* (Wellington), *New Zealand Listener* (Wellington), *Outlook* (Dunedin), *Round Table* (London), *Truth* (Wellington), *Weekly News* (Auckland).

PUBLISHED SECONDARY SOURCES

(i) Books:

Acheson, Dean, *Present at the Creation*, New York, 1969.

Albinski, Henry S., *Australian Policies and Attitudes toward China*, Princeton, 1965.

Ball, W. Macmahon, *Australia and Japan: Documents and Readings in Australian History*, Sydney, 1969.

Ball, W. Macmahon, *Japan: Enemy or Ally?*, London, 1948.

Beaglehole, Ann, *A Small Price to Pay: Refugees from Hitler in New Zealand 1936–1946*, Wellington, 1988.

Bennett, Bruce S., *New Zealand's Moral Foreign Policy 1935–1939*, Wellington, 1988.

Bentley, Geoffrey, *RNZAF: A Short History*, Wellington, 1969.

Bercovitch, Jacob (ed.), *ANZUS in Crisis: Alliance Management in International Affairs*, London, 1988.

Bertram, James, *The Shadow of a War: A New Zealander in the Far East*, London, 1947.

Blakeslee, George H., *The Far Eastern Commission: A Study in International Cooperation 1945–1952*, Washington, 1953. (Department of State Publication No. 5138).

Brackman, Arnold C., *The Other Nuremburg: The Untold Story of the Tokyo War Crimes Trials*, New York, 1987.

Brown, Bruce, *New Zealand Foreign Policy in Retrospect*, Wellington, 1970.

Buckley, Roger, *Occupation Diplomacy: Britain and Japan 1945–1952*, Cambridge, 1982.

Burkman, Thomas W., *The Occupation of Japan: The International Context*, Norfolk, Virginia, 1982.

Burnett, Alan, *The A-NZ-US Triangle*, Canberra, 1988.

Condliffe, J. B., *New Zealand in the Making*, Wellington, 1959.

Coox, Alvin and Conroy, Hilary, *China and Japan: A Search for a Balance Since World War I*, Oxford, 1978.

Cox, Brian, *Too Young To Die*, Auckland, 1987.

Daniels, Gordon (ed.), *Proceedings of the British Association for Japanese Studies*, Sheffield, 1979. vol. 4, Part 1.

Daniels, G. and Lowe P., (eds.) *Proceedings of the British Association for Japanese Studies*, Sheffield, 1977. vol. 2, Part 1.

Darby, Charles, *The RNZAF: The First Decade 1937–1946*, Melbourne, 1978.

Davidson, J. W., *Samoa mo Samoa: the Emergence of the Independent State of Samoa*, Oxford, 1967.

Dennett, R. and Johnson, J., (eds.), *Negotiating with the Russians*, Boston, 1951.

Dilkes, David (ed.), *The Diaries of Sir Alexander Cadogan 1938–1945*, London, 1971.

Drifte, Reinhard, *The Security Factor in Japan's Foreign policy 1945–1952*, Ripe, Sussex, 1983.

Dower, J. W., *Empire and Aftermath; Yoshida Shigeru and the Japanese Experience, 1978–1954*, Harvard, 1979.

Dulles, John Foster, *War or Peace*, London, 1950.

East, M. A., Salmore, S. A. and Hermann, C. F., *Why Nations Act*, London, 1978.

Evatt, H. V., *Australia and World Affairs*, Sydney, 1946.

Gillespie, Oliver A., *New Zealand in the Second World War 1939–1945: The Pacific*, Wellington, 1952.

Gold, Hyam (ed.), *New Directions in New Zealand Foreign Policy*, Auckland, 1985.

Gordon, Bernard K., *New Zealand becomes a Pacific Power*, Chicago, 1960.

Gukin, Michael A., *John Foster Dulles: A Statesman and his Times*, New York, 1972.

Gustafson, Barry, *From the Cradle to the Grave: a Biography of Michael Joseph Savage*, Auckland, 1986.

Hamill, Ian, *The Strategic Illusion: The Singapore Strategy and the Defence of Australia and New Zealand*, Singapore, 1981.

Hancock, Kenneth R., *New Zealand at War*, Wellington, 1946.

Harries, Merion and Harries, Susie, *Sheathing the Sword: the Demilitarisation of Japan*, London, 1987.

Hasluck, Sir Paul, *The Government and the People*, Canberra, 1970.

Hastings, Max, *The Korean War*, New York, 1987.

Hawke, G. R., *Between Government and Banks. A History of the Reserve Bank of New Zealand*, Wellington, 1973.

Hearn, T. J., *New Zealand and Japan*, Dunedin, 1981.

Henderson, J., Jackson K. and Kennaway, R. (eds.), *Beyond New Zealand: The Foreign Policy of a Small State*, Auckland, 1980.

Holland, B. F., *Britain and the Commonwealth Alliance 1918–1939*, London, 1981.

Iriye, Akira, *The Cold War in Asia: A Historical Introduction*, New Jersey, 1974.

Kay, Robin, *Chronology: New Zealand and the War 1939–1946*, Wellington, 1968.

Kenan, George, *Memoirs 1925–1963*, London, 1968–73.

Larkin, T. C., *New Zealand and Japan in the Post-War World*, Wellington, 1969.

Larkin, T. C. (ed.), *New Zealand's External Relations*, Wellington, 1962.

Lissington, M. P., *New Zealand and Japan 1900–1941*, Wellington, 1972.

Lissington, M. P., *New Zealand and the United States 1940–1944*, Wellington, 1972.

Livingston, J., Moore, J. and Oldfather, F., *The Japan Reader*, Harmondsworth, 1976. vol. 2.

Lochore, R. A., *From Europe to New Zealand*, Wellington, 1951.

Louis, W. Roger, *Imperialism at Bay*, Oxford, 1977.

Lowe, Peter, *Britain in the Far East: A Survey, 1819 to the Present*, London, 1981.

Lowe, Peter, *Great Britain and the Origins of the Pacific War*, Oxford, 1977.

Lowe, Peter, *The Origins of the Korean War*, London, 1986.

McCarthy, Edwin, *Wool Disposals 1945–52: The Joint Organisation*, [Canberra (?)], 1967.

McGibbon, I. C., *Bluewater Rationale: The Naval Defence of New Zealand 1914–1942*, Wellington, 1981.

McIntyre, W. David, *New Zealand Prepares for War*, Christchurch, 1988.

McIntyre, W. David, *Neutralism, Non-alignment and New Zealand*, Wellington, 1969.

McIntyre, W. David, *The Rise and Fall of Singapore*, London, 1979.

Masahide, Shibusawa, *Japan and the Asian Pacific Region*, London, 1984.

Milner, Ian F. G., *New Zealand's Interest and Policies in the Far East*, New York, 1940.

Minear, Richard H., *Victor's Justice*, Princeton, 1971.

Munz, Peter (ed.) *The Feel of Truth: Essays in New Zealand and Pacific History*, Wellington, 1969.

Nagai, Y. and Iriye, A. (eds.), *The Origins of the Cold War in Asia*, New York, 1977.

New Zealand Army Board, *Guadalcanal to Nissan: With the Third Division through the Solomons*, Wellington, 1945.

New Zealand Army Board, *Pacific Story: A Survey of the Early History of the Third New Zealand Division*, Wellington, 1945.

New Zealand Department of Defence, *Defence Review*, Wellington, 1978.

New Zealand Institute of International Affairs, *Must We Trust Japan?*, Wellington, 1952.

New Zealand Institute of International Affairs, *New Zealand in World Affairs* vol. 1, Wellington, 1977.

New Zealand Institute of International Affairs, *The Commonwealth, its Past, Present and Future*, Wellington, 1972.

Nish, Ian (ed.), *Anglo-Japanese Alienation*, Cambridge, 1982.

Nish, Ian (ed.), *Aspects of the Allied Occupation of Japan*, London, 1986.

Nish, Ian (ed.), *Aspects of the Korean War*, London, 1987.

Nish, Ian (ed.), *The British Commonwealth and the Occupation of Japan*, London, 1983.

Nish, Ian (ed.), *The East Asian Crisis 1945–1951: the Problem of China, Korea and Japan*, London, 1982.

Official History of New Zealand in the Second World War, 1939–1945, Wellington, 1949. vol. I *Episodes and Studies*.

Oliver, W. and Williams, B., *The Oxford History of New Zealand*, Oxford, 1981.

O'Neill, Robert, *Australia and the Korean War 1950–1953*, Canberra, 1981. vol. I *Strategy and Diplomacy*.

Pal, R. *International Military Tribunal for the Far East*, Calcutta, 1953.

Pritchard, J. and Zaide, S., *The Tokyo War Crimes Trial. Proceedings of the Tribunal*, London 1981. vol. I.

Reese, Trevor R., *Australia, New Zealand and the United States 1951–1968*, Oxford, 1969.

Reischauer, E. O., *The Japanese Today*, Harvard, 1988.

Rennie, Frank, *Regular Soldier*, Auckland, 1986.

Rix, Allan, *Coming to Terms*, Sydney, 1986.

Rix, Allan (ed.), *Intermittent Diplomat*, Melbourne, 1988.

Rosecrance, R. N., *Australian Diplomacy and Japan 1945–1951*, Melbourne, 1962.

Roskill, Stephen, *Hankey: Man of Secrets*, London, 1974.

Ross, Angus, *New Zealand Aspirations in the Pacific in the Nineteenth Century*, Oxford, 1964.

Ross, Angus, *New Zealand in the Pacific World*, Wellington, 1965.

Ross, J. M. S., *Official History of New Zealand in the Second World War 1939–1945: The Royal New Zealand Airforce*, Wellington, 1955.

Sinclair, Keith, *A Destiny Apart: New Zealand's Search for National Identity*, Wellington, 1986.

Sinclair, Keith, *History of New Zealand*, Harmondsworth, 1959.

Sinclair, Keith (ed.), *Tasman Relations: New Zealand and Australia 1788–1988*, Auckland, 1987.

Sinclair, Keith, *Walter Nash*, Oxford, 1976.

Singh, R., *Official History of the Indian Armed Forces in the Second World War, 1939–1945: Post-War Occupation Forces: Japan and South-East Asia*, Kanpur, 1958.

Smith, Bradley F., *Reaching Judgment at Nuremberg*, London, 1977.

Spender, Sir Percy, *Exercises in Diplomacy*, Sydney, 1969.

Spurdle, Bob, *The Blue Arena*, London, 1986.

Taylor, Nancy M., *Official History of New Zealand in the Second World War 1939–1945: The Home Front*, Wellington, 1986. vols. I and II.

Templeton, Malcolm, *Defence and Security: What New Zealand Needs*, Wellington, 1986.

Templeton, Malcolm, *Top Hats Are Not Being Taken: A Short History of the New Zealand Legation in Moscow*, Wellington, 1989.

Thakur, R., *In Defence of New Zealand: Foreign Policy Choices in a Nuclear Age*, Wellington, 1984.

Thompson, Richard, *Race Relations in New Zealand*, Christchurch, 1963.

Thorn, James, *Peter Fraser, New Zealand's Wartime Prime Minister*, London, 1952.

Thorne, Christopher, *Allies of a Kind*, Oxford, 1978.

Thorne, Christopher, *The Issue of War: States Societies and the Far Eastern Conflict of 1941–1945*, London, 1985.

Trotter, Ann (ed.), *New Zealand and China*, Dunedin, 1986.

Wevers, Maarten, *Japan, Its Future and New Zealand*, Wellington, 1988.

Wood, F. L. W., *New Zealand and the Big Powers*, Wellington, 1967.

Wood, F. L. W., *New Zealand in the World*, Wellington, 1940.

Wood, F. L. W., *Official History of New Zealand in the Second World War 1939–1945: The New Zealand People at War*, Wellington, 1958.

Wood F. L. W., *This New Zealand*, Hamilton, 1952.

(ii) Articles

Bagish, M. and Conroy, H., 'Japanese Aggression against China: the Question of Responsibility', in Alvin Coox and Hilary Conroy (eds.), *China and Japan: A Search for Balance since World War I*, Oxford, 1978.

Bell, Roger, 'Australian-American Disagreement over the Peace Settlement with Japan 1944–1946', *Australian Outlook*, XXX No. 2 August, 1976.

Blakeslee, George H., 'Negotiating to Establish the Far Eastern Commission', in R. Dennett and J. Johnson, *Negotiating with the Russians*, Boston, 1951.

Bolton, Geoffrey, 'Australia and the Occupation of Japan', in I. Nish (ed.), *The British Commonwealth and the Occupation of Japan*, London, 1983.

Buckley, Roger, 'British Diplomacy and the Allied Control of Japan' in G. Daniels and P. Lowe (eds.), *Proceedings of the British Association of Japanese Studies*, vol. II, Sheffield, 1977.

Buckley, Roger, 'Working with MacArthur: Sir Alvary Gascoigne, UKLIM and British Policy towards Occupied Japan, 1945–52', in Ian Nish (ed.), *Aspects of the Allied Occupation of Japan*, London, 1986.

Chapman, Robert, 'From Labour to National', in *The Oxford History of New Zealand*, W. H. Oliver and B. Williams, (eds.), Oxford, 1981.

Cunninghame, R. R., 'The Development of New Zealand's Foreign Policy and Political Alignments', in T. C. Larkin (ed.), *New Zealand's External Relations*, Wellington 1962.

Daniels, Gordon, 'From Benevolence to Enmity: Britain and Japanese Communism, 1945–50', *Zinbun: Memoirs of the Research Institute for Humanistic Studies*, Kyoto, 1985.

Daniels, Gordon, 'Nationalist China in the Allied Council: Policies towards Japan 1946–52, *The Hokkaido Law Review*, (1976) XXVII (2).

Daniels, Gordon, 'New Zealand and Occupied Japan 1945–48' in Ian Nish (ed.), *The British Commonwealth and the Occupation of Japan*, London, 1983.

Dingman, Roger, 'The Diplomacy of Dependency: The Philippines and Peace-Making with Japan 1945–1952', *Journal of South East Asian Studies*, (1986) XVII (2).

Dingman, Roger, 'The View from Down Under: Australia and Japan 1945–1952', in Thomas Burkman (ed.), *The Occupation of Japan: the International Context*, MacArthur Foundation, Norfolk, Virginia, 1982.

Dingman, Roger, 'Truman, Attlee and the Korean War Crisis', in Ian Nish (ed.), *The East Asian Crisis, 1945–1951: The Problem of China, Korea and Japan*, London, 1982.

Dulles, John F., 'Security in the Pacific', *Foreign Affairs* (Jan. 1952) XXX.

Elder, C. J., and Green, M. F., 'New Zealand and China', in Ann Trotter (ed.), *New Zealand and China*, Dunedin, 1986.

Gibbons, P. J. 'The Climate of Opinion', in W. H. Oliver and B. Williams (eds.), *The Oxford History of New Zealand*, Oxford, 1981.

Goodman, Grant, 'MacArthurian Japan: Remembered and

Revised', in Ian Nish (ed.), *The British Commonwealth and the Occupation of Japan*, London, 1983.

Hall, D. O. W., 'Prisoners of Japan' in *Official History of New Zealand in the Second World War*, Wellington, 1948. vol. I *Episodes and Studies*.

Harland, Bryce, 'New Zealand, the United States and Asia: The background to the ANZUS Treaty', in Peter Munz (ed.), *The Feel of truth: Essays on New Zealand and Pacific History*, Wellington, 1969.

Hawke, G. R., 'The Growth of the Economy' in W. H. Oliver and B. Williams (eds.), *The Oxford History of New Zealand*, Oxford, 1981.

Henderson, J., 'The Foreign Policy of a Small State', in J. Henderson, K. Jackson and R. Dennaway (eds.), *Beyond New Zealand: The Foreign Policy of a Small State*, Auckland, 1980.

Hosoya, Chichiro, 'Dulles-Yoshida Talks 1950–1951', in Ian Nish (ed.), *The East Asian Crisis 1945–1951: The Problem of China, Japan and Korea*, London, 1982.

Iriye, Akira, 'Continuities in US-Japanese Relations 1941–49', in Y. Nagai and A. Iriye (eds.), *The Origins of the Cold War in Asia*, New York, 1977.

Larkin, T. C., 'Japan: Changing Problems', in J. Henderson, Jackson K. and Kennaway, R. (eds.), *Beyond New Zealand: The Foreign Policy of a Small State*, Auckland, 1980.

Larkin, T. C., 'The Place, Directions and Future Needs of New Zealand Relations with Japan' in T. J. Hearn (ed.), *New Zealand and Japan*, Dunedin, 1981.

McGibbon, Ian C., 'New Zealand's Intervention in the Korean War, June-July 1950', *The International History Review*, (1989) XI (2).

McGibbon, Ian C., 'The Defence of New Zealand 1945–1957', in New Zealand Institute of International Affairs, *New Zealand in World Affairs*, Wellington, 1977. vol. I.

McGibbon, Ian C., 'The History of New Zealand Defence', Erik Olssen and Bill Webb (eds.), *New Zealand Foreign Policy and Defence*, Dunedin, 1977.

McGibbon, Ian C., 'The Origins of the Alliance', *New Zealand International Review*, (1988) XIII (3).

McIntosh, Alister, 'The Origins of the Department', in New Zealand Institute of International Affairs, *New Zealand in World Affairs*, Wellington, 1977. vol. I.

McIntosh, Alister, 'Working with Peter Fraser in Wartime', *New Zealand Journal of History*, (1976) XX (1).

McIntyre, W. David, 'Labour Experience in Foreign Policy', in Hyam Gold (ed.), *New Directions in New Zealand Foreign Policy*, Auckland, 1985.

McIntyre, W. David, 'Peter Fraser's Commonwealth: New Zealand and the Origins of the new Commonwealth in the 1940s', in New Zealand Institute of International Affairs, *New Zealand in World Affairs*, Wellington, 1977. vol. I

McKinnon, M., *'Costs and Continuity: New Zealand's Security and the United States'*, Political Science (1978) XXX (1).

McLean, Dennis, 'Defence Policies in a Small State', in J. Henderson, K. Jackson and R. Kennaway (eds.), *Beyond New Zealand: The Foreign Policy of a Small State*, Auckland, 1980.

Munro, L. K., 'New Zealand and the Pacific', *Foreign Affairs*, (1953) XXXI (4).

Nish, Ian, 'Britain and the Occupation of Japan – Some personal Recollections' in Gordon Daniels (ed.), *Proceeding of the British Association of Japanese Studies*, vol. 4 pt. 1, Sheffield, 1979.

Nish, Ian, 'India and the Occupation of Japan', in Ian Nish (ed.), *The British Commonwealth and the Occupation of Japan*, London, 1983.

Nish, Ian, 'The Occupation of Japan: Some British Perspectives', in Ian Nish (ed.), *The East Asian Crisis, 1945–1951: The Problem of China, Korea and Japan*, London, 1982.

O'Connor, P. S., 'Keeping New Zealand White 1908–1920', *New Zealand Journal of History* (1968) XXII (1).

Ross, Angus, 'New Zealand and the Commonwealth to 1939' in New Zealand Institute of International Affairs, *The Commonwealth, its Past, Present and Future*, Wellington, 1972.

Schaller, M. 'Securing the Great Crescent: Occupied Japan and the Origins of Containment in South East Asia', *Journal of American History* (1982) LXIX (2).

Strazar, Marie D., 'Japanese Efforts to Influence a Peace Settlement 1945–1951', in T. W. Burkman (ed.), *The Occupation of Japan: The International Context*, Norfolk Va., 1984.

Tamchina, R., 'In Search of Common Causes: The Imperial Conference of 1937', *Journal of Imperial and Commonwealth History* (1972) I (1).

Thorne, Christopher, 'Racial Aspects of the Far Eastern War of 1941–1945', *Proceedings of the British Academy* (1980), LXVI.

Trotter, Ann, 'New Zealanders and the International Military Tribunal for the Far East', *New Zealand Journal of History*, XXIII, No. 2.

Trotter, Ann, 'Personality in Foreign Policy; Sir Carl Berendsen in Washington', *New Zealand Journal of History*, (1986) XX (2).

Trotter, Ann, 'Sir Carl Berendsen and Japan' in Ian Nish (ed.), *Aspects of the Allied Occupation of Japan*, London, 1984.

Wilson, J. V., 'New Zealand's Participation in International Organisations' in T. C. Larkin, *New Zealand's External Relations*, Wellington, 1962.

Wood, F. L. W., 'Foreign Policy 1945–1951' in New Zealand Institute of International Affairs, *New Zealand in World Affairs*, Wellington 1977. vol. I.

Wood, F. L. W., 'The Anzac Dilemma', *International Affairs* (1953) XXIX (2).

UNPUBLISHED THESES AND PAPERS

Angus, Barbara, 'Public Opinion towards Japan 1939–1945', War History Narrative, (compiled for the *Official History of New Zealand in the Second World War*), National Archives.

Baker, Terence C., 'New Zealand and the Genesis of the ANZUS Treaty', M. A. thesis, Victoria University of Wellington, 1971.

Borden, William S., 'The Pacific Alliance: The United States and Japanese Trade Recovery 1947–1954', Ph.D. thesis, University of Wisconsin, Madison, 1981.

Caird, Felicity, 'The Strategic Significance of the Pacific Islands in New Zealand's Defence Policy 1935–1939', M. A. thesis, University of Canterbury, 1987.

Eaddy, Robert R, 'New Zealand and the Korean War: the First Year', M. A. thesis, University of Otago, 1983.

Gray, Earl C., 'The Gag Again – J. T. Paul and Press Censorship during World War Two', B. A. Hons. thesis, University of Otago, 1986.

Harvey, Sharon L. A., 'The Third Dimension – Cultural relations between New Zealand and Japan in the Post-War Period', M. A. thesis, University of Auckland, 1988.

Kennaway, Richard N., 'New Zealand's Relations with Japan', Paper presented to the Foreign Policy School, University of Otago, 1970.

Lissington, M. P., 'Allied Control of Japan', War History Narrative, (compiled for the *Official History of New Zealand in the Second World War*), National Archives.

McDonald, Melanie, 'New Zealand and the Far Eastern Commission 1945–1951', B. A. Hons. thesis, University of Otago, 1985.

McGibbon, Ian C., 'New Zealand and the Korean War', Paper presented at the Pacific Coast Branch of the American Historical Association Annual Meeting, Hawaii, 1986.

Templeton, Malcolm, 'Some notes on the development of the Prime Ministers Department', War History Narrative, (compiled for the *Official History of New Zealand in the Second World War*), National Archives.

Templeton, Nina ' A Coming Man', B.A. Hons. thesis, University of Otago, 1981.

Trotter, Ann, 'New Zealand's Alliance Diplomacy: Sir Carl Berendsen in Washington', Paper presented at the Pacific Coast Branch of the American Historical Association Annual Meeting, Hawaii, 1986.

Witheford, H., 'Attitudes to the War in the New Zealand Labour Party', War History Narrative, (compiled for the *Official History of New Zealand in the Second World War*), National Archives.

Witheford, H., 'Censorship of the Press', War History Narrative, (compiled for the *Official History of New Zealand in the Second World War*), National Archives.

Index